For Mari

with thanks for helping
with Audrey's legacy

Clifton

AMS STUDIES IN MUSIC
ISSN 1941-7861
Series ISBN-13: 978-0-404-64600-4

No. 1
AUDREY EKDAHL DAVIDSON

ASPECTS OF EARLY MUSIC AND PERFORMANCE

ISBN-13: 978-0-404-64601-1

Above and on cover: Drawing by Linda Judy after a woodcut in an incunabulum in the British Library.

Aspects of Early Music and Performance

Audrey Ekdahl Davidson

AMS Press, Inc.
New York

Library of Congress Cataloging-in-Publication Data

Davidson, Audrey Ekdahl-
  Aspects of Early Music and Performance / Audrey Ekdahl Davidson.
    p. cm. – (AMS Studies in Music, ISSN 1941-7861 ; no. 1)
    Includes index.
    ISBN-13: 978-0-404-64601-1 (cloth: alk. paper)
    1. Vocal music—Europe—History and criticism. 2. Music and literature. 3. Performance practice (Music). I. Title.
ML1400.D38   2008
780.9'02—dc22   2008026127
                                                                   CIP

All AMS books are printed on acid-free paper that meets the guidelines for performance and durability of the Committee on Production Guidelines for Book Longevity of the Council on Library Resources.

Copyright © 2008 by AMS Press, Inc.
All rights reserved

AMS Press, Inc.
Brooklyn Navy Yard, 63 Flushing Ave-Unit #221
Brooklyn, NY 11205-1073, USA
www.amspressinc.com

MANUFACTURED IN THE UNITED STATES OF AMERICA

Contents

Illustrations vi

Preface vii

Acknowledgments xi

I

Music and Performance: Hildegard of Bingen's *Ordo Virtutum* 3

The Cividale *Planctus Mariae* for Modern Performance 31

Music in the Beauvais *Ludus Danielis* 49

Alma redemptoris mater: The Little Clergeon's Song 61

High, Clear, and Sweet: Singing Early Music 75

II

Palestrina and Mannerism 91

Five Settings of Songs Attributed to Sir Philip Sidney 101

Milton's Encomiastic Sonnet to Henry Lawes 123

George Herbert and the Celestial Harmony 133

III

The Origin and Development
of Quasi-Dramatic Passion Music 155

The Roskilde St. John Passion and Its Suppression 177

IV

Vocal Production and Early Music 187

Index 213

Illustrations in Text

1. The Devil chained. Detail from an illumination in lost manuscript of Hildegard of Bingen's *Scivias* (Wiesbaden, Hessische Landesbibliothek, Cod. 1). Drawing by Marianne Cappelletti Lutes 25

2. Crucifix created for a demonstration performance of Cividale *Planctus Mariae* at the International Congress on Medieval Studies, 2006, in Western Michigan University's Kanley Chapel 40

3. The Cosmic Monochord. Robert Fludd, *Utriusque Cosmi maioris scilicet et minoris Metaphysica, Physica, atque Technica Istoria* (1617–18) 141

4. The Roskilde Passion. Manuscript in the Danish National Archives (Copenhagen, Rigsarkivet, MS. DK D 21 Indlæg og koncepter til Sjællandske Tegnelser 1736 13/4, nr. 179) 178

5. The Larynx. Drawing by Marianne Cappelletti Lutes 191

6. The lower respiratory system and larynx. Athanasius Kircher, *Musurgia Universalis* (1650) 199

7. The Sinuses. Diagram showing the forehead cavity, nasal cavity, and palate used in singing in high, middle, and low ranges 201

Preface

This selection of studies by Audrey Ekdahl Davidson (1930–2006) represents a sampling of her interests through a busy lifetime in music. The earliest were the articles that developed out of her fascination with Renaissance English songs, beginning with Dowland and Campion but later extending to Henry Lawes and the poets of the period. She had been introduced to these as a singer by a voice coach, Robert Holliday, when she was in her mid-twenties and continued to value them always. These then led to broader interests in early music generally when she was a professional soprano soloist in Detroit in the early 1960s. After she and I moved to Kalamazoo, Michigan, to teach at Western Michigan University those interests only grew. She founded her own early music group, initially to perform in 1966 at the small medieval conference which eventually grew to become the university's annual International Congress on Medieval Studies. She continued as director for twenty-five years and frequently, over the course of preparing an average of three concerts each year, showcased a considerable amount of music that had never been heard before on this side of the Atlantic Ocean. One of her specialties was the staging of medieval music-dramas, as reported in a monograph, *Performing Medieval Music Drama*, on which we collaborated in 1998.

The articles that are offered here are not in the order in which they were written, and some of them were left without their finishing touches by the author and hence were never offered for publication. For these, it was necessary to decipher rough drafts and to supply footnotes and documentation, not always fully identified—for example, a page number, but referring to an unspecified reference that had to be tracked down. I have tried to retain the sources cited (or intended to be cited) by her, sometimes where later editions are available, as in the case of *The New Grove Dictionary of Music and Musicians* (1980), now published in a second edition, and I have been as faithful as possible to her texts as she left them. In a few instances I have included additions, which have been enclosed in brackets. It was inevitable that some problems should emerge during my efforts, however. Her paper on the Roskilde Passion, for example, had been largely incorporated in her book *The Quasi-Dramatic St. John Passions from Scandinavia*, but I have been able to reclaim nearly intact the original paper that she read at a meeting of the American

Musicological Society in Denver. Less effort was usually required for previously published studies, with the exception of her paper on the Cividale *Planctus Mariae*, which had been offered as a conference paper for a colloquium sponsored by the Société Internationale pour l'Etude du Théâtre Médiéval in Perpignan, France, and thereafter appeared in print but with some errors. For the study of the music of the Beauvais *Daniel*, transcriptions she had prepared for a performance by her own troupe in conjunction with the university's Collegium Musicum in 1990, along with other examples approximating her intent insofar as possible that were provided by her colleague Matthew Steel, replaced those by Marcel Zijlstra which she had been asked to use in her article when it was initially published.

In addition to Professor Steel, I owe a special debt of gratitude to Eric Strand, who prepared the musical examples for publication and otherwise was supportive. Drew Minter and Timothy McGee kindly read a portion of the manuscript dealing with performance practice. Marianne Cappelletti Lutes offered her graphic skills, and many others also encouraged or helped me in the course of asembling the essays for publication. I am of course grateful to Ashlie Sponenberg and Gabriel Hornstein of AMS Press for their interest in seeing the project through. Those to whom Audrey would have expressed gratitude are certainly far too many to be listed here, and in any case I am not in a position even to have any knowledge about many of them. However, I know that, in addition to others named in this preface, Clyde Brockett, Richard Rastall, Larry Syndergaard, John Cutts, Fletcher Collins, Jr., Herbert Schueller, Margery Selden, Barbara Thornton, Jon Higgins, Johannes Riedel, Sister M. Patricia, and Otto Gründler are among those whom she would have identified in her list as providing various kinds of assistance or encouragement over the years.

Though Audrey was born with a congenital bone disease that left her wheelchair-bound for most of her adult life, her achievement was substantial. Serious scholarship of course became extremely difficult in the final decade of her life, but even then she was able at last substantially to revise and update her doctoral dissertation. The result, *Olivier Messiaen and the Tristan Myth* (2001), was fortunately in press when she was hospitalized and suffering a severe decline in her health. The Messiaen book, which treated his trilogy of songs, symphony, and choral work inspired by the Tristan legend, excited her because it brought together several topics that particularly interested her, including of course medieval legend. She was also attracted to the project because it necessarily extended to Messiaen's use of non-Western music, to which Audrey had been introduced so many years ago by Bruno Nettl. This included Indian rhythms derived from the thirteenth-century theorist Śarngadeva and Quechua melodies from Peru. Only a little more than a month before her death she checked preliminary proofs for her transcription of the *Planctus Mariae*, which was treated to a demonstration performance for the International Congress on Medieval Studies at Western Michigan University in 2006. This transcription will be included in a memorial issue of *Comparative Drama*, which will honor her for her contribution to the medieval music-drama.

In spite of her disability, osteogenesis imperfecta or "brittle bone disease," Audrey was not afraid of travel, and much of her research was done in libraries abroad. In England she was indebted to the resources of the British Library, the Bodleian, and the library of Christ Church, Oxford, as well as others; in Germany to the Hessische Landesbibiothek in Wiesbaden; in Scandinavia to libraries and archives in Copenhagen, Lund, Stockholm, Uppsala, and Vadstena. It was among the Scandinavian collections that she obtained information for her work not only on Scandinavian Passion music but also on the extant music-dramas of the medieval period in that region, work which resulted in her *Holy Week and Easter Dramas and Ceremonies from Medieval Sweden* (1990). It was, needless to say, her tribute to her Swedish heritage, of which she was inordinately proud.

A word needs to be said about the two articles on voice production and early music in the present collection. "High, Clear, and Sweet: Singing Early Music" was written for a Festschrift, *Sacra/Profana: Studies in Sacred and Secular Music for Johannes Riedel* (1985), which she co-edited as a tribute to her dissertation advisor upon his retirement from the University of Minnesota. "Vocal Production and Early Music" was intended to be part of much more ambitious project, a projected book on singing. This essay, incorporating her knowledge of the subject gained from experience and work with remarkable vocal coaches, particularly Avery Crew of Detroit, as well as early music practitioners was to follow an introductory chapter that was only vaguely sketched out. The second chapter alone was reasonably complete. Subsequent chapters were envisioned on style and interpretation, including regional practice; early and late styles, sacred and secular; gender, children as singers; articulation and ornaments; treatment of melodic and rhythmic structures; reading early notation. Recently, many aspects of singing and performing early music have been covered in publications by Timothy McGee and others, but her completed segment on voice production still fills a need with regard to the topic and hence is included here.

Audrey was, until her last years, a work-three-jobs type of person, sometimes *pro bono*, as was the case with her early music group and her role as director of music at St. Martin of Tours Church. There was always music to be edited or written, for example providing service music for church, an occasional anthem, and, for a time, weekly antiphons—and, of course, fighting the good fight for standards in sacred music. One of her colleagues in her university's School of Music insists that she should have devoted her life to composing. She was always busy and productive in so many ways, including scholarship carried out mostly in summers away from teaching. She received support from Western Michigan University in the form of numerous summer research fellowships and sabbaticals as well as from the American Society of Learned Societies, which awarded her a generous travel grant in 1983. When she retired in 1993 on account of her health her colleagues surprised her with a publication, a selection of her transcriptions of early music, and the legislature of the state of Michigan honored her with a citation for special service to the university, the scholarly community, and the arts and for being "an example to us all."

Clifford Davidson

Acknowledgments

The following essays are reprinted by permission of Medieval Institute Publications: "Music and Performance: Hildegard of Bingen's *Ordo Virtutum*," from Audrey Ekdahl Davidson, ed., *The Ordo Virtutum of Hildegard of Bingen: Critical Studies* (1992); "Music in the Beauvais *Ludus Danielis*," from Dunbar H. Ogden, ed., *The Play of Daniel: Critical Essays* (1997); "The Origin and Development of Quasi-Dramatic Passion Music," and portions of her original conference paper incorporated in "The Roskilde Passion and Its Suppression," from Audrey Ekdahl Davidson, *The Quasi-Dramatic St. John Passions from Scandinavia and Their Medieval Background* (1981). "The Cividale *Planctus Mariae* for Modern Performance" is reprinted from *Fifteenth-Century Studies* (1988), by permission of the editor, Edelgard E. DuBruck. "*Alma redemptoris mater*: The Little Clergeon's Song," "Palestrina and Mannerism," and "Milton's Encomiastic Sonnet to Henry Lawes" are reprinted from Audrey Davidson, *Substance and Manner: Studies in Music and the Other Arts* (Hiawatha Press, 1977). For the use of illustrations, the Danish National Archives gave permission to use fig. 4, and fig. 5 was used with permission of Georg Olms. Fig. 3 is published by permission of the Special Collections division of the University of Michigan Libraries.

I

Music and Performance: Hildegard of Bingen's *Ordo Virtutum*

The Latin music-drama *Ordo Virtutum* (c.1151) is one of the most important dramatic works of the Middle Ages. Written by a seeress noted for her powerful imagery, its remarkable text is set to music which is no less powerful in its aesthetic effect. And the music-drama is all the more remarkable since its author, Hildegard of Bingen, denied ever having been formally taught or having "learnt musical notation or any kind of singing."[1]

It is strange that Hildegard's *Ordo Virtutum* was so thoroughly neglected prior to the publication in 1970 of Peter Dronke's *Poetic Individuality in the Middle Ages*[2] and even for some time thereafter. Though the play was known to German scholars in the early part of this century,[3] Karl Young's monumental *The Drama of the*

---

[1] Hildegard, *Vita*, as quoted in translation by Peter Dronke, *Women Writers of the Middle Ages* (Cambridge: Cambridge University Press, 1984), 145; for the Latin text, see ibid., 232.

[2] Peter Dronke, *Poetic Individuality in the Middle Ages* (Oxford: Clarendon Press, 1970), 169–92.

[3] The text (but not the music) of the *Ordo Virtutum* had been edited by Joannes Baptista Pitra (*Analecta Sacra* [1882; reprint, Farnborough: Gregg Press, 1966], 8:457–65). Josef Gmelch published a facsimile of the *Symphonia*, including the *Ordo Virtutum*, from the *Riesenkodex* in 1913 (*Die Kompositionen der heil. Hildegard nach dem grossen Hildegardkodex in Wiesbaden* [Düsseldorf, 1913], 37–47). See also especially Ludwig Bronarski, *Die Lieder der hl. Hildegard: Ein Beitrag zur Geschichte der geistlichen Musik des Mittelalters* (Leipzig: Breitkopf und Härtel, 1922), and Der heiligen Hildegard von Bingen, *Reigen der Tugenden: Ordo Virtutum: Ein*

Medieval Church (1933) does not mention the *Ordo*, but more disturbing is the reluctance of more recent scholars to take notice of this music-drama. William L. Smoldon's *The Music of the Medieval Church Dramas* (1980) has no listing in its index for Hildegard, although there is an entry for Hilarius (followed by one for *Hodie cantandus est*). Even Susan Rankin's recent and otherwise admirable discussion of liturgical drama in the revised volume *The Early Middle Ages to 1300* in the New Oxford History of Music fails to treat Hildegard or her *Ordo Virtutum*.[4]

To be sure, until recently there was no usable performing edition of the *Ordo Virtutum* which would make it accessible to performers and those scholars not comfortable with early notation.[5]

Singspiel, ed. Maura Böckeler (Berlin: Sankt Augustinus Verlag, 1927).

[4] Karl Young, *The Drama of the Medieval Church*, 2 vols. (Oxford: Clarendon Press, 1933); William L. Smoldon, *The Music of the Medieval Church Dramas*, ed. Cynthia Bourgeault (London: Oxford University Press, 1980); Susan Rankin, "Liturgical Drama," in *The Early Middle Ages to 1300*, ed. Richard Crocker and David Hiley, New Oxford History of Music 2 (London: Oxford Univ. Press, 1990), 310–56. It should be noted in all fairness that Smoldon was working on his book at the time of his death in 1974 and that he left the notes to the volume essentially unfinished. In contrast, a study which takes full account of the *Ordo Virtutum* is Richard Axton, *European Drama of the Early Middle Ages* (London: Hutchinson, 1974), 94–99.

[5] See my performing edition: Hildegard von Bingen, *Ordo Virtutum*, ed. Audrey Ekdahl Davidson (Kalamazoo: Medieval Institute Publications, 1984); citations to the play (abbreviated *OV*) in this study are for convenience to this edition (references are to item numbers, with the addition of line numbers from Dronke's edition in *Poetic Individuality*, 180–92), though I have in some cases re-transcribed the musical notation on the basis of an on-site examination of the manuscript. My performing edition was first prepared for the Society for Old Music production, which I directed in May of 1984, and has been used for a number of performances by other troupes, including a performance at Lincoln Center and by the Atlanta Camerata. [A second edition was issued in 2002 by the Hildegard Publishing Company of Bryn Mawr, Pennsylvania.] A beautiful and affecting recording of the play has been recorded by Sequentia (Harmonia

There had been a 1927 edition of the text of the play by Maura Böckeler in Der heiligen Hildegard von Bingen, *Reigen der Tugenden: Ordo Virtutum*, which included a transcription of the music into modern notation by Sr. Pudentiana Barth of St. Hildegard's Abbey at Eibingen.[6] Sr. Pudentiana's transcription, however, departs significantly from the unique manuscript, the so-called *Riesenkodex*, Codex 2 in the Hessische Landesbibliothek, Wiesbaden (hereafter identified as R), fols. 478^v–481^v.[7] Since Sr. Pudentiana transposes the various characters' melodic phrases up or down in pitch in order to keep the music within an extremely limited range, her transcription gratuitously alters in range many of the sung dramatic speeches, thus destroying any possibility of tonal coherence. While she does not actually try to justify her use of transpositions, she nevertheless indicates that she has attempted to choose "keys" (an anachronistic term) that will go harmoniously together: "Da die Tonarten der einzelnen Antiphonen beständig wechseln . . . waren wir bestrebt, die Transposition so zu wählen, daß sich die Melodien harmonisch anschliessen."[8] She does not acknowledge the fact that medieval pitch was relative rather than ab-

---

Mundi 1C165-00), which has also staged the play in both Europe and the United States. The voices (especially Barbara Thornton as the Soul) are most convincing, but the instrumental interludes are somewhat too "south European" to seem right for the Rhine valley. [Sequentia's re-recording of the *Ordo Virtutum* (Harmonia Mundi 05472-77394-2) revises Thornton's approach to some aspects of performance practice, and is generally preferred over the earlier version. For a tribute by Rick Johnson to the late Barbara Thornton in the context of a review of an Ann Arbor performance of this production of the *Ordo*, see *The Dramatic Tradition of the Middle Ages*, ed. Clifford Davidson (New York: AMS Press, 2005), 84–86.—Ed.]

[6] For the musical transcription, see Hildegard von Bingen, *Reigen der Tugenden*, 105–35.

[7] For a reduced facsimile, see Audrey Ekdahl Davidson, ed., *The* Ordo Virtutum *of Hildegard of Bingen: Critical Studies*, Early Drama, Art, and Music Monograph Series 18 (Kalamazoo: Medieval Institute Publications, 1992)

[8] Ibid., 100–101.

solute or that the note as written may not be the pitch to be sung. In actuality, the beginning note was only a relative point from which the singer(s) could launch the song once he, she, or they had determined what was the most comfortable range for the said singer(s). Also, Sr. Pudentiana may have believed that neither medieval nor modern singers would be able to encompass the range in R which is from a below c' (middle c) to a" above c".[9] The notes from a to a" constitute a spread of two octaves. What Sr. Pudentiana does not take into account is that not all voices need to sing the entire range of possible notes; at the beginning of the *Ordo Virtutum* (*OV* 1/1, 3/6–8), the Patriarchs and Prophets, for example, sing from a to c", with the possibility of the baritones emphasizing the lower tones and the tenors taking over more strongly at the upper tones. Done skilfully, there need be no break in sound, only a seamless passage from lowest to highest tones. However, while the notes as found in the manuscript are reasonable for both baritones and tenors, Sr. Pudentiana's transcription nevertheless provides two different transpositions for (1) the question by the Patriarchs and Prophets (*OV* 1/1)—transposed into a "key" with the signature of four sharps—a question to which the Virtues answer in *OV* 2/2–5 in a "key" with the signature of two sharps; and (2) the statement by the Patriarchs and Prophets (*OV* 3/6–8)—using the same "key" signature as in no. 2 (two sharps). Likewise the manuscript presents the women's voices singing no lower than a, while only Mercy (*OV* 49/137–39) and Victory (*OV* 80/236) sing as high as a". The collective Virtues occasionally do rise to g", but a musical director can utilize a two choir system that separates altos and mezzo-sopranos into a lower, richer choir (although any good mezzo-soprano should be able to sing at least a b") and that places sopranos into an upper, lighter choir. Thus there is no valid reason for Sr. Pudentiana's erratic transposition practice either for men's or for women's voices. This practice is particularly irksome at *OV* 55/152–53 when Patience's speech is transposed down a fourth, moving her singing into a darker, heavier range instead of the bright, clear one shown in the manuscript.

In spite of the idiosyncracies of Sr. Pudentiana's transpositions,

---

[9] For a convenient explanation of the letter notation that I have adopted, see Willi Apel, *Harvard Dictionary of Music*, 2nd ed. (Cambridge: Harvard University Press, 1969), 467. In this system, middle c is labeled c'.

the number of actual notational errors will be seen to be few. At *OV* 2/4 she renders the word "illo" as b–c'–a (with a key signature of two sharps); the notes at this word should be rendered a–b–a. Also, at *OV* 47/133 at the syllable "-ti-" of "spurcitias" (R: "spurcicias") there is a variation from the manuscript (Example 1). But generally Sr. Pudentiana is faithful to the notes as found in R.

Example 1

However, the editorial division of the drama in this edition into six discrete sections should be carefully scrutinized. The Böckeler-Barth edition divides the play into *Vorspiel* (Prologue), three "scenes," *Nachspiel*, and *Epilog*. These divisions are not found in R, though in my own study of the organization of the play I have arrived at a similar structure with a slightly different rationale behind it (see below). However, while helpful for study, such divisions should not be introduced into the performance itself since the action must be continuous and not interrupted.[10] The manuscript (R) also does not divide the Virtues into two choruses, nor does it combine both choruses into one larger chorus (*Gesamtchor*) as the Böckeler-Barth edition directs. Nevertheless, splitting the chorus into lower and higher voices—a practice suggested above—could have been useful or even necessary, and such an arrangement also provides contrast; the two choruses, separately and then brought together, are a commonsensical and sound theatrical solution to the monotony of a single large chorus singing constantly, albeit broken up with many solo sections. Although we

---

[10] See Cynthia Bourgeault, "Liturgical Dramaturgy," *Comparative Drama*, 17 (1983), 125–28, regarding the need to allow a liturgical drama space and time to "breathe" back and forth between ritual and theater.

do not have any evidence in R for the use of divided choruses which amalgamate into a larger one, such practice would have been consistent with the liturgical practice of Hildegard's monastery.

The transcription of the *Ordo Virtutum* into square-note musical notation by Pudentiana Barth, Maria-Immaculata Ritscher, and Joseph Schmidt-Görg as recently as 1969[11] might be presumed to be more accurate than the earlier transcription of Sr. Pudentiana. However, such is not the case; the transcription slips the traces at several points, most notably at *OV* 71/199–200, where several musical phrases are found to be transposed exactly one note higher than in R (see the music accompanying the words "in te non amisisti, sed acute previdisti"). The same type of error happens at the words "quomodo eos" and at "quam prius illorum causa fuisset," except that for the latter phrase the editors conclude on an e, which is the note found in R at this point. What has happened is that the 1969 editors have thrown several passages into totally new modal relationships; while Hildegard herself might be found beginning an item in one mode and moving to another mode within it, this was her prerogative as composer. It is much harder to rationalize the rather inconsistent treatment of her tonality in the 1969 edition.

The *Ordo Virtutum* is found in three manuscripts, if we count the abbreviated version of the text preserved in the *Scivias*.[12] But the music appears in only two manuscripts, though one of these, a transcription dated 1487 and copied for the humanist Johannes Trithemius (British Library Add. MS. 15,102), is musically

---

[11] Hildegard von Bingen, *Lieder*, ed. Pudentiana Barth, Maria-Immaculata Ritcher, and Joseph Schmidt-Görg (Salzburg: Otto Müller, 1969), 165–205.

[12] Hildegard, *Scivias*, ed. Adelgundis Führkötter and Angela Carlevaris, Corpus Christianorum, Continuatio Mediaevalis, 43–43A (Turnhout: Brepols, 1978), 2:621–29; *Scivias*, trans. Columba Hart and Jane Bishop, introd. Barbara Newman (New York: Paulist Press, 1990), 529–33. For the miniatures, see also Adelgundis Führkötter, *The Miniatures from the Book Scivias of St. Hildegard of Bingen from the Illuminated Rupertsberg Codex* (Turnhout: Brepols, 1977).

unreliable.[13] The only reliable copy is preserved in R, to which reference has been made above. While, as Robert Potter has speculated, the *Ordo* may possibly have been completed in time for performance at Rupertsberg coinciding with the occurrence of the dedication of the nuns' new abbey church[14] (though Pamela Sheingorn argues for another specific occasion, the ceremony of the Dedication of Virgins, and Gunilla Iversen has proposed an even more plausible theory[15]), the manuscript R containing the only extant twelfth-century version of the music of the *Ordo* was apparently itself not copied until the decade after Hildegard's death in 1179.[16] The work of copying R—a large, thick manuscript measuring 11 1/2 x 18 inches, containing 481 folios, and handsomely bound in leather— was under the direction of her nephew Wezelin.[17] The placement of the *Ordo* in this manuscript is at the very end, following sixty-seven songs and sequences of her *Symphonia*, each of which has musical notation. The neumes in the musical settings of the songs and the play are typical of Upper Rhenish notation—a system descended from St. Gall neumes—in

---

[13] See Audrey Ekdahl Davidson, "Another Manuscript of the *Ordo Virtutum* of Hildegard of Bingen," in C. Davidson, ed., *The Dramatic Tradition of the Middle Ages*, 79–83.

[14] Robert Potter, "The *Ordo Virtutum*: The Ancestor of the English Moralities?" in A. E. Davidson, ed., *The* Ordo Virtutum *of Hildegard of Bingen: Critical Studies*, 31–42, 51–57. See also Newman, Introduction, in *Scivias*, trans. Hart and Bishop, 26.

[15] Pamela Sheingorn, "The Virtues of Hildegard's *Ordo Virtutum*," in A. E. Davidson, ed., *The* Ordo Virtutum *of Hildegard of Bingen: Critical Studies*, 43–63, and Gunilla Iversen, "*O Virginitas, in regali thalamo stas*; New Light on the *Ordo Virtutum*: Hildegard, Richardis, and the Order of the Virtues" [in C. Davidson, ed., *The Dramatic Tradition of the Middle Ages*, 63–78].

[16] Marianna Schrader and Adelgundis Führkötter, *Die Echtheit des Schrifttums der heiligen Hildegard von Bingen* (Cologne: Böhlau-Verlag, 1956), 154–79.

[17] Ibid., 177–78; see also Dronke, *Poetic Individuality*, 152.

use in the twelfth century prior to the development of gothic or *Hufnagel* notation.[18] The neumes are placed on four-line staves with the text residing on a red line, which occasionally is also utilized as an extra line for neumes.

Hildegard's music has not been sufficiently subjected to analysis, and yet it would seem that such analysis is required if her work is to be understood and performed. First, the Hildegardian "thumbprint" in her *Symphonia* and especially in her *Ordo Virtutum* needs to be recognized. Her "thumbprint," which seems unique in medieval music-drama, consists of more or less formulaic structures built on frequently appearing intervals combined in an uncodified but yet not random fashion. What makes this process special for Hildegard is that the most frequently used intervals are the melodic ascending fifth followed either by an upper ascending fourth built on the top note of the fifth *or* by an upper ascending fifth built on the top note of the fifth (see Example 2).

Example 2

Commenting on Hildegard's music in general in his article in *The New Grove Dictionary of Music and Musicians*, Ian Bent compares her use of small mosaics of melody to the melodic practice of Adam of St. Victor, but he believes that the Victorine com-

---

[18] On St. Gall and related neumes, see Dom Eugène Cardine, *Gregorian Semiology*, trans. Robert M. Fowels (Solesmes: Abbaye Saint Pierre de Solesmes, 1982), 11–16 and passim. Bronarski, *Die Lieder der hl. Hildegard*, 14, designates the neumes as "gothic," but I now recognize that term as properly reserved for a later style of notation. For a brief and useful description of Hildegard's neumes as they occur in the Dendermonde manuscript, see Peter van Poucke's Introduction to Hildegard of Bingen, *Symphoniae Harmoniae Caelestium Revelationum* (Peer: Alamire, 1991), 11–12.

poser is closer to a centonization practice than is Hildegard.[19] Robert Cogan, who seems to have more confidence in Hildegard's unitary structures and the additive method with which she creates her melodies, has made reference to these units as "cells," capable of being joined to other cells in various permutations.[20] Thus Hildegard's method, in Cogan's useful system, comes very near to being a true centonization process. Further mathematical analysis would verify more precisely how often a particular unit is joined to another particular unit—or if there is a virtually endless variety of permutations.

Other characteristics of Hildegard's music include: (1) the alternation of solo and chorus material, and (2) melodies rendered both melismatically and syllabically. The narrative segments of the *Ordo* are set in simple syllabic neumes—segments which are juxtaposed with expansive melismatic settings of the more lyrical passages. Ludwig Bronarski cannot resist calling the syllabic material "recitative" and the melismatic material "aria"—terms from modern opera not especially appropriate to medieval music-drama.[21] There is also a structural factor since the entire work is organized to culminate in a final climactic melismatic section which enters an ecstatic realm of poetry, music, and theology, all three blending to evoke a mystical state.

The subject matter of the play possesses genuine dramatic interest. The drama itself is no mere copy of the narrative related by Prudentius in his *Psychomachia*, although there are obvious resemblances since the Virtues in Hildegard's drama are part of a

---

[19] Ian Bent, "Hildegard of Bingen," in *The New Grove Dictionary of Music and Musicians*, ed. Stanley Sadie, 20 vols. (London: Macmillan, 1980), 8:554. It should be noted that Bent erroneously cites the *Ordo Virtutum* as being excluded from the Wiesbaden manuscript (R) when, as the present article indicates, R is in fact the only authentic source extant for the *Ordo*. [This error has been corrected in the second edition of *The New Grove*.—Ed.]

[20] Robert Cogan, "Hildegard's Fractal Antiphon," in *Wisdom Which Encircles Circles*, ed. Audrey Ekdahl Davidson (Kalamazoo: Medieval Institute Publications, 1996), 93–104.

[21] Bronarski, *Die Lieder der hl. Hildegard*, 44–45.

long tradition extending back to Prudentius' personified figures. In the *Psychomachia*, the battle is drawn between Virtues and Vices, and both are mostly portrayed as feminine.[22] For example, Prudentius' Queen of the Virtues, Faith, is shown as a female in rough, disordered dress in deadly combat with Worship-of-the-Old-Gods, also a feminine figure:

> Lo, first Worship-of-the-Old-Gods ventures to match *her* strength against Faith's challenge and strike at her. But she [Faith], rising higher, smites her foe's head down, with its fillet-decked brows, lays in the dust that mouth that was sated with the blood of beasts, and tramples the eyes under foot, squeezing them out in death.[23]

Hildegard, who does not, to be sure, illustrate the battling against the Vices that is present in Prudentius and in the visual arts described by Adolf Katzenellenbogen,[24] depicts almost all of the drama's characters as female. Indeed, except for the figures of the Patriarchs and Prophets at the beginning of the play, the only significant male role is that of the Devil, who in the original production could have been played by a priest or monk.[25]

---

[22] *Prudentius*, ed. and trans. H. J. Thomson, Loeb Classical Library (Cambridge: Harvard University Press, 1949), 274–343; see also Adolf Katzenellenbogen, *Allegories of the Virtues and Vices in Mediaeval Art*, trans. Alan J. P. Crick (1939; reprint, New York: Norton, 1964), 1–13, 42–44, and passim.

[23] *Prudentius*, trans. Thomson, 281 (italics mine).

[24] Katzenellenbogen, *Allegories of the Virtues and Vices*, passim.

[25] For the playing of male roles Hildegard could have drawn on one of her several male amanuenses, including Guibert of Gembloux, who promulgated the notion that Hildegard was the tenth child in her family and thus the one to be given to the Church as a tithe (see Sabina Flanagan, *Hildegard of Bingen, 1098–1179: A Visionary Life* [London: Routledge, 1989], 23); Volmar, first her teacher and later her secretary, pictured with Hildegard in what is undoubtedly the best known of the miniatures from *Scivias*; and Wezelin, her nephew, who, in the decade following Hildegard's death,

Hildegard's drama also differs from Prudentius' undramatized narrative in that her work establishes the struggle of the Virtues and the Devil for one single Soul who represents all souls—an Everysoul as in the medieval drama *Everyman*—and who is shown in both happy and unhappy modes.[26] This particular but universal Soul is thus the center of a conflict between the Devil and the Virtues. What the music must therefore express is the struggle against the wiles of the Devil, whose aim is the permanent seduction of the Soul, who wavers, goes astray, and returns penitently. Hildegard's musical setting must also help to individualize and personalize the Virtues, especially Humilitas or Humility, the Queen of the Virtues. In contrast, the Devil (*OV* 17/48–49, 19/59–62, 29/84–85, 72/209–11, and 83/235–37) has no music but makes his characterization clear through growls, howls, and other disgusting noises.[27] The Patriarchs and Prophets, who at the very begin-

---

oversaw the copying of the Wiesbaden manuscript, which includes the *Symphonia* and the *Ordo Virtutum*.

[26] In his 1972 translation of the *Ordo Virtutum*, Bruce Hozeski suggested that there are two Souls, one happy and one sad ("'Ordo Virtutum': Hildegard of Bingen's Liturgical Morality Play," *Annuale Mediaevale* 13 [1972]: 45–69). Instead, the Soul should be seen as one, and she simply is shown in different guises: as happy, sad, penitent, and being healed by the medicine that the Virtues offer and through the blood of the Son of God. The Virtues then are able to receive the Soul back into their fellowship (*OV* 65–71). The welcoming-helping scene can be interpreted as the feminist ideal of the way women ought to assist other women, but I prefer to leave ideology aside and to remain with a purely musicological-dramatic analysis in the present study. On the point of the single vs. double Soul, see Peter Dronke, "Problemata Hildegardiana," *Mittellateinisches Jahrbuch* 16 (1981): 102–03.

[27] Reinhold Hammerstein, *Diabolus in Musica* (Bern: Francke Verlag, 1974), 17 and passim. According to Hammerstein, devils "are either silent or they can shriek, scrape, hiss, and, if need be, speak, but they can never sing" (17; translation mine); he thus notes the appropriateness of the non-singing Devil in the *Ordo Virtutum*. Cf. Bronarski, *Die Lieder der hl. Hildegard*, who thinks that the absence of music for the Devil is due to Hildegard's inability to find suitable music (46). A somewhat more

ning of the play have rather small roles (but who may also be brought back at the end of the drama to add strength to the final procession, *In principio* ["In the beginning," *OV* 87/252–69]), need far less care in musical differentiation.

The shape of the drama may be described in rough outline as follows:

1. An introduction (*OV* 1–3) in which the Virtues are introduced to the Patriarchs and Prophets. (This section is identified as *Vorspiel* in Böckeler's edition.)

2. The complaints of the Souls Imprisoned in Bodies are heard; they contrast with the joyful sounds of the Soul. Though at first happy (*Felix Anima*), she shortly will fall into discouragement and will be seduced through the influence of the Devil (*OV* 4–21).

3. A section (*OV* 22–57) in which the Virtues define themselves. The Devil remains present to espouse views diametrically opposed to those of the Virtues. (Peter Dronke suggests that this portion of the play includes a dance by the Virtues.[28])

4. A section (*OV* 58–71) in which the Soul returns, weakened and stained by her experience, and repents.

5. A penultimate section (*OV* 72–86) in which the Devil is bound and God the Father is praised.

6. The closing, a strange and mystical passage (*OV* 87) which contains the voice of Christ speaking to God the Father and describing his wounds from the Crucifixion.

---

complicated picture emerges in the later vernacular drama; see Richard Rastall, "The Sounds of Hell," in *The Iconography of Hell*, ed. Clifford Davidson and Thomas Seiler, Early Drama, Art, and Music, Monograph Series 17 (Kalamazoo: Medieval Institute Publications, 1992), 102–31.

[28] Dronke, *Poetic Individuality*, 174.

This section has all the marks of a procession, which would provide an appropriate conclusion to the play.

The drama begins, then, with the male voices of the Patriarchs and Prophets, who actually have very little to sing. Their question—"Qui sunt hi, qui ut nubes?" ("Who are these, who come like clouds?" *OV* 1/1)—will be answered by the Virtues, who say that they are those who "shine with him" ("et ideo fulgemus cum illo," *OV* 2/4). There are seventeen female personifications of abstract qualities; counting these and the Soul, there are eighteen female roles in all—very nearly the number of nuns (twenty) brought by Hildegard from Disibodenberg to her new convent at Rupertsberg.[29] The function of the Virtues is to serve as the handmaidens of God whose glory they share and to introduce the light imagery which Dronke has noted as connecting them to divinity.[30] The Patriarchs and Prophets sing in the Dorian mode, utilizing the fourth below the *finalis*, while the Virtues, using the same mode, emphasize the five notes above the final along with the upper fourth leading to the octave, a setting which places the combined melodies into an expanded form of the Dorian mode in the manner of certain early medieval sequences (see, for example, *Victimae paschali* in the *Liber usualis*, p. 780) which defy encapsulation within the so-called normal limits of the mode. When the Patriarchs and Prophets reply to the Virtues, they once again underline the latter's importance and the interrelatedness of Virtues and Patriarchs and Prophets: "Nos sumus radices et vos rami,/ fructus viventis oculi" ("We are the roots and you the branches, the fruit of the living bud [or eye]," *OV* 3/6–7).

The Virtues assert their cosmic importance and their spiritual roles: though they are personifications of abstractions, they are also attributes inhering in God and Christ, whom they serve. Yet their own strength and independence are shown in their melody at *OV* 2/2–5, since they are unwilling to sink to the lower extremity of the Dorian mode except for briefly touching on the low *a* near the end of the rejoinder. The Patriarchs and Prophets' reply to the Virtues in which they make reference to the imagery of root and branch

---

[29] Dronke, *Women Writers of the Middle Ages*, 153.

[30] Ibid., 171.

("Nos sumus radices et vos rami," *OV* 3/6) will then be in the Phrygian mode, wandering between the lower parts of the mode and the upper—a pattern which is characteristic of Hildegard's compositions.

Certain motifs are repeated in this introductory section: the melismatic motif d'–c'–d' c'–a c'–d' e'– f''–d' at the very first word "Qui" (sung by the Patriarchs and Prophets) is echoed by the Virtues at "antiqui" and the syllables "-poris" from the word "corporis" (*OV* 2/5). Twice in their short passage the Virtues present the Hildegardian thumbprint of the rising fifth, in which they alight on the fifth note of the scale and thus, rising by the interval of a fourth to the octave, create a motivic coherence right from the start.

The second section opens with the introduction of a group of souls imprisoned within their bodies and complaining. The musical characterization of these complaining Souls Imprisoned in Bodies is done with consummate skill, for they are delineated by a melody which stays close to the e' final but which moves stepwise up and down, back and forth meanderingly to show their wavering and querulous nature. They insist that they ought to be daughters of the King, but now have fallen into the shadow of sin ("sed in umbram peccatorum cecidimus," *OV* 4/12). The presentation of the Complaining Souls probably means that at least three more voices (the minimum needed to make a blend for the passage) would have been required at the original presentation. Since the total number of twenty nuns brought to Rupertsberg would be nearly exhausted by the number of singers needed for portraying the Virtues and the Soul, extra voices would very likely have been needed for these roles.

In contrast to the complaints of these unhappy souls is the happy singing of the rejoicing Soul, the protagonist of the drama, who at first praises God: "O dulcis Divinitas, et O suavis vita . . . ad te suspiro, et omnes Virtutes invoco" ("O sweet Divinity, O delightful life . . . to you I sigh, and invoke all Virtues," *OV* 5/16). Her joyful, positive statements, set in the Dorian mode, are embodied in motifs using the rising fifth at "O dulcis" and the characteristically Hildegardian hallmark of the ascending fifth, followed by the fourth rising to the octave at "O suavis. . . ." When the Soul's mood begins to change and she complains about "gravis labor" ("hard labor") and "durum pondus" ("heavy weight") that she carries "in veste huius vite" ("in the garment of this life," *OV*

9/26–27), her singing remains in a low tessitura, near the *finalis*, to reflect the downward pressure of her mortal flesh which she is forced to endure. The melody introduces the interval of an ascending fourth at "O gravis labor" ("O what hard labor"), at "habeo" from "quod habeo in veste huius vite" ("[O what a heavy weight] that I carry in the garment of this life"), and finally at "-a" of "quia nimis grave michi est contra carnem pugnare" ("because it is so hard for me to fight against my body"). However, when the Troubled Soul actually arrives at the last segment of that phrase, those few rising intervals are not merely balanced but are also quite negated by the meandering pattern which travels both downward and upward but mainly stays in a low tessitura, indicating just how indecisive and confused the Soul really is. The Soul's present emotional state as depicted in the musical setting for her words contrasts sharply with the musical settings representing the Soul as *Felix Anima*, when the ascending fifth and the interval of the rising fourth or fifth placed above and adjacent to the first fifth dominated the musical material. Now, as the Soul asks to be helped to stand (*OV* 11/33), she sings a beautifully undulating line made up of two groups of five notes rising stepwise (e'–e'–f' quilisma–g'–a', and g'–a'–a' quilisma–b'–c") and a third group of four notes descending stepwise (a'–g'– f'–e'). Knowledge of God (*OV* 12/35) urges the Soul to stand firm—"esto stabilis et numquam cades" ("Be firm and you will never fall"). In performance, it should be made obvious that the early efforts of Knowledge of God and the other Virtues are to be of little avail. The Soul's ambivalence is seen: on the one hand, she wants to be helped to resist the Devil, but on the other hand she wants to know the delights of the world (*OV* 16/45–47) and, by extension, the pleasures of the flesh and of the Devil.

After the Soul has expressed her wish to enjoy the world, the Devil speaks in a loud and rude voice. He does not sing his words of advice (as already noted, the Devil has no music): "Fatue! fatue! quid prodest tibi laborare?/ Respice mundum, et amplectetur te magno honore" ("Foolish! foolish! what do you gain by exerting yourself in vain?/ Turn your attention to the world, and it will embrace you with great honor," *OV* 17/48–49). It is entirely appropriate that the Devil should not be provided with music since this unharmonious and discordant principle of evil should never be represented by harmonious concords. Here the Neoplatonism pointed out in the play by Richard Axton is especially apparent, since the order associated with heaven and the heavenly spheres would be regarded in terms of harmonious tuning, while in contrast hell's sounds are typically dissonant, discordant, and disgusting noises—growling, howling, and other sounds of wild animals.[31]

The Soul's fall from grace into sin and degradation is not here made explicit in the text; yet it does indeed take place, for the remainder of the action of the play hangs on this fact. In the foreground at this time instead is the conflict between the Virtues and the Devil, the latter offering to give all things to whoever will follow him. Later, the Devil charges (*OV* 19/59–62) that the Virtues do not know themselves, the implication being that sexual knowledge, which the Virtues lack, is required for self-knowledge. His argument, however, is irrelevant, as Humility implies when she refutes the adversary's claims with the statement that they *do* know with whom they are speaking—"ille antiquus draco" ("that old dragon") whom God threw into the abyss. Their music therefore serves to separate the Virtues, whose dwelling is on high, from the non-musical—and therefore unconvincing—representative and source of depravity who, as Lucifer, fell from the heights of heaven.

The next section (*OV* 22–57), in which the Virtues introduce themselves and explain their characteristics, is marked by movement and activity. It includes the segment that Dronke identifies as a "dance."[32] The text defines some of the movements: movement toward, as in Humility's "Venite ad me, Virtutes" ("Come to me, Virtues," *OV* 22/69); movement away, as in Innocence's "Fugite, oves, spurcicias diaboli!" ("Flee, you sheep, from the filth of the Devil!" *OV* 39/112); the activity of trampling the world under foot in the statement by the Virtues to Contempt of the World: "O

---

[31] Axton, *European Drama of the Early Middle Ages*, 96. Two illustrations in Hildegard's *Scivias* show the sounding of the heavenly harmony; see Führkötter, *The Miniatures*, pls. 9, 35. See also John Hollander, *The Untuning of the Sky* (Princeton: Princeton University Press, 1961), passim, for a study which demonstrates how such ideas extended to the seventeenth century.

[32] Dronke, *Poetic Individuality*, 174–75; see also Axton, *European Drama of the Early Middle Ages*, 96–97.

magna virtus, que mundum conculcas" ("O great Virtue, you tread the world under your foot," *OV* 42/120); and of similar treatment for the old serpent by Victory: "serpentem antiquum conculco" ("I tread the old serpent under my foot," *OV* 51/143); and movement which encircles and embraces, described by one of the Virtues (probably Discipline, though the name has been scratched out in R):[33] "sed semper in regem regum aspicio, et amplector eum in honore altissimo" ("but I always look upon the King of Kings, and I embrace him in the highest honor," *OV* 45/127–29).

The music for this section includes some of the richest and most melismatic of the entire play, as is befitting the exposition and development of the characterization of the Virtues. When Humility announces herself—"Ego Humilitas, regina Virtutum" ("I, Humility, queen of the Virtues," *OV* 22/68)—the syllable "E-" of the word "Ego" is given a melismatic setting of six notes (d'–e'–f'–e'–d'–c'), with the remaining syllables of the verbal phrase set relatively syllabically, as if to compensate for the richness and possible immodesty of naming one's self. Humility calls the other Virtues to their coronation in a melodic line which proceeds for the most part syllabically but which elaborates in another display of richness on the syllable "-nan-" (f'–g'–f') of the word "coronandum" ("[to] crown"). When Humility speaks of the "royal bedchamber" in which the daughters (i.e., the Virtues) are kept, the melodic line again blossoms into richly ornamented phrases, "filie" being set to ten notes and "regalia" to eleven (*OV* 24/74–75).[34]

But in this section the song *Flos campi* ("The flower of the

---

[33] "Disciplina" is silently inserted in the edition of Böckeler and Barth (*Reigen der Tugenden*, 118); this figure seems to be the most likely of the Virtues to sing at this point in the play. In the copy of the *Ordo Virtutum* in British Library Add. MS. 15,102 the speaker is identified as "Caritas"; Dronke rightly notes that "she, like Castitas [Pitra's emendation], has already declared herself" (*Poetic Individuality*, p. 186n).

[34] Richness and ornamentation in music should not surprise us since we know that in dress Hildegard's nuns were not at all restrained by their holy order; they were accused of wearing ostentatious finery, including crowns and tiaras. See the comments of Potter, Pamela Sheingorn, and Julia Bolton Holloway, in A. E. Davidson, ed., *The* Ordo Virtutum *of Hildegard of Bingen: Critical Studies*, 34–35, 55–56, 67.

field," *OV* 38/109–11)³⁵ is the one for which Hildegard has reserved her most lavish and florid setting. Clyde Brockett believes that this song appears to be entirely in the transposed Dorian mode "in the manner of certain graduals, most notably *Haec dies*, where b♮ and b♭ seem to be virtually interchangeable."³⁶ This piece, resonant with echoes of the *Song of Songs*, compares virginity to "a sweet flower of the field which will never dry up" ("suavis flos qui numquam aresces"). No word or phrase is untouched by melismas. Since *Flos campi* comes almost at the center of the *Ordo Virtutum* (as thirty-eighth in a series of eighty-seven items), the piece not surprisingly stands as a high point of the drama. With its rich musical ornamentation like embroidery or interlace ornamentation and its vivid floral imagery, *Flos campi* is placed within the structure of the drama like the capstone of an arch.

In this scene the trampling images, as in the Virtues' "que mundum conculcas" ("you tread the world under your feet," *OV* 42/120) and Modesty's "atque conculco omnes spurcicias diaboli" ("and tread under my feet all the dirt of the Devil," *OV* 47/132–33), are set to notes proceeding in a determined manner, soberly and syllabically in stepwise fashion. When one of the Virtues, probably Discipline,³⁷ refers to embracing "the king of kings in highest honor" (*OV* 45/128–29), the setting for the word "amplector" ("I embrace"), descending to c', does not seem to embody any attempt at word painting, but the setting for "in honore altissimo" begins by soaring to the octave (g'–a'–c"), then descends through the entire octave (c"–b'–a'), hesitating (a'–g'), returning to a', then descending again and finally resolving from below by means of a whole tone: g'–f'–e' d'–c'–d' e' (see Example 3).

Example 3

⁳⁵ Bronarski insists upon calling this piece an "aria" (*Die Lieder der hl. Hildegard*, 44).

³⁶ Unpublished remarks (personal correspondence).

³⁷ See n. 32, above.

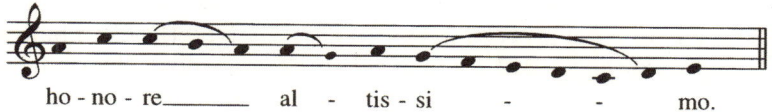
ho - no - re___ al - tis - si - - mo.

The scene closes with a triumphantly joyful song sung by Humility, in which the Hildegardian thumbprint appears in the setting for "O filie Israhel, sub arbore suscitavit vos Deus; unde in hoc tempore recordamini plantationis sue./ Gaudete ergo, filie Sion!" ("O daughters of Israel, God lifted you up from under the tree; whence you at this time remember your own planting./ Rejoice therefore, daughters of Zion!" *OV* 57/156–58). Although the words are set in a rather low tessitura, there is no mistaking that this is an exuberant, intense, melismatic melody with a triumphant final cadence.

When the Soul returns from her wandering into sin in the fourth section (*OV* 58–71), she is repentant. Her melody wanders up and down in the Phrygian mode, and, coupled with the lamenting words, is affectingly sorrowful. There must be no mistaking the repentance in her manner (and this is the task of the actress-singer and the director to make sure that the proper attitude of penitence is established[38]). The Virtues, who mourned her departure and subsequent fall, are still mourning her ("Heu! Heu!" at *OV* 58/159) at the beginning of this "scene." However, she now evinces true repentance (*OV* 59/165): "O ve michi, quia a vobis fugi" ("O woe is me, because from you I fled"). There is an about-face in their attitude of mourning, and they are now willing to accept her back into their fellowship. However, they still want her to make the movement towards them, and they first advise her, saying, "O fugitive, veni, veni ad nos" ("O fugitive, come, come to us") and if she does that, God will raise her up ("et Deus suscipiet te," *OV*

---

[38] In the Society for Old Music production in 1984, I depended on the dramatic director for all blocking, movement, gestures, and acting decisions. While this production was intentionally stylized, influenced strongly by the liturgy in which Hildegard was steeped, the singer-actresses at times very much identified themselves with the parts they were portraying. Some effects occurred naturally and without planning; for example, more than one member of the audience commented on the tears in the eyes of the singer-actress who played the Soul.

60/165). But the Soul still feels guilty because of her past sins and fears to enter the circle of the Virtues (*OV* 61/166–67). This is one of the two instances (see also *OV* 18/51) in which the play slips into the vernacular. The Soul, rather than saying "Heu! Heu!" says, "Ach! Ach! Fervens dulcedo absorbuit me in peccatis et ideo non ausa sua intrare" ("Alas! Alas! A fiery sweetness absorbed me in my sins, and therefore I dared not enter").[39] The Virtues, continuing to encourage her, use the words "Noli timere" ("Fear not, *OV* 62/168) that echo the synoptic Gospel accounts of Christ's Resurrection.[40] At *OV* 63/170–72, the Soul pleads with the Virtues to lift her up because her wounds have weakened her; the activity suggested in her plea—"suscipiatis"—is represented by a melismatic phrase beginning with the familiar and once again appropriate rising fifth. However, the Virtues, instead of going to help the Soul immediately, advise her to run to them ("Curre ad nos," *OV* 64/173), perhaps at this point following the good therapist's rule of having the patient do as much for himself or herself as possible.

In spite of the encouraging words of the Virtues, the Soul is still too weak to stand alone, as she relates her tale of woe to the Virtues (*OV* 65/176–82). Continuing to delay, they tell the Soul to "clothe yourself in the armor of light" ("indue te arma lucis," *OV* 66/184). The Soul pleads once again (*OV* 67/185–88), and in this instance she speaks directly to Humility, queen of the Virtues. Humility thereupon addresses the Virtues to ask them to lift or to

---

[39] In *OV* 18 it is the Virtues rather than the Soul who use the German "Ach! Ach!"

[40] The Virtues' words, "Noli timere" ("Fear not," *OV* 62/168), resonate with tones from the Resurrection accounts in the synoptic Gospels. In *Matthew* 28:5, the angel (in this case a single angel) says to the two women, Mary Magdalene and "the other Mary": "nolite timere vos" ("Fear not you"); and again, in *Matthew* 28:10, the women meet Jesus, who says to them, "Nolite timere" ("Fear not"). At *Mark* 16:5–6, "a young man . . . clothed with a white robe," presumably an angel, says to Mary Magdalene, Mary the mother of James, and Salome, "nolite expavescere" ("Be not affrighted"). *Luke* 24:4–10 identifies "two men" (presumably angels) and three women (in this instance Mary Magdalene, Joanna, and Mary [the mother of] James), but there are no words explicitly telling the women not to be afraid.

receive the formerly wayward Soul: "O omnes Virtutes, suscipite lugentem peccatorem" ("O all you Virtues, receive the mourning sinner," *OV* 68/189). Since a request from Humility has the weight of a command, the Virtues agree to lead the Soul back to blessedness: "Volumus te reducere" ("We are willing to lead you back"). Humility then says, "O misera filia, volo te amplecti, quia magnus medicus dura et amara vulnera propter te passus est" ("O miserable daughter, I wish to embrace you, because the great physician [Christ] has suffered painful and bitter wounds on account of you," *OV* 70/195–97). Significantly, all is done in the name of the Great Physician, but the female hands of the Virtues are required to carry out the principles of Christ.

The musical settings for each of these passages are as follows: when the Virtues lament over the temptation of the Soul (*OV* 58/159), their words—"Heu! Heu!" ("Alas! Alas!")—are set to a familiar pattern (e'–f'–e' d'–c' d'–e' e'), now taking on the characteristics of a wail. The Soul's rejoinder to the Virtues (*OV* 59/161) is in the form of an invocation; the rubric, one of very few such, describes "Querela animam penitentis et uirtutes inuocantis" ("The Soul, lamenting and penitent, invoking the Virtues," *OV* 59/161 *s.d.*). Her invocation demands that she sing in an extremely wide range (d' to g") and that her voice remain in a high tessitura for much of that passage; perhaps she is representing a strongly emotional reaction produced by her guilt over what she has done and her fear that she will not be accepted—feelings which battle with her hope that she will be forgiven.

In contrast, the first tentative invitation of the Virtues to the now penitent Soul is set to a meandering pattern of e'–e'–f' quilisma–g'–f'–d' at the syllables "O fu-gi-" of "O fugitive" (*OV* 60/165), while the phrases denoting "running" and "lifting" begin with rising fifths—for example, with d'–a' at "Curre" ("run," *OV* 64/173). Again, the rising fifth is used at Humility's "O omnes Virtutes, suscipite lugentem peccatorem in suis cicatricibus propter vulnera Christi" ("O all you Virtues, receive the mourning sinner with her scars for the sake of the wounds of Christ," *OV* 68/189). In an alternative musical manner, the idea of "leading" is represented by a rising fourth from a' to d" outlining the high range of the authentic form of the Dorian mode at "Volumus te reducere" ("We are willing to lead you back," *OV* 69/192). Once the Soul is on the way to rehabilitation, the Virtues sing a *paean* of joy in the

Phrygian mode: "O vivens fons, quam magna est suavitas tua" ("O living fountain [i.e., Christ as Savior and fountain of life], how great is your sweetness," *OV* 71/198). The rising fifth joined to the upper fourth outlining the octave (as noted before, one of Hildegard's trademarks) appears in the fourth section several times: twice at *OV* 62/168–69, when the Virtues tell the Soul not to be afraid; twice at *OV* 64/173–75, when the Virtues advise the Soul to run to them; and seven times at *OV* 71/188–208: "O vivens fons" ("O living fountain").

In the penultimate section (*OV* 72–86), the Devil, trying to recapture the Soul, insists that he does not understand the Soul's turning against him: "Sed nunc in reversione tua confundis me" ("But now in your turning back you confuse me") and threatens to harm her bodily: "Ego autem pugna mea deiciam te!" ("But I will hurl you down with my assault," *OV* 72/210–11). As usual these words are emitted (not sung) as a growl, a howl, or a shrieking shout. The penitent Soul then resists bravely with the words "o illusor, pugno contra te" ("O deceiver, I fight against you," *OV* 73/213)—words set syllabically to underline the new determination of the Soul. Humility will now address Victory directly regarding the action that is to come: "O Victoria, que istum in celo superasti, curre cum militibus tuis, et omnes ligate diabolum hunc" ("O Victory, who conquered that one [the Devil] in heaven, hasten with your knights, and all of you bind that Devil," *OV* 75/215–17). Although rubrics providing stage directions are lacking here, these words are clearly indicative of the action that Hildegard had in mind. But there is something a trifle odd about this particular directive: the Virtues are referred to as "knights" (in the phrase "cum militibus tuis"); then, at *OV* 76/218–19, Victory also addresses the Virtues as "milites" ("knights") as she enlists their aid in binding the Devil. The Virtues reply to Victory that they will join the battle against the Devil, but in their affirmation they address Victory as "O dulcissima bellatrix" ("O fairest warrior," feminine gender, *OV* 77/220).[41]

---

[41] On the question of Hildegard's ambivalence toward the female gender, see Barbara Newman, *Sister of Wisdom: St. Hildegard's Theology of the Feminine* (Berkeley: University of California Press, 1987), 1–41, esp. 2, 37.

Hildegard of Bingen's Ordo Virtutum

Fig. 1. The Devil chained. Detail from an illumination in a lost manuscript of Hildegard of Bingen's *Scivias* (Wiesbaden, Hessische Landesbibliothek, Cod. 1). Drawing by Marianne Cappelletti Lutes.

The music for this scene is marked by the rising fifth–added upper fourth "thumbprint" at Humility's "O Victoria" (*OV* 75/215) and by the rising fifth at the first word, "O" of the phrase "O fortissimi et gloriosissimi milites, venite, et adiuvate me istum fallacem vincere," Victory's address to the Virtues to invite them to the battle ("O you most brave and most glorious knights, come and help me to conquer that deceitful one," *OV* 76/218–19). The last word, "vincere," of the latter phrase is given a final-sounding Dorian cadence, the c' resolving to the d' a whole step above it; this musical setting shows Victory's resoluteness in her effort to vanquish the Devil. With the words "nos libenter militamus tecum contra illusorem hunc" ("we willingly fight with you against that deceiver," *OV* 77/222–23) the Virtues demonstrate their singleness of purpose in the fight against the Evil One. That phrase of affirmation ends with a d'–e' Phrygian cadence, again showing resolve. The rising fifth appears again at the beginning of Humility's speech when she orders the "shining Virtues" to bind the Devil ("Ligate ergo istum, o virtutes preclare!" *OV* 78/224). And at the end of Humility's speech is found an f'–e'–d'–c'–d' cadence, an ornamented yet strong cadence ending a stirring speech which not only gives the Virtues license to bind the Devil but actually compels them to do so. The next item (*OV* 79/225–26), in which the Virtues affirm their obedience, also ends with the strong f'–e'– d'–c'–d' cadence. At the binding of the Devil (see fig. 1),[42] Victory's song of rejoicing (*OV* 80/227) rings out freely in a high tessitura; sung at the written pitch as adjusted for female voices, this is one of the most glorious moments in all of medieval music-drama. The mood here is that of unrestrained joy, high and "lifted up" in ecstatic exultation. In this passage of praise and thanksgiving for the final defeat of the Devil, the words and the notes setting the words are transcribed in Example 4. This entire passage outlines the G mode (VII) transposed up a fourth. The manuscript adds one b♭, and I have added editorially a b♭ to the b nearest it since it is in the same system.

Example 4

Gau - de - te, o___ so - ci - i,

qui - a___ an-ti - quus ser- pens li - ga - tus___ est.___

In the remainder of the scene the level of tension is clearly reduced after that climactic point of Victory's joyful shout. There is, however, one more ugly outburst from the bound Devil, who has been rendered ineffectual by reason of his chains. His outburst repeats his earlier diatribe against the chaste Virtues because of

---

[42] For a color reproduction, see Führkötter, *The Miniatures from the Book of Scivias*, pl. 17.

their empty wombs:

> Tu nescis quid colis,
> quia venter tuus vacuus est pulcra forma de viro sumpta,
> ubi transis preceptum quod Deus in suavi copula precepit:
> unde nescis quid sis. (*OV* 83/235–37)

> You know not what you bring forth,
> because your womb is empty of any fair form taken from man,
> wherein you transgress the command of pleasant intercourse
> which God commanded;
> wherefore you know not what you are.

Again, as noted above, the Devil cannot sing, and so one proof of the Virtues' worth comes in their ability to sing and to plead the correctness of their chastity through music. Celibacy was, of course, regarded from the earliest period of Christianity to be superior to marriage,[43] and the chaste life was a monastic ideal which Hildegard and her nuns intended unquestioningly to affirm in the *Ordo Virtutum*.

The final section of the play is a single item (*In principio*, *OV* 87/252–69), which appears to be processional in nature. The text, which almost defies explanation, begins with an invocation of the beginning of time when "all creatures grew and flourished." The musical setting uses melismata extensively with the object of providing an appropriate and even impressive setting for the mystical words closing the play. The concluding words of the drama, especially the final word, "porrigat" ("to reach out," or "to stretch out"), are set to music which may be described as early word-painting. Hildegard attempts to provide melodic form which reflects words that describe the reaching out of Christ to his people in love—words that simultaneously remind us of his being stretched out on the cross, fatigued, as he says, "Nam me fatigat, quod omnia membra mea in irrisionem vadunt" ("Now it wearies me, so that all my members become a mockery"), and with all of his wounds exposed: "Pater, vide, vulnera mea tibi ostendo"

---

[43] See "Matrimony," *The Oxford Dictionary of the Christian Church*, 2nd ed., ed. F. L. Cross and E. A. Livingstone (Oxford: Oxford University Press, 1974), 889.

("Father, see, I show my wounds to you").

When we turn from the music to the question of the staging of the *Ordo Virtutum*, we are able to appreciate even more fully the visionary power of Hildegard. The key to her concepts of staging and costuming would seem to be found in her own work—to be specific, in her *Scivias*.[44] In this book she describes her visions of the City of God and those arrayed on the side of the deity, including the Virtues. In the miniatures which illustrate the *Scivias* (drawn from descriptions therein and produced contemporaneously with the book), each of the Virtues is depicted with her own special garment and/or attributes—e.g., Fear of God has a garment made all of eyes, Discipline has a purple garment which protects her from sinful lusts, Victory is armed, and Humility wears a golden crown.[45] Humility also wears a mirror on her breast in which Christ's image is reflected.[46] From the standpoint of staging it may be asserted that there should be no reason for rejecting Hildegard's own conceptions concerning the appearance of the Virtues and their costumes. In modern productions of the *Ordo* it would seem utterly perverse to set aside these ideas in favor of, for example, garbing the Virtues in American Civil War uniforms, although recently there have been such trendily perverse productions of early drama and of operas based on classical tales.

For other aspects of staging we again look to Hildegard herself, who was not without definite ideas about the appearance of her mystical landscape. Here the leap from the *Scivias* is not a large one, as the subject matter of this work will show. In her introductory vision in the *Scivias*, she shows a hill on which God is enthroned, with one of the Virtues, Timor Dei (Fear of God), standing at the bottom. Later, Hildegard sees the structure of God's domain also as a city, with walls corresponding to the various epochs in history since the Creation and towers which represent spiritual entities and within which some of the Virtues are residing.

---

[44] See n. 11, above.

[45] Katzenellenbogen, *Allegories of the Virtues and Vices*, 43; Führkötter, *The Miniatures from the Book Scivias*, pls. 2, 27, 29, 31, and passim

[46] Noted by Katzenellenbogen, *Allegories of the Virtues and Vices*, 44.

Thus the director of the play would seem to have a choice with regard to the basic set, which might be a simple "mound" or raised area with Humility seated on it, or a more elaborate construction resembling walls and towers. A third possibility emerges from another vision which involves a ladder descending from God's abode, by means of which the Virtues are able to come down to the earthly level or to re-ascend.[47] Indeed, the whole drama could be staged at the bottom of the spiritual ladder, with the Soul approaching the ladder when she is in her happy condition and fleeing from the area of the ladder when she is in the unhappy condition of going astray. Such a view is, however, admittedly speculative, and in our Society for Old Music production a more simple approach to staging was adopted because of budgetary restrictions and careful consideration of the architectural setting that served as *locus* for the play.[48]

Mention has been made above of some of the actions suggested by the text of the drama which include the Soul's leaving the scene to signify her downfall, the motions signifying the trampling down of the world in the so-called dance of the Virtues along with some circling, embracing motions also in that section, and the capturing and binding of Satan. Otherwise it seems to me that a rather classical and static staging would be entirely appropriate, utilizing the calm, stately motions of liturgical practice.

Even these brief and sketchy suggestions, indicating a close relationship between the visions of the *Scivias* and the staging of the *Ordo*, will reveal the depth of Hildegard's imagination—an imagination that crafted music, poetry, drama, and word-pictures into a coherent vision of the condition of humankind. Her musical settings, carefully reflecting the characterizations of her *dramatis*

---

[47] Führkötter, *The Miniatures from the Book Scivias*, pl. 29. See also Katzenellenbogen, *Allegories of the Virtues and Vices*, who shows a twelfth-century drawing from Herrad of Landsberg's *Hortus Deliciarum* which illustrates the Ladder of Virtue (fig. 25). For further commentary, see Gérard Cames, *Allegories et symboles dans l'Hortus Deliciarum* (Leiden: E. J. Brill, 1971), 88–90.

[48] See Clifford Davidson, "The *Ordo Virtutum*: A Note on Production," in A. E. Davidson, ed., *The* Ordo Virtutum *of Hildegard of Bingen: Critical Studies*, 111–22.

personae as well as the dramatic situation of the play, were a very important part of this artistically integrated vision. In short, we find in the *Ordo Virtutum* a work that is strong in every sense—visually, musically, theatrically—and hence it is a work worthy of further scholarly scrutiny and especially of being realized in performance before modern audiences.

The Cividale *Planctus Mariae* for Modern Performance

Both the text and music of the *Planctus Mariae* from Cividale in Northern Italy have been previously edited by scholars, both in the nineteenth century and the twentieth. However, it is my belief that a new non-metrical transcription may better capture the liturgical context of the play. The present study accompanies my work toward such a transcription, and has as its purpose the reopening of various aspects of the play as well as noting problems which appear in the manuscript.

I

The Liturgical Context. Karl Young raised the question of why there are no dramatic Passions earlier than the thirteenth century and why even following that date they were exceedingly rare.[1] (Young, however, did not know about the existence of the Montecassino Passion Play[2] of the twelfth century, for which the text but not the music survives.) In supporting his argument regarding the rarity of the Passion drama genre, Young stated that "in comparison with the multitude of medieval Church plays treating events relating to the Resurrection, the number of dramatic

---

[1] Karl Young, *The Drama of the Medieval Church*, 2 vols. (Oxford: Clarendon Press, 1933), 1:492.

[2] See Sandro Sticca, *The Latin Passion Play* (Albany: State University of New York Press, 1970), and "The Literary Genesis of the Latin Passion Play and the *Planctus Mariae*: A New Christocentric and Marian Theology," in *The Medieval Drama*, ed. Sandro Sticca (Albany: State University of New York Press, 1972), 39–68; Robert Edwards, *The Montecassino Passion and the Poetics of Medieval Drama* (Berkeley: University of California Press, 1977).

representations of the Crucifixion is astonishingly small." He indicates that it may be surmised "that for bringing vividly before the medieval worshipper the great Immolation, the Mass itself was felt to be sufficiently effective."[3] Yet Young admitted that there are several ceremonies connected with the Mass on Good Friday which need only "a mere touch of impersonation" to make them into actual Passion plays.[4] These ceremonies include, among others, the chanting of the Gospel lesson in the proper location in the Mass which will be discussed elsewhere in the present book.

The other ceremonies connected with the Good Friday Mass of the Pre-sanctified, each of which can also properly be termed quasi-dramatic, include in order: (1) the Veneration of the Cross accompanied by the chanting of the *Improperia*; and (2) the *Depositio*, the Burial of the Cross. The *Depositio* was sometimes performed within the structure of the Mass of the Pre-sanctified, sometimes along with the Veneration, or following the Mass and preceding Vespers.[5] The *Improperia*, which consisted of twelve reproaches as spoken by Christ on the cross to his people, were removed from the ceremony by Vatican II because of the anti-Semitic content.[6] The *Depositio*, on the other hand, involved "a solemn procession, followed by the placing of a cross in a *sepulchre* to commemorate the death and burial of Christ. Sometimes instead of a cross, a consecrated Host or an image of Christ was used, or sometimes both a cross and a Host."[7]

An interesting account of the ceremony from the monastic

---

[3] Young, *The Drama of the Medieval Church*, 1:492.

[4] Ibid.

[5] Ibid., 1:113, 129–30.

[6] See Ruth Steiner, "Reproaches," *The New Grove Dictionary of Music and Musicians*, ed. Stanley Sadie, 20 vols. (London: Macmillan, 1980), 15:750–51.

[7] Richard B. Donovan, *Liturgical Drama in Medieval Spain* (Toronto: Pontifical Institute of Mediaeval Studies, 1958), 8. [See also Audrey Ekdahl Davidson, *Holy Week and Easter Ceremonies and Dramas from Medieval Sweden* (Kalamazoo: Medieval Institute Publications, 1990), passim.]

The Cividale Planctus Mariae for Modern Performance

cathedral church at Durham describes the manner in which the Veneration of the Cross and the *Depositio* were performed following the singing of the St. John Passion:

> Two of the eldest Monkes did take a goodly large CRUCIFIX, all of gold, of the picture of our Saviour Christ nailed uppon the crosse, lyinge uppon a velvett cushion, havinge St. Cuthbert's armes uppon it all imboydered with gold, bringinge that betwixt them uppon the said cushion to the lowest greeces [steps] in the Quire; and there betixt them did hold the said picture of our Saviour, sittinge of every side [kneeling], of that, and then one of the said Monkes did rise and went a pretty way from it, sittinge downe uppon his knees, with his shooes put of, and verye reverently did creepe away uppon his knees unto the said Crosse, and most reverently did kisse it. And after him the other Monke did so likewise, and then they did sitt them downe on every side of the Crosse, and, holdinge it betwixt them, and after that the Prior came forth of his stall, and did sitt him downe of his knees, with his shooes off, and in like sort did creepe also unto the said Crosse, in the mean time all the whole quire singinge an himne. The seruice being ended, the two Monkes did carrye it to the SEPULCHRE with great reverence, which Sepulchre was sett upp in the morninge, on the north side of the Quire, nigh to the High Altar, before the service time; and there lay it within the said Sepulchre, with great devotion, with another picture of our Saviour Christ, in whose breast they did enclose, with great reverence, the most holy and blessed Sacrament of the Altar, sencinge it and prayinge unto it upon theire knees, a great space, settinge two tapers lighted before it, which tapers did burne unto Easter day in the morninge, that it was taken forth.[8]

The details such as the removal of shoes and the creeping to the cross as well as the use of "props" such a the crucifix with the image of Christ placed on an elaborately embroidered cushion make this rite a nearly dramatic one at the same time that they help to set the tone for the ceremonies which celebrate Good Friday.

One further item, the *planctus Mariae*, or lament of Mary, with which we are concerned in this study, could also be a part of the

---

[8] *A Description or Breife Declaration of All the Ancient Monuments, Rites, and Costumes belonginge or beinge within the Monastical Church of Durham before the Suppression*, Surtees Society 15 (London: J. B. Nichols and Son, 1842), 9–10.

ceremonies on Good Friday; in the later Middle Ages its logical location among these ceremonies would seem to be attached to the Veneration of the Cross, following the chanting of the *Improperia.* According to Young, a rubric in a fourteenth-century missal from Friuli gives its location in this position.[9] That this location was not inevitable is, however, indicated by evidence from thirteenth-century Toulouse, where the *planctus* was sung as part of the *Tenebrae* service at Matins and Lauds.[10]

The theological and literary background for the presence of the *planctus* in the liturgy is complex and controversial. The scene at the cross, with the Virgin Mary and the beloved disciple John present, is described in John 19:25–27, but in that account there is no mention of Mary's laments or of those of any other of her friends. The most direct source for the *planctus* would seem to be the Greek version of the Apocryphal Gospel of Nicodemus, probably dated in the fifth century, which uniquely sets forth the sorrow of Mary: here the Virgin (*theotokos*) is seen at the foot of the cross where she swoons and then recovers.[11] There at the cross, she speaks sorrowfully to Jesus, to her companions, and to bystanders. Although the laments were lost when the Greek text was translated into Latin, nevertheless through other and less direct routes the laments found their way into the medieval Latin liturgy. Young notes the presence of "sentences assumed to be spoken by Mary at the cross . . . in the liturgy by the ninth or tenth century," and cites as an example of such a speech one that is attributed to Mary in the Roman *Liber responsalis.*[12]

In Western tradition there are, of course, the laments uttered by Mary and two women companions in the various versions of the *Visitatio Sepulchri,* and a number of attempts have been made to

---

[9] Young, *The Drama of the Medieval Church,* 1:503n.

[10] Ibid., 1:101, 503.

[11] *The Apocryphal New Testament,* trans. M. R. James (Oxford: Clarendon Press, 1924), 116; the Virgin's swooning here seems unique in early literature.

[12] Young, *The Drama of the Medieval Church,* 1:494, citing *Paléographie musicale,* 5:243–44.

connect these laments to the *planctus Mariae* form. E. K. Chambers and Young even saw the *planctus* as a prior form leading to the *Visitatio Sepulchri* drama, but Sandro Sticca refutes this evolutionary view.[13]

It is possible also that beyond the probable sources of the *planctus* cited above we will need to recognize some kind of relationship to the popular practice of the ritual lament for the dead in Greek and Byzantine tradition. As Margaret Alexiou has noted, such ritual laments go back as far as classical and even pre-classical Greece, but are alive in popular Greek culture to this day.[14]

Whatever pathways were followed in the development of the liturgical tradition, interest in the dramatic *planctus* in the later Middle Ages appears to have been stimulated by two movements of the twelfth through fourteenth centuries: the tendency to humanize Christ, and increased emphasis on the cult of Mary. The emphasis on Christ's humanity appears especially in the writings of St. Anselm (1033–1109) and St. Bernard of Clairvaux (1090–1153) as well as in a work which was attributed to St. Bonaventure (c.1217–74). St. Anselm's *Cur Deus Homo* (*Why God Became Man*) emphasizes God's compassion, which makes him concerned about sinners, who would otherwise be doomed to damnation. Anselm stresses the fact that Christ is God but is also man; Christ's having been born of a woman and having suffered and died on a tree give "a certain indescribable beauty to our redemption thus procured."[15] St. Bernard, in turn, points out Christ's "humility, gentleness, [and] self-surrender revealed by the Lord of majesty in assuming human nature, in accepting the punishment of death, the

---

[13] E. K. Chambers, *The Mediaeval Stage*, 2 vols. (London: Oxford University Press, 1903), 2:39–40; Young, *The Drama of the Medieval Church*, 2:538; Sticca, "The Literary Genesis of the Passion Play," 73.

[14] Margaret Alexiou, *The Ritual Lament in Greek Tradition* (Cambridge: Cambridge University Press, 1973), 4, 24–35.

[15] St. Anselm, *Basic Writings*, ed. S. N. Deane, 2nd ed. (La Salle, Illinois: Open Court, 1962), 183; see also Audrey Ekdahl Davidson, *The Quasi-Dramatic St. John Passions from Scandinavia and Their Medieval Background* (Kalamazoo: Medieval Institute Publications, 1981), 12–23.

shame of the cross."[16] And in the Franciscan *Meditations on the Life of Christ*, which was believed to have been written by St. Bonaventure, the Passion of Christ is depicted in great detail and with an unusual degree of realism.[17] The humanization of Christ, which includes the fact of his having been born of a woman who herself can grieve over his death, is a salient feature in the development of Passion literature, and as Sandro Sticca and others have observed,[18] it is part of the web of influences which have at least indirect bearing upon the *planctus*. The Man of Sorrows is a blood relative to the Sorrowing Mother.

An even more important influence upon the *planctus* was the cult of Mary, which also increased in popularity in the twelfth century and thereafter. Young notes that, as far as antecedents and influences are concerned, "we shall be sufficiently near the truth if we regard the *planctus Mariae* as merely one manifestation of the abundant cult of the Blessed Virgin. . . ."[19] The importance of St. Bernard and the Cistercian Order in the development of this emphasis on the Virgin was pointed out long ago by Henry Adams in his *Mont-Saint-Michel and Chartres*.[20] Bernard, as a recent writer on the Virgin Mary has reminded us, preached that "Mary was martyred, not in body but in the spirit, and that the sword Simeon prophesied would pierce her soul drew forth spiritual graces for mankind."[21]

However, it apparently was the Franciscan Order which most closely identified Mary with the subject and with the suffering

---

[16] Bernard of Clairvaux, *On the Song of Songs*, trans. Kilian Walsh (Kalamazoo: Cistercian Publications, 1971), 74–75.

[17] See Davidson, *The Quasi-Dramatic St. John Passions*, 33.

[18] Sticca, "The Literary Genesis of the Latin Passion Play," 55.

[19] Young, *The Drama of the Medieval Church*, 1:495.

[20] Henry Adams, *Mont-Saint-Michel and Chartres* (1905; reprint, Boston: Houghton Mifflin, 1913), 91–92 and passim.

[21] Marina Warner, *Alone of All Her Sex: The Myth and Cult of the Virgin Mary* (1976; reprint, London: Pan Books, 1985), 210.

aspect of women generally.²² As Marina Warner notes, while the humility of Mary had been praised by the Church Fathers and "the Cistercian mood of intimate meditation created the climate in which Mary could be brought down from her plinth, . . . the translation of the spiritual state into a physical and social condition was accomplished by the peculiar, inflamed genius of the founder of the Franciscans, Francis of Assisi (1186–1226)."²³ The literary expression of the particularly heightened Franciscan response may be observed in the poem *Donna del Paradiso*, written by Jacopone da Todi (c.1230–1306). This poem describes Mary at the scene of the Crucifixion, being addressed by Christ and, in turn, addressing him in language which is extremely intimate.²⁴ But the most poignant picture of the sorrowing mother at the scene of the Crucifixion is found in the great Franciscan sequence of the thirteenth century, *Stabat Mater dolorosa*, long attributed also to Jacopone.²⁵ In this poem, an eyewitness at the event describes Mary's suffering:

> Quis est homo qui non fleret
> Matrem Christi si videret
> In tanto supplicio?
>
> Who is he who would not weep to see
> the mother of Christ in such torment?²⁶

Such works as these elaborate upon the details that are found in Scripture, in apocryphal writings, and in devotional literature such

---

[22] David L. Jeffrey, *The Early English Lyric and Franciscan Spirituality* (Lincoln: University of Nebraska Press, 1975), 60–64.

[23] Warner, *Alone of All Her Sex*, 179.

[24] See ibid., 213.

[25] John Caldwell, "Stabat mater dolorosa," *New Grove Dictionary of Music and Musicians*, 18:36.

[26] Text and music in *Liber usualis* (Tournai: Desclee, 1961), 1424; translation from Warner, *Alone of All Her Sex*, 214.

as that of the Cistercians, and help to create, rather than the picture of the Queen of Heaven, a view of Mary as the humble, suffering mother. This complex cultural matrix was an incubator for liturgical drama—in particular, the special framework for the *planctus* form.[27] The scene of Mary at the foot of the cross, lamenting, is found depicted both dramatically and musically in the *Planctus Mariae*, the example from Cividale being the focus of the present study. This dramatization impressively makes specific reference to Christ's suffering and death as the sword piercing the soul of the Virgin.

II

The Cividale Planctus Mariae. The *Planctus Mariae* from Cividale del Friuli is not unique, but rather is one example of the form, as Young indicates.[28] The Cividale play is, however, of the greatest interest, since it preserves its music and is much more fully dramatized than the dialogue *Planctus ante nescia* (twelfth century) or *Flete, fideles animae* (thirteenth century), both characterized by the fact that the Virgin alone speaks.[29] The *Planctus Mariae* from Cividale, on the other hand, has four speakers—the Blessed Virgin (Mary Major), Mary Magdalen, Mary Jacobi, and the apostle John—and appears with musical notation which, as Fletcher Collins notes, makes this example "the only surviving produceable version in the form of a music-drama."[30] What also makes this work special are its extremely detailed rubrics, which include elaborate directions for hand gestures.

This *Planctus Mariae* appears in Cividale, Reale Museo

---

[27] See Sandro Sticca, *The* Planctus Mariae *in the Dramatic Tradition of the Middle Ages*, trans. Joseph R. Berrigan (Athens: University of Georgia Press, 1988).

[28] See Young, *The Drama of the Medieval Church*, 1:496–506.

[29] Ibid., 1:496–99.

[30] Fletcher Collins, Jr., *The Production of Medieval Church Music-Drama* (Charlottesville: University Press of Virginia, 1972), 90.

The Cividale Planctus Mariae *for Modern Performance* 39

Archeologico Nazionale, MS. CI, fols. 74r–76v, a manuscript transcribed in the fourteenth century.[31] It is written in a neat hand, with the rubrics added in smaller script. The music appears in easily decipherable square-note notation. The manuscript is a processional of local provenance.[32]

Cividale del Friuli was known for its liturgical music in the Middle Ages, with a *scola* established there in the Collegiate Church of S. Maria Assunta under a *scolasticus* by the thirteenth century. In 1338, the *scolasticus* was replaced by a cantor who was selected from the canons. In additon to the *Planctus Mariae*, three other examples of liturgical drama survive.[33] The fact that these plays at Cividale were produced not in a monastic but in a *scola* setting is important, since the production would probably have differed considerably from that of a Benedictine foundation. The rubrics which indicate gestures should therefore be taken seriously as stage directions intended for use in production.

The setting for the *Planctus Mariae*—the scene at the foot of the cross—is an emotional one, which is further heightened through the plaintive words of the women and by the gestures specified in the rubrics. These gestures include beating of the breast (seventeen times!), bowing the head, and various hand movements, including gesturing toward Christ on the cross, who is

---

[31] I am grateful to Fletcher Collins, Jr., for supplying me with photographs of the leaves of the manuscript which contain the *Planctus Mariae*. Previous editions which contain transcriptions of the music are: E. de Coussemaker, ed., *Drames Liturgique du Moyen Age* (Rennes, 1860), 285–97; William L. Smoldon, ed., *Planctus Mariae (The Lament of Mary): An Acting Version of a 14th Century Liturgical Music-Drama* (London: Oxford University Press, n.d.); Fletcher Collins, Jr., ed., *Medieval Church Music-Dramas* (Charlottesville: University Press of Virginia, 1976), 43–62.

[32] See William L. Smoldon, *The Music of the Medieval Church Dramas*, ed. Cynthia Bourgeault (London: Oxford University Press, 1980), 376.

[33] Pierluigi Perobelli, "Cividale de Friuli," in *The New Grove Dictionary of Music and Musicians*, 4:423. Other liturgical plays extant from the Cividale repertoire include the *Visitatio Sepulchri* (Young, *The Drama of the Medieval Church*, 1:267–68, 378–80, 597–98) and *Annnciation* (ibid., 2:247–48).

40   *The Cividale* Planctus Mariae *for Modern Performance*

Fig. 2. Crucifix created for demonstration performance of Cividale *Planctus Mariae* at the International Congress on Medieval Studies, 2006, in Western Michigan University's Kanley Chapel.

represented by a crucifix (see fig. 2). Collins criticizes the abundance and elaborateness of the gestures, and speculates that the clergy might have wanted them for performance before an audience unlearned in Latin in order that the gestures might communicate the meaning by functioning as sign language. Alternatively, the gestures might have been added, he believes, by a scribe without theatrical experience in this kind of drama.[34] These stage directions, however, are useful to a modern director attempting to perform the work in a manner consistent with the original performance practice at Cividale,[35] and certainly their use within reason would add to the poignancy of the play's atmosphere.

The play opens with an address by Mary Magdalen to the crowd, "O fratres et sorores." The audience plays the role of the crowd in the drama, and hence its members are brought into the play as participants. Mary's speech is mainly interrogative: "Where is my hope? Where is my consolation? Where is my whole salvation, O my Master?" There are borrowings here from the earlier dialogue *planctus*, *Flete, fideles animae*, which has been noted above. The melody is largely stepwise, wandering up and down, and seems to move from the Ionian mode to Aeolian mode to Dorian; these modes, along with the Phrygian mode, are used in the melodic material in the rest of the drama. Such use of modal changes adds to the sadness and indecision expressed by the sorrowing women.

The principal melody of the drama occurs first of all in the second item, Mary Major's speech: "Ergo quare, fili care,/ Pendes ita" ("Why, therefore, do you hang there so?").

Example 1

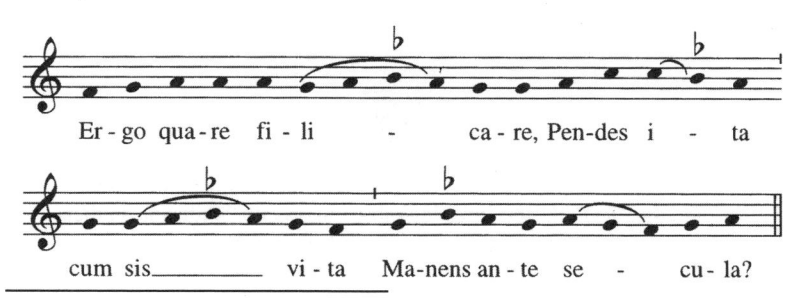

[Musical notation: Er-go qua-re fi-li — ca-re, Pen-des i-ta cum sis___ vi-ta Ma-nens an-te se - cu-la?]

---

[34] Collins, *The Production of Medieval Church Music-Drama*, 94–95.

[35] Smoldon, *The Music of the Medieval Church Dramas*, suggests oddly that "the director was apparently trying to arrange for the drama to produce itself" (378). [In comments following the production of the *Planctus Mariae* at the International Congress on Medieval Studies in 2006 (see note at conclusion of the present essay), Thomas Campbell proposed a new and very plausible theory—that is, the addition of the rubrics to aid in the recovery of a past tradition of acting.—Ed.]

The melody is repeated throughout the play, either literally or with additions and changes, in the following speeches:

> 4 (Mary Jacobi): at the words "Munda caro, mundo cara" ("Cleansing of flesh, caring for the world").
>
> 10 (Mary Major): "Mi Johannes, planctum move" ("My John, be moved to lament").
>
> 11 (John): "O Maria, mater mea" (O Mary, my mother").
>
> 15 "Ubi sunt discipuli" (Mary Major): at the words "Et tu solum, fili mi" ("And you alone, my Son").
>
> 17 (Mary Major): "O vos omnes qui transitus" ("O all you who pass by").

W. L. Smoldon, using rather nineteenth-century terminology, calls the insistent melody an *idée fixe*.[36] The repetition of this theme undoubtedly heightens the mood of sadness in the drama, just as in the Fleury *Raising of Lazarus* where the same tune returns again and again.[37] Even today, audiences at the *Lazarus* regularly are overcome with emotion as the nearly hypnotic melody draws them into the action of the drama.

Further musical coherence is achieved through the use of paired melodies setting the words at items 5 and 6 (John's words "Fleant materna viscera" and Mary Major's "Flete fideles anime") 13 and 14 (Mary Major's "O Maria Magdalena" and Mary Magdalen's reply "Mater Yhesu crucifixi").

There does not seem to be a great deal of opportunity for stage movement in this play; like the first speech of Mary Magdalen, most of the rest of the dialogue is cast in the interrogative mode— who, where, why—and such questions could be posed by singers standing in a stationary position. Many of the questions are, of course, directed reproachfully or even accusingly at the crucified

---

[36] Ibid., 379.

[37] For a practical edition of this play, see Collins, ed., *Medieval Church Music-Dramas*, 189–239.

One in a blame-the-victim fashion. John calls Christ "Rex celestis" and asserts that he has freed others from their guilt—a statement spoken with the despairing implication that "he has saved others but himself he cannot save." Mary Jacobi also questions Christ: "Why do you thirst upon the altar of the cross, a victim for sinners . . . ?" These complaints, which often should seem unfair to the audience, are psychologically understandable in the light of the speakers' grief and perhaps local conventions of lamenting the dead.

The dramatic tension rises and falls with the laments of the Virgin followed by the consolations of the other Marys. For example, item 17, Mary Major's lament "O vos omnes," which repeats *Lamentations* 1:12, is followed in the next by Mary Magdalen's consoling words, "Consolare, Domina,/ Mater et regina."

Musical climaxes (if such terminology may be used) seem to be found at the point of the last three speeches, those by Mary Major, John, and the Virgin again. In item 19, Mary Major questions Christ's presence on the cross once more; here, the gestures indicated in the manuscript seem absolutely essential to her point, for at "Fili mi carissime" she gestures toward Christ, as she also does at "Dulcis amor meus." At the words "cruce," "latrones," "Spinis coronatum," and "Latus" she indicates in turn the cross, the thieves, the crown of thorns, and Christ's wounded side. Concluding, she laments "Heu" and beats her breast—a very frequent gesture, as noted above.

In item 10, John again questions Christ's presence on the cross and beats his breast. Finally, in item 21, Mary Major denounces the members of the crowd ("mentes perfidas" and, speaking of them as lying or double-tongued ("linguas duplices"), she accuses the witnesses and judges alike and insists that they should be hanged for their crimes. To some viewers of the drama, the vehemence, even violence, of the Virgin's words may seem uncharacteristic of the medieval music-drama. In a play she should not need to suffer in silence simply on the basis of the authority of John 19, since her laments have been established in tradition. But the bitterness and unforgivingness of her words surprise us.

Another unexpected element is the suddenness with which the drama would seem to end—i.e., with these unmitigatedly harsh words of the Virgin. The final section of the play is in fact lost on account of a defect in the manuscript, and editors normally have supplied the missing text from *Flete, fideles animae*.[38] Smoldon felt that the drama needed a less abrupt ending, and in his performing edition he added a *Stabat Mater*. Collins does not furnish a concluding item, but recommends the use of *Crux fidelis*, which follows the Regensburg *Planctus*.[39] In modern performance, some kind of concluding piece is needed to round out the presentation of the drama since the play very likely will not be surrounded by the medieval Good Friday ceremonies which conclude with the *Depositio*.

In addition to the defective conclusion, a number of other problems appear in the copy of the Cividale *Planctus Mariae* in the manuscript. There are small lacunae—missing words and music—and puzzling attributions of speeches. For example, Young, on the basis of comparison with the text of *Flete, fidelis animae*, believed that there is a missing word and some lost notes at item 5, "Fleant materna viscera / Marie [matris] vulnera."[40] Both Smoldon and Collins have taken the music for this word from the setting for the word "sorores" in item 7 since the surrounding notes there are identical to the material in item 5.[41] The manuscript has the following:

Example 2

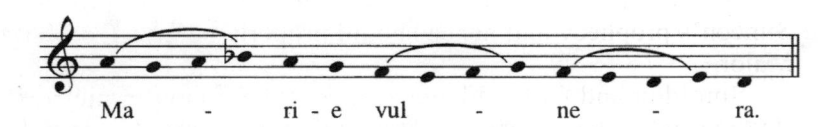

Ma - ri - e vul - ne - ra.

With the emendation, the passage appears:

---

[38] Young, *The Drama of the Medieval Church*, 1:499, 512.

[39] Collins, *Medieval Church Music-Dramas*, 45.

[40] Young, *The Drama of the Medieval Church*, 1:508; cf. ibid., 1:498. Only Coussemaker, *Drames Liturgiques*, fails to emend the passage (286).

[41] Collins, ed., *Medieval Church Music-Dramas*, 49; Smoldon, ed., *Planctus Mariae*, 5.

Example 3

Ma - ri - a ma - tris vul - ne - ra

Further flaws are present in the manuscript copy of the play at item 13, where there are notes missing or unreadable at the words "Magdalena," "Filii," and "mecum." Collins's solutions at these points seem very sensible to me.[42] There is even a puzzling attribution—"*Maria sola*"—at item 18 which Coussemaker thought meant a fifth speaker, Salome.[43] Smoldon and Collins give the speech, correctly in my opinion, to Mary Magdalen.

A puzzling rubric has Mary Major pointing to an angel ("Hic ostendat angelum") at item 9 in association with her reference to the sword that shall pierce her soul. Smoldon can only speculate that maybe "the sworded angel was a nearby effigy; but, in any case, it was Simeon, not an angel, who made the prophecy."[44] An angel without a solo role could, of course, easily have been added in production. Less likely to be questioned is the solution to another problem due to a peculiarity in the manuscript, an odd capital seemingly indicating a new speech. Collins hence attributes a portion of item 9 to St. John,[45] but the text refers to the sword of Simeon's prophecy and hence should properly be given to Mary Major.

Smoldon and Collins have rendered the drama in metrical rhythms, while the nineteen-century editor, Coussemaker, merely presented, without interpretation, the work in square-note notation. The argument for rhythmic notation is based on the fact that the

---

[42] See Collins, ed., *Medieval Church Music-Dramas*, 54.

[43] Coussemaker, *Drames Liturgiques*, 290.

[44] Smoldon, *The Music of the Medieval Church Dramas*, 380.

[45] Collins, ed., *Medieval Church Music-Dramas*, 45, 51.

poetry is in the Victorine double 8 8 7 form,[46] a characteristic that Smoldon and Collins believe indicates a music setting in a rhythmic mode. Each has chosen the first rhythmic mode for his edition. Another argument suggests that it may be easier to memorize a role when the work is notated in regular rhythms.

However, I believe an argument can also be made for rendering this late medieval *Planctus Mariae* in the equalized, non-metrical rhythms of plainchant. Obviously, such a transcription gives the play a more timeless atmosphere and helps it to "breathe" in the way that Cynthia Bourgeault suggests between liturgy and drama.[47] Furthermore, it is now recognized that the assigning of rhythms to monophonic Latin music is more complicated than formerly realized, and some scholars tend to think that the sacred music of the later medieval period favored equalized rhythms while monophonic secular music was rendered metrically.[48] While the matter is hardly settled, I have chosen to provide a transcription in equalized rhythms in preparing my performing edition of the Cividale *Planctus Mariae*.

[Note: The promised performing edition of the Cividale *Planctus Mariae* was not completed until some time after the present study was first published. It was to be used for the first time for a demonstration-

---

[46] Patrick S. Diehl, *The Medieval European Religious Lyric* (Berkeley: University of California Press, 1985), 88.

[47] Cynthia Bourgeault, "Liturgical Dramaturgy," *Comparative Drama* 17 (1973): 126.

[48] See Walther Durr and Walter Gerstenberg, "Rhythm," *The New Grove Dictionary of Music and Musicians*, 15:811–14. For an extremely skeptical view, see Hendrik van der Werf, *The Emergence of Gregorian Chant*, 2 vols. (Rochester, N.Y., 1983), 1:22–42; he notes: "According to Johannes de Grocheio, writing ca. 1300, some people had come to distinguish between measurable and immeasurable music, with plain chant belonging to the latter and the polyphonic motet to the former" (1:23). [To the end of her life the author was undecided about the matter of rhythm, and came to different conclusions than the above when engaged with the Beauvais *Ludus Danielis*. See "Music in the Beauvais *Ludus Danielis*, below.—Ed.]

performance at the forty-second International Congress on Medieval Studies, and is scheduled to be published in a forthcoming issue of *Comparative Drama* along with essays by various scholars in memory of the transcriber, Audrey Ekdahl Davidson.—Ed.]

Music in the Beauvais *Ludus Danielis*

The *Ludus Danielis* from Beauvais Cathedral has been a remarkably popular work ever since its modern revival by Noah Greenberg and the New York Pro Musica in 1958; the principal reasons for its popularity are clearly its melodic inventiveness and the coherence achieved by its musical structure. The play, preserved in the unique manuscript, British Library Egerton MS. 2615, fols. 95^r–108^r, and known to scholars since it was first edited by Edmond de Coussemaker in 1860, was, according to the statement in the first item at the beginning of the play, devised and presumably presented by youths at the Cathedral of Beauvais.[1] Associated with the Christmas octave, it apparently was, as Margot Fassler has argued, part of a reform movement determined upon supplanting the lewd frivolity and even sacrilege of the Feast of Fools when secular clergy and minor orders traditionally engaged

---

[1] See Henry Copley Greene, "The Song of the Ass," *Speculum* 6 (1931): 535n, for the observation that British Library, Egerton MS. 2615 was probably written "during the pontificate of Gregory IX (1217–41) and before the marriage of Louis IX to Marguerite of Provence in 1234." This conjecture is based on the fact that the *Officium* included in the same manuscript gives prayers for Pope Gregory and King Louis, but there are no prayers for Queen Marguerite. For the contents of the manuscript, see *Catalogue of Additions to the Manuscripts in the British Museum in the Years 1882–1887*, pp. 336–37, and Augustus Hughes-Hughes, *Catalogue of Manuscript Music in the British Museum* (London: British Museum, 1906), 1:242, 253; see also Richard Emmerson, "Divine Judgment and Local Ideology in the Beauvais *Ludus Danielis*, in Dunbar H. Ogden, ed., The Play of Daniel: *Critical Essays*, Early Drama, Art, and Music Monograph Series 24 (Kalamazoo: Medieval Institute Publications, 1996), 54, n. 6, for further references.

in role reversal and other outlandish behavior—e.g., drinking wine before the church door, bringing an ass into the cathedral, and censing the altar with pudding and sausage.[2] These rites were celebrated as a culmination of the ceremonies belonging to deacons (Feast of St. Stephen, on 26 December), to priests (Feast of the Apostle St. John, on 27 December), to acolytes and boys of the cathedral (Feast of the Innocents, on 28 December), and to subdeacons (Feast of the Circumcision, ordinarily on 1 January).[3] The *Ludus Danielis* quite plausibly can be seen as part of the design to bring some order out of the chaotic yearly celebrations of youths and minor clerical orders, in particular of the subdeacons.

As a play written by and for the boys and minor clergy of Beauvais, the drama is a blending of two stories regarding the prophet Daniel. The first concerns the downfall of King Balthasar (Belshazzar) because of his and his father's desecration of the sacred vessels taken from the temple at Jerusalem; coincidentally, these reflect the liturgical vessels normally in the care of the subdeacons.[4] The second focuses, during the time of King Darius, on Daniel's incarceration in the lion's den for refusing to relinquish the worship of his own God. The biblical sources for these episodes are *Daniel*, chapters 5–6, and the apocryphal *Bel and the Dragon*, the latter supplying the Habakkuk incident. These actions are framed by a series of processions which, in their one note–one syllable melodic form and their nearly hypnotic repetitions, drive the action forward and contribute to the power that Jerome Taylor noted when he said that even amateur groups

---

[2] Margot Fassler, "The Feast of Fools and *Danielis Ludus*: Popular Tradition in a Medieval Cathedral Play," in *Plainsong in the Age of Polyphony*, ed. Thomas Forrest Kelly (Cambridge: Cambridge University Press, 1992), 72, 87–88, 97; cf. E. K. Chambers, *The Mediaeval Stage*, 2 vols. (London: Oxford University Press, 1903), 1:287, who cites a mock procession from Beauvais in the thirteenth century.

[3] Fassler, "The Feast of Fools," 69.

[4] Ibid., 88.

are able "to evoke a moving religious experience"[5] through the play. The dramatic effect emphasizes the prophetic element in the drama, for, appropriately with regard to the Christmas season, the events are linked to the prophecy of Christ's birth.[6]

The notation, characteristic for late twelfth- and early thirteenth-century Northern France, is marked by the canted *punctum*, a rhomboid shape.[7] It is written on a staff of four red lines, and, while clearly showing individual pitches, the notation leaves room for more than a single interpretation with regard to rhythmic values; however, as John Stevens observes, a number of "melodies with their strongly accentual Latin verse texts seem to invite the metrical interpretation that most editors give them."[8] Medieval theorists such as Guido of Arezzo provide corroboration for the metrical interpretation of plainchant and, by extension, of plainchant in liturgical drama; Guido says: "I speak of chants as metrical because we often sing in such a way that we appear almost

---

[5] See Jerome Taylor, "Prophetic 'Play' and Symbolist 'Plot' in the Beauvais *Daniel*," *Comparative Drama* 11 (1977): 192.

[6] Ibid., 199.

[7] See John Stevens, "Medieval Drama," *The New Grove Dictionary of Music and Musicians*, ed. Stanley Sadie, 20 vols. (London: Macmillan, 1980), 12:31.

[8] Ibid., 31. The regular rhythmic interpretation of the music in *Ludus Danielis* is given support by David Hiley in *Western Plainchant: A Handbook* (New York: Oxford University Press, 1993), p. 270, who comments: "In the first half of the piece nearly every entrance or exit of characters is accompanied by vigorously rhythmic conductus." See also Hiley's discussion of medieval rhythmic theories in "Notation, III, I: Western, plainchant," *The New Grove Dictionary of Music and Musicians*, 12:351. Hiley cites, among others, Aurelian of Réôme (d. 850) and Guido of Arezzo (c. 1030), whose works point toward the metrical rendering of chant and the music of liturgical drama.

to scan verses by feet, as happens when we sing actual meters."[9]

The processions which frame the action are related to the liturgical conductus, the purpose in the liturgy being that of bringing the reader of the lesson to the lectern.[10] In *Ludus Danielis* suitable processions, usually labeled *conductus*, are introduced for each character as he or she proceeds to his or her destination. The strongly accented *prosa, Astra tenenti cunctipotenti* (5–34),[11] though not marked in the rubric as a conductus, nevertheless functions similarly for the entrance of Balthasar's princes; it also serves to identify the Beauvais singers as "virilis et puerilis." The piece consists of nine appearances of the A melody; the hypnotic repetition coupled with the driving, strongly accented rhythm combine to emphasize the ideas of the text: the heavenly might and

---

[9] Guido of Arezzo, *Micrologus*, trans. Warren Babb, in *Hucbald, Guido, and John on Music: Three Medieval Treatises*, ed. Claude V. Palisca (New Haven: Yale University Press, 1978), 72. It seems probable that the medieval composers of liturgical music set the Latin metrical verse to music governed by the rhythmic modes. Both Fletcher Collins, Jr. and William L. Smoldon have argued for the use of the rhythmic modes in transcribing liturgical drama. Collins remarks, "The metric units of nearly all verse in the plays are either trochaic, iambic, or dactyllic, which have musical analogues in what are called rhythmic modes" (*Medieval Church Music-Dramas: A Repertory of Complete Plays* [Charlottesville: University Press of Virginia, 1976], xi). Smoldon presents a similar position: "As the centuries passed, the admission into Church music-drama libretti of more and more rhyming Latin poetry of regular scansion made it obvious that settings of such lyrical compositions, though written in plainchant notation, were more than likely to have been interpreted . . . through some kind of use of the 'rhythmic modes,' or at least, in something other than 'free rhythm'" (*The Music of the Medieval Church Dramas*, ed. Cynthia Bourgeault [London: Oxford University Press, 1980], 36n).

[10] John Stevens, *Words and Music in the Middle Ages: Song, Narrative, Dance, and Drama, 1050–1350* (Cambridge: Cambridge University Press, 1986), 56.

[11] Line numbers in parentheses in my text refer to the edition of Karl Young, *The Drama of the Medieval Church*, 2 vols. (Oxford: Clarendon Press, 1933), 2:290–301.

Music in the Beauvais Ludus Danielis 53

power of the Creator of the firmament, King Balthasar's earthly and temporal power, and Daniel's sagacity, which will prevail beyond that of Balthasar's reign. The Latin verse of this item is seen by John Stevens as being particularly apt for a metrical musical rendering[12] (see Example 1).

Example 1

A-stra te-nen-ti cunc-ti po-ten-ti Tur-ba vi-ri-lis et pu-er-i-lis Con-ti-o plau-dit

The Satraps' processional song, *Iubilemus Regi nostro*, accompanying the bringing of the purloined vessels to the King (40–59) is a liturgical item which also appears in the Laon Epiphany office as *Jubilemus cordis voce*.[13] The song as it appears in the *Ludus Danielis* opens with the following melodic progression:

Example 2

Ju-bi-le-mus Re-gi no-stro ma-gno ac po-ten-ti, Re-so-ne-mus lau-de di-gna vo-ce com-pe-ten-ti!

---

[12] Stevens, "Medieval Drama," 31.

[13] Hiley, *Western Plainchant*, 270.

This melody, which is syllabic, proceeds stepwise with the addition of two short leaps of a major third. The strong resemblance of the piece to *Orientis partibus* (*Prose of the Ass*, from the Beauvais Circumcision Office also contained in Egerton MS. 2615, fols. 1^r–2^r and 43^r–44^v) has been observed by Fassler, who comments that "[t]he use of this melody both within a special Office designed for the subdeacons at Laon and in the Beauvais Daniel play points to the association the piece had for this particular tripudium and strengthens the argument that the Babylonians in *Ludus Danielis* were meant to be recognized as subdeacons in disguise."[14] Thus there is additional evidence for the subdeacons as the ones impersonating those characters in the play who brought out the ill-gotten vessels in order to drink from them in an improper and possibly even blasphemous celebration. For the audience, the echoes of the *Song of the Ass* also would have established a secular, even satiric context for *Iubilemus Regi nostro*; coupled with the accents of the poetry which drive the piece into a metrical rhythmic rendition, the piece achieves a kind of youthful vitality. Conversely, Taylor has perceived this item as being "jingly" and even silly.[15]

The conductus *Cum doctorum et magorum* that accompanies the Queen's entrance and passage to the King (75–98) is marked by a beautiful melody which first falls and then rises. The melody fits the description of the Queen as "prudent" or "sagacious" (*prudens*) and as having power (*cum potentia*). Her wisdom is more fully displayed in the next item when she suggests that the prophet Daniel be consulted to interpret the words written on the wall; nevertheless, the conductus that brings her in foreshadows her active role in the play. The melody is marked by melismas strategically placed (four notes on the syllable "-rum" of *doctorum* and four notes on the syllable "ma-" of *magorum*), notes which ripple downward gracefully (Example 3).

---

[14] Fassler, "The Feast of Fools," 89.

[15] Taylor, "Prophetic 'Play' and Symbolist 'Plot'," 203.

Example 3

Cum doc - to - rum___ et ma - go - rum__ om - nis ad - sit___ con - ti - o,

Interestingly, the first four notes of the beautiful melody which signifies the Queen—the g g–e f motif—are borrowed from her conductus and are used for Daniel's procession at *Hic verus Dei famulus* (122–26);[16] Daniel then sings the motif as, setting out to meet the King, he describes his exiled condition in a macaronic statement: "Pauper et exulans envois al Roi par vos" (l. 127). The use of the vernacular French for "I go with you to the King" marks Daniel as a man of the people. Ultimately, the motif from the Queen's conductus will be echoed six times as Daniel processes. The individuality of the melody and its ability to distinguish character may be blunted, but the qualities of dignity and wisdom, possessed by both the Queen and Daniel, are underlined.

Daniel's speech to the King—*Rex tua nolo munera* (147–76)—although not strictly accompanying a procession, still has the one syllable–one note pattern which is characteristic of the conductus. It is as if Daniel were pacing as he speaks to the King. He refuses the immense gifts offered by the King, and then identifies Balthasar's culpability when he lists the crimes of his father Nebuchadnezzar; concluding the catalogue of sins, he finally reveals the meaning of the mysterious message on the wall. The musical setting includes numerous appearances of a pervasive melody with its transpositions and variants, all obviously related. These repetitions build up suspense for the elucidation of the riddle which appears in the last three appearances of the melody.

Daniel's message having been heard, the Queen takes her

---

[16] Hiley notes that *Hic verus Dei famulus* "has the same melody as the Benedicamus song *Postquam celorum dominus* in Paris 1139" (*Western Plainchant*, 270).

leave. Perhaps because her entrance music has been used by Daniel and the princes, a different conductus, *Solvitur in libro Salomonis*, is used for her exit (181–94). The piece, again praising her wisdom, has fourteen lines of verse paired in an *ouvert-clos* manner, as Mathias Bielitz has noted.[17] The rhythm of the text falls into a triple meter which should be taken at a dignified but not solemn pace (see Example 4). Any seeming satisfaction that the text conveys can only be ironic, since the message as deciphered by Daniel holds no happy results in store for either the Queen or the King.

Example 4

Sol - vi - tur in li - bro Sa - lo - mo - nis

Di - gna laus et con - gru -

a ma - tro - - nis.

Following the departure of the Queen, the conductus *Regis vasa referentes*, accompanying the act of bringing the vessels before Daniel (195–215), praises the prophet in a repeated refrain: "Gaudeamus, laudes sibi debitas referamus." Its poetic structure, shaping the musical form, seems related to the litany as transformed into a secular strophic *laisse* with refrain. The strophes in this song are irregular, with new material inserted at the second and fourth strophes. Here the poetic meter can be fitted to a

---

[17] My discussion of forms in *Solvitur in libro Salomonis*, *Regis vasa referentes*, and *Congaudentes celebremus* is indebted to Mathias Bielitz's analysis in *Hilarii Aurelianensis: Versus et Ludi: Epistolae: Ludus Danielis Belouacensis*, ed. Walther Bulst and M. L. Bulst-Thiele (Leiden: E. J. Brill, 1989).

strongly duple musical rhythm, and the song moves along with vigor. The refrain is strengthened when the notes setting the text "Gaudeamus" are lengthened to emphasize their importance. The jubilant text, steady rhythm, and words of praise and rejoicing are, in the light of Balthasar's fate, ironic.

The arrival of the triumphant King Darius and Balthasar's subsequent expulsion also could occasion another procession, although not strictly labeled such. In *Ecce Rex Darius* (216–45), the mentioning of musical instruments, citharas and organs, does not necessarily indicate that these would have been used in a liturgical context, though they are not by nature to be seen as decadent in themselves. However, in connection with the entrance of the Persian king and his princes, who are said to be dancing (*tripudia*), these instruments could well have been played in such a way as to be signs of the depravity of the Medes and Persians.

Daniel, having been recommended to the new King, is led to Darius with *Congaudentes celebremus*, which has a melody that moves along in what must be triple metered rhythm (270–84). The text, celebrating both the prophet Daniel and the birth of Christ, credits Daniel with foretelling the new Christian era; in his wisdom and faithfulness to God, Daniel is revealed as a type of Christ.[18] The structure of the song is comprised of six repeated A sections (with variants in higher and lower ranges), labeled 5a, and three B sections, labelded 5b, at the center, and then six A sections with variants to close—an ABA or arch form.[19]

This joyous moment is, of course, not to last. The envious counsellors advise Darius to create a law prohibiting the worship of any gods other than the King Darius; Daniel, praying to the God of Judea, is the one deliberately caught in their trap. Daniel is led to the lions' den; realizing his plight, the prophet laments: "Heu, heu, heu" (342–49). The repetition of the words on a single note in this instance is particularly affecting.

The depiction of the Angel's protection of Daniel in the lion's den is not marked by any framing conductus, nor can the music for another Angel's message to Habakkuk—*Abacuc, tu senex pie*—be

---

[18] Taylor, "Prophetic 'Play' and Symbolist 'Plot'," 205.

[19] Bielitz, no. 34, in *Hilarii Aurelianensis*, ed. Bulst and Bulst-Thiele.

Example 5a

Con - gau - den - tes ce - le - bre - mus na - ta - lis so - le - mni - a Jam de mor - te nos re - de - mit de - i sa - pi - en - ti - a Ho - mo na - tus est in car - ne qui ce - a - vit o - mni - a Na - sci - tu - rum quem prae - di - xit pro - phe - tae fa - cun - di - a

Example 5b

In hoc na - ta - li - ti - o, Da - ni - el, cum gau - di - o, te lau - dat haec con - ti - o.

construed as rhythmically measured (358–61). Habakkuk's rejoinder *Novit Dei cognitio quod Babylonem nescio* (362–65) is a straightforward melody, for the most part syllabic and chant-like in the logic of its intervals, moving up and down the Dorian mode in seconds and thirds. The Angel's action of seizing Habakkuk by the hair and forcing him to go to the lions' den would seem to be a comic detail, but there is nothing inherently humorous in the music. Habakkuk's words to Daniel in the item *Surge, frater, ut cibum capias* (366–69) are set to mostly syllabic music with several four-note melismas interspersed: the melismas occur on *Sur-* of *Surge*, on *gra-* of *gratias*, and on *qui*. A kind of word-painting appears on the rising notes setting the syllable *Sur-*.

The movement of the characters near the close of the play is accompanied by less elaborate music, not to be construed as full-scale processions. King Darius goes to the den and laments, then finds Daniel alive. The envious counsellors are led to the den, and their words are remarkable for their recognition of their responsibility for their fate. King Darius rejoices, Daniel prophesies, and the Angel announces the birth of Christ in Bethlehem with a hymn, *Nuntium vobis fero de supernis* (389–92).[20] After the long, elaborate processions in the earlier part of the play, the relative calm of the ending is almost surprising. The *Te Deum*, suggesting performance at Matins in Beauvais Cathedral, concludes what remains today a most satisfying drama. Then as now one comes away from a performance of the play quite aware of the overarching pattern of the music. The music both accompanies and carries the action in the drama from moment to moment, from unrest to climactic tension to this finale in rest and revelation.

---

[20] See Susan Rankin, "Liturgical Drama," in *The Early Middle Ages*, ed. Richard Crocker and David Hiley, New Oxford History of Music 2 (Oxford: Oxford University Press, 1990), 350.

Alma redemptoris mater:
The Little Clergeon's Song

I should like to re-open the vexed question of the song the "litel clergeon" sings in Chaucer's *Prioress' Tale*. My interest is to weigh questions of text and tune, and I also wish to propose some suggestions for Chaucer's choice of the little boy's song in preference to other Marian antiphons.[1]

Questions of text seem to be easiest to answer. We can say with certainty that we do know what text Chaucer had in mind when he tells of the little "innocent" singing *Alma redemptoris* "wel and boldely" each day as he passes through the Jewry "To scholeward and homward." In his notes on the *Prioress' Tale* in volume 5 of the Oxford Chaucer, W. W. Skeat erroneously identifies *Alma redemptoris* as the sequence which begins with the words *Alma redemptoris mater, quam de caelis misit pater . . .* ("Blessed mother of the redeemer, who was sent from heaven by the Father").[2] The song which the boy sings is called an "antheme" which, as Carleton Brown has noted, "is in itself decisive, for this

---

[1] [Since its initial publication, the present study has come to be part of the mainstream of Chaucer criticism; see Beverly Boyd, ed., *A Variorum Edition of Geoffrey Chaucer*, 2: *The Canterbury Tales*, pt. 20 (Norman: University of Oklahoma Press, 1959), 15–17.—Ed.]

[2] W. W. Skeat, *Prioresses Tale*, Oxford Chaucer, 5:77, as cited in Carleton Brown, *A Study of the Miracle of Our Lady, Told by Chaucer's Prioress*, Chaucer Society, 2nd series 45 (London, 1910), 122. As Brown notes, however, Skeat contradicts himself by correctly identifying the little clergeon's song as *Alma redemptoris mater, quae pervia caeli* in vol. 3 of the Oxford Chaucer. The text and music of the sequence are found in Peter Wagner, *Einführung in die Gregorianischen Melodien*, 3 vols. (Leipzig: Breitkopf und Härtel, 1911–21), 3:497.

is a term which could not properly be applied to a Sequence."³ The word "antheme" specifically indicates that the song is an antiphon.⁴ *Alma redemptoris mater* therefore unquestionably is the Marian antiphon which reads as follows:

> Alma redemptoris mater, quae pervia caeli
> Porta manes et stella maris, succurre cadenti,
> Surgere qui curat populo, tu quae genuisti
> Natura mirante tuum sanctum genitorem,
> Virgo prius ac posterius, Gabrielis ab ore
> Sumens illud Ave, peccatorum miserere.⁵

Kind Mother of the Redeemer—heaven's open door and the star of the sea—assist your fallen people who are attempting to rise up again. You who, while Nature wondered, gave birth to your own sacred Creator and yet remained a virgin afterward as before receiving that "Hail" from the lips of Gabriel, have mercy on us sinners.

Both text and tune have been ascribed to Hermannus Contractus (c.1013–54), monk at the Abbey of Reichenau. Brown notes that in the thirteenth century Bishop Durandus (Guillaume Durand) of Mende in his *Rationale divinorum officiorum* and Jacobus de Voragine in his *Sermones aurei* accepted him as the author of the antiphon, but we can no longer concur with the assertion that "modern authorities are agreed in regarding it as the work of

---

³ Brown, *A Study of the Miracle of Our Lady*, 123.

⁴ The *Oxford English Dictionary* [1st ed.] correctly identifies the medieval term "antheme" as "antiphon." A second meaning, which became current in the Renaissance, is given: "a composition in unmeasured prose (usually from the Scriptures or Liturgy) set to music." The *OED* incorrectly lists the word "antheme" in the *Prioress' Tale* under this second definition.

⁵ *Analecta Hymnica Medii Aevi*, 55 vols. (1886–1922), 50:317, as quoted in F. J. E. Raby, *A History of Christian-Latin Poetry from the Beginnings to the Close of the Middle Ages*, 2nd ed. (Oxford: Clarendon Press, 1953), 226–27.

Hermannus Contractus, the celebrated author of Latin hymns."[6] F. J. E. Raby pronounces the evidence in favor of Hermannus insufficient.[7] The earliest manuscript to credit the writing of the antiphon to him is from the twelfth century—a date sufficiently removed from Hermannus' lifetime to cast some doubt on the validity of the ascription. We can only say that the chant does not appear before Hermannus' time and that it is present with great frequency in manuscripts which date from the twelfth century and later.[8]

The question of the tune is far more tangled. The temptation is to be content with the chant as it is presented in the *Liber usualis*. This is a trap into which both Gustave Reese and Raymond Preston have fallen in their discussions of the song in the *Prioress' Tale*.[9] The *Liber usualis* is certainly a respectable practical compilation, but *Alma redemptoris* as found there is not perfectly satisfactory for a discussion that involves the English rites of Chaucer's time. Unfortunately, English medieval antiphonals are rare, thanks to the zeal of the reformers in the sixteenth century. No London service books are extant,[10] but we do possess this antiphon in the

---

[6] Brown, *A Study of the Miracle of Our Lady*, 123. See also Heinrich Hüschen, "Hermannus Contractus," in *Die Musik in Geschichte und Gegenwart*, 6:229–30, and Leonard Ellinwood, *Musica Hermannus Contracti* (Rochester, N.Y.: Eastman School of Music, 1936), neither of whom has serious doubts about Hermannus' authorship.

[7] Raby, *A History of Christian-Latin Poetry*, 227.

[8] Hüschen, "Hermannus Contractus," 229.

[9] Gustave Reese, *Music in the Middle Ages* (New York: Norton, 1940), 128; Raymond Preston, *Chaucer* (London: Sheed and Ward, 1952), 209–09.

[10] Beverly Boyd, *Chaucer and the Liturgy* (Philadelphia: Dorrance, 1967), 5–6. Professor Boyd notes that Chaucer's life was "closely connected with London, the Diocese of St. Paul's, and it is to this diocese that one should expect to look for the liturgy as he knew it best." However, as she points out, the Use of St. Paul's "must be written off as lost" and we must turn to the Use of Sarum (including antiphonals, breviaries, and legendaries) for evidence of the way the Roman rite was adapted to English practice.

following: (1) the thirteenth-century Cambridge University Library MS. Mm IIg,[11] (2) the thirteenth-century Worcester Cathedral Library MS. F.160,[12] and (3) the *Sarum Antiphonal* printed at Paris in 1519–20.[13] These three sources, when collated and compared, will give us a far more authentic idea of what the chant sounded like in the English churches of Chaucer's age.

Since the derived rite of Salisbury, known as the Use of Sarum, was most widespread in medieval England,[14] any reconstructed version of *Alma redemptoris mater* must depend mainly on the Sarum versions contained in Cambridge University Library MS. Mm IIg and in the printed *Sarum Antiphonal*. The Worcester manuscript version will be used only for purposes of comparison. Thus the reconstructed English version of the chant will follow the Sarum practice of presenting it in the transposed Vth mode on C. Other English compositions which make use of the chant, such as

---

[11] *Antiphonale Sarisburiense*, ed. W. H. Frere, 6 vols. (London: Plainsong and Mediaeval Music Society, 1901–26), 5:529. See also Frere's Inroduction in ibid., 1:77: "The MS. is not strictly speaking of Sarum Use pure and simple, but was written for an Augustinian House, probably St. Giles Abbey, Barnwell, near Cambridge.... [T]he Austin Canons followed for the most part the secular service of the diocese: so this MS. can be taken, more or less trustfully, as evidence for Sarum Use."

[12] *Codex F.160 de la Bibliothèque de la Cathédral de Worcester (XIIIe Siècle) Antiphonaire monastique*, Paleographie musicale 12 (1922–25), 303.

[13] A. W. Pollard and G. R. Redgrave, *Short Title Catalogue of Books Printed in England, Scotland, and Ireland and of English Books Printed Abroad, 1475–1640* (reprint London: Bibliographical Society, 1969), nos. 15790–15790a. See Frere, ed., *Antiphonale Sarisburiense*, 1:81–82, for a description of this edition, the only known version of the Sarum antiphonal.

[14] See Frank Ll. Harrison, *Music in Medieval Britain* (London: Routledge and Kegan Paul, 1963); Archdale A. King, *Liturgies of the Past* (London: Longmans, 1959), 292–98.

Alma redemptoris mater: *The Little Clergeon's Song* 65

Dunstable's motet *Alma redemptoris mater*[15] and the carol found in Cambridge, Trinity College MS. 0.3.58, present the chant in this manner,[16] strongly suggesting that the performance of the chant in the transposed Vth mode is the usual manner in England. In the discussion which follows, I have attempted to avoid confusion when treating the transposed chant and the untransposed version in the Worcester manuscript by referring to scale degrees rather than to actual pitches. The reconstructed chant also is here presented in modern notation to make it accessible to specialists in fields other than music.

The reconstructed version differs both in some of its pitches and in rhythm from the form found in the *Liber usualis*. The notation of rhythms in plainchant is a controversial question beyond the scope of this study;[17] suffice it to say that the *Liber usualis* illustrates many instances in which a punctum or virga is dotted, probably indicating some lengthening of the dotted note. There are no dotted notes in any of the English sources and only a few points at which an oriscus or pressus occurs. The note values, then, in the reconstructed version generally will be rendered as eighth notes, and the infrequent appearance of two eighths tied together or a quarter note is determined by the presence of an oriscus or pressus in the English sources.

The most significant differences in pitch between the English sources and the *Liber usualis* appear at the words *Alma redemptoris mater, genitorem, ore,* and *illud*. In the *Liber usualis*, the syllable of *-ma* of *Alma* is rendered by three notes, scale steps 3–2–3, instead of by scale step 3 alone as in the English sources. At the syllable *ma-* of *mater*, the English antiphonals shows scale steps 4–3–2–1. At the word *genitorem*, no agreement is found among the English sources. The use of scale steps 4–2–1–6–1–1 at

---

[15] John Dunstable, *Complete Works*, ed. Manfred Bukofzer, Musica Britannica 8 (London: Stainer and Bell, 1953), 106–07.

[16] *Mediaeval Carols*, ed. John Stevens, 2nd ed., Musica Britannica 4 (London: Stainer and Bell, 1958), 3.

[17] For convenient summary of the different views on Gregorian rhythm, see Carl Parrish, *The Notation of Medieval Music* (New York: Norton, 1957), 31–38, and Reese, *Music in the Middle Ages*, 140–48.

Example 1

this point seems peculiar to the Worcester manuscript since it is found in no other English source, including the composed pieces which use the chant literally. If we reject the Worcester reading as a variant, we must look to the Sarum versions for clarification. The Cambridge manuscript gives the passage as 4–3–2–1–flat 7–1–1; the printed *Sarum Antiphonal* presents it as 4–3–2–7–1–1. It appears that the flatted seventh, a tone not proper to the mode,[18] may have been dropped before the sixteenth century, the date of the printed *Sarum Antiphonal*. However, the flatted scale step appears as late as c.1475, when it is utilized in Edmund Sturton's *Gaude virgo mater Christi*, a composed work based on *Alma redemptoris mater*.[19] The flatted seventh therefore seems required in the reconstructed version of the chant since it must have been sung that way in England during the latter part of the fourteenth century. At *ore*, the Sarum sources give scale steps 4–3–2–1, while the Worcester manuscript and the *Liber usualis* show 5–4–2–1. At *illud*, the Sarum versions have scale steps 3–2–1, whereas Worcester has 4–3–2–1 and the *Liber usualis* prints 4–2–1.

Why does Chaucer choose *Alma redemptoris mater* for his *Prioress' Tale* in preference to other Marian antiphons? The reasons here are multiple. It is the antiphon that appears in the version of the story that is most closely related to Chaucer's direct source, which appears now to be lost.[20] The chant, used very widely in the liturgy and also commonly employed as the basis for composed pieces in the fourteenth and fifteenth centuries, was demonstrably extremely popular. The words and the music are also especially appropriate to the tale.

Among the analogues to the *Prioress' Tale*, those most similar to Chaucer's version are members of the C group. However, each

---

[18] Harrison, *Music in Medieval Britain*, 327.

[19] Sturton's *Gaude virgo mater Christi* is contained in *The Eton Choirbook*, ed. Frank Ll. Harrison, Musica Britannica 9–11 (London: Stainer and Bell, 1956–61), 1:110–12; see also Harrison, *Music in Medieval Britain*, 317, 327.

[20] Carleton Brown, "The Prioress's Tale," in *Sources and Analogues of Chaucer's Canterbury Tales*, ed. W. F. Bryan and Germaine Dempster (New York: Humanities Press, 1958), 460–64.

of the three groups of analogues shares certain features.[21] Common to groups A, B, and C is the little boy himself, who must walk through the ghetto daily. As he passes through the Jewish community, he sings a Christian liturgical song. This so inflames the Jews that they kill the boy, usually by slashing his throat. His body is then cast into a pit, buried under the house, buried in the garden, hidden under a pile of manure, or, as in the *Prioress' Tale* and all the other versions belonging to Group C, cast into a privy.[22] The miracle then happens. Usually the voice of the child is heard singing from his burial place.[23] It is the Blessed Virgin who has effected the miraculous happening; in Group C, she often utilizes a magical object such as a pearl, a lily, a precious stone, or, as in Chaucer's tale, a grain which is placed under the boy's tongue.[24] Thus he is enabled to sing throughout an elaborate funeral service.

Like most of the analogues of the C group, Chaucer's tale chooses *Alma redemptoris mater* for the walk through the ghetto. Unlike most of the analogues, the *Prioress' Tale* chooses the same antiphon for the funeral service. In four versions of the C group,[25] the priest begins the Requiem Mass, but the child rises up and interrupts by singing *Salve sancte parens*, the Introit for the Lady Mass (*Sollemnis missa de beata Maria*).[26] Chaucer, however, achieves a higher level of unity by insisting upon the same chant in

---

[21] Ibid., 447–51.

[22] The Prioress here shows her nicety by calling the place where the boy is thrown a "wardrobe," which, in Chaucer's time was a euphemism for "privy"; see John W. Draper, "Chaucer's Wardrobe," *Englische Studien* 60 (1926): 249.

[23] In some B versions, the boy, a chorister, is miraculously restored to his place in the choir where he continues singing.

[24] In the later C version, preserved in C 9 and C 10, there is the gruesome detail of the boy's tongue having been cut out and then replaced by the magical object which enables him to sing.

[25] C 3, C 4, C 5, and C 7 contain the detail.

[26] On the Lady Mass, see Harrison, *Music in Medieval Britain*, 77–80.

the concluding portion of the funeral service as was used in the beginning of the tale. When he had a chance to improve upon his source material, he did so.

The antiphon *Alma redemptoris mater* is appropriate to the *Prioress' Tale* since the story is heavily laden with liturgical overtones. Marie Padgett Hamilton claims that "*The Prioress' Tale* and Prologue taken together, either quote or refer to all the chief portions of the Mass for 28 December, Childermas or the Feast of the Holy Innocents."[27] For example, the Prioress' first words in the Prologue—"O Lord, oure Lord, thy name how merveillous/ Is in this large world ysprad"—echo Psalm 8:2–3, the Introit for Mass on that day. The Gospel for Holy Innocents, Matthew 2:13–18, which speaks of "Rachel bewailing her children, and would not be comforted, because they are not," is recalled in the Prioress' reference to the boy's grieving mother as a "newe Rachel." The Epistle, Apocalypse 14:1–5, again is subtly echoed in the tale; the 144,000 followers of the Lamb, mentioned in the lesson, were identified in the Middle Ages with the children or Innocents slain by Herod's soldiers.[28] And not only is the passage in the Apocalypse recalled in the tale of the Prioress, but the boy himself is a kind of innocent, martyred by Herod's kin. Unfortunately, Hamilton's crowning argument—her claim that *Alma redemptoris mater* is the proper antiphon for Holy Innocents—holds only for the modern Roman rite[29] and not for the medieval use of Sarum. Frank Ll. Harrison notes that the four Marian antiphons were not necessarily sung in medieval England according to the present rigid seasonal use.[30] And Sarum missals and breviaries do not list *Alma*

---

[27] Marie Padgett Hamilton, "Echoes of Childermas in the Tale of the Prioress," in *Chaucer: Modern Essays in Criticism*, ed. Edward Wagenknecht (New York: Oxford University Press, 1959), 88.

[28] Ibid., 91–92. J. C. Wenk, "On the Sources of *The Prioress's Tale*," *Mediaeval Studies* 17 (1955): 214–19, also points out further verbal echoes from the Feast of the Holy Innocents.

[29] Hamilton, "Echoes of Childermas," 97n.

[30] See Harrison, *Music in Medieval Britain*, 81.

redemptoris mater as part of the service for 28 December.[31]

While Hamilton's discussion is very illuminating concerning the tale's relation to Childermas, it has otherwise had the effect of limiting our understanding of other liturgical aspects. As a miracle of the Virgin, the *Prioress' Tale* could altogether use a Marian antiphon without regard to its seasonal use. We should remember that *Alma redemptoris mater* was very widely utilized in the English rite. The Sarum breviary lists the antiphon at First Vespers on the first Sunday after the Feast of the Holy Trinity. It was used as a processional at Vespers from the second Sunday after Easter until Ascension Sunday, and it sometimes was chosen as a processional during the Nativity of the Blessed Virgin Mary when it was used as the second of two antiphons.[32] In English secular use, the daily singing of one or another of the Marian antiphons was prescribed at Vespers and Compline, and this practice then grew into a separate devotion to the Blessed Virgin.[33] Thus, as Beverly Boyd has pointed out, Chaucer's tale and the song which rings through it are actually more closely related to the canonical hours than to the Holy Innocents Mass.[34]

The fact is that *Alma redemptoris mater* was not only ubiquitous in liturgical practice, but also was popular as the basis for composed pieces by English composers in the late fourteenth and fifteenth centuries. Like the continental composers Dufay and Ockeghem, the Englishmen John Dunstable, Edmund Sturton, Forest, Leonel Power, and "Anglicanus" made use of the chant in motets and polyphonic settings of the Mass. The amount of freedom with which each composer treats the tune varies widely,

---

[31] *Sarum Breviary* (Paris, 1531), fols. 37–39; see also *The Sarum Missal in English*, trans. Frederick E. Warren, 2 vols. (London: A. Moring, 1911), 110–12.

[32] *Sarum Breviary*, fols. 71, 132, 137. See also Brown, *A Study of the Miracle of Our Lady*, 124.

[33] Harrison, *Music in Medieval Britain*, 82.

[34] Boyd, *Chaucer and the Liturgy*, 64–68, and Beverly Boyd, "Young Hugh of Lincoln and Chaucer's 'Prioress's Tale'," *Radford Review* 14 (1960): 1–5.

of course. "Anglicanus" uses the melody quite literally but not slavishly in his *Credo*,[35] and the same may be said of Forest in his *Ascendit Christus*,[36] Sturton in his *Gaude virgo mater Christi*, and Ockeghem in his motet *Alma redemptoris mater*. Dunstable opens his motet *Alma redemptoris mater* with a fairly straightforward statement of the melody but shortly introduces so many additional notes that it becomes a game to find the notes of the chant. On the other hand, Dufay's motet begins with a very free treatment of the melody of the antiphon, but concludes with a section which quotes the chant literally.[37] Leonel Power's *Missa alma redemptoris* uses the chant as an isorhythmic tenor and disregards the natural phrasing of the antiphon.[38] The artistry with which each of these composers treats the antiphon demonstrates their high regard for the beautiful *Alma redemptoris mater*.

The beauty of the text and tune and the way both fit the story are reasons for Chaucer's decision to retain the antiphon in the *Prioress' Tale*. It emphasizes the motherliness of the Blessed Virgin Mary rather than qualities of the distant Queen of Heaven which are stressed in *Ave regina caelorum* or *Regina caeli laetari*. In *Alma redemptoris mater* she is said to be the open door to heaven, and thus she appears in her role as intermediary between the ordinary person and the Lord of heaven. This antiphon calls upon the Blessed Mother to help her fallen people, who are striving again to rise (*succurre cadenti / Surgere qui curat populo*). These phrases are highly appropriate when we consider the fate of the fallen and struggling boy who, like all of us, is in need of "sucour whan we deye." *Gaude Maria*, the responsorium used in most

---

[35] Rudolf Fischer, ed., *Sieben Trienter Codices: Geistliche und Weltliche Kompositionem des XV. Jhs.*, Denkmäler der Tonkunst in Österreich 61 (Graz: Akademische Druck- und Verlagsanstalt, 1960), 92–93.

[36] In John Dunstable, *Complete Works*, ed. Manfred Bukofzer, Musica Britannica 8 (London: Stainer and Bell, 1953), 148–49.

[37] Guillaume Dufay, *Opera Omnia*, ed. Henrik Besseler, 5 vols. (Rome: American Institute of Musicology, 1947–66), 5:117–19.

[38] *Documenta Polyphoniae Liturgicae*, ed. L. Feininger, ser. 1, no. 2 (Rome, 1947).

analogues of the A group, has been called suitable because of its anti-Semitic *erubescat*,[39] which is roughly translated as follows: "Let the unfortunate Jews blush, who say that Christ was born from the seed of Joseph."[40] Professor Boyd, however, correctly notes that the *erubescat* is lost in the Sarum version of *Gaude Maria*, making it less appropriate and opening the way for another Marian song.[41] My own view is the *Gaude Maria*, even if it had contained the *erubescat*, would not have been as appropriate for the tale of the Prioress as *Alma redemptoris mater*. The anti-Semitic details of the story are simply never associated in any way with the Virgin. She only appears in order to aid the lad who had so faithfully demonstrated his devotion to her. The cruel punishment of the murderers is decreed by the provost, a secular authority unrelated to the Blessed Virgin who represents mercy but not vengeance.[42]

---

[39] See Brown, *A Study of the Miracle of Our Lady*, 126.

[40] The versicle for this responsorium concludes: *erubescat iudaeus infelix qui dicit Christum ex Joseph semine esse natum*. See Wagner, *Einführung in die Gregorischen Melodien*, 1:293.

[41] Beverly Boyd, "The Little Clergeon's 'Alma Redemptoris Mater,'" *Notes and Queries* 202 (1957): 277.

[42] Much debate has been devoted to the question of the Prioress' fitness to be a religious person, in the light of the cruelty and anti-Semitism in the tale which she tells. Florence Ridley agrees that the tale is ugly and anti-Semitic, but refuses to judge either the Prioress or her creator, Chaucer, for relating the tale (*The Prioress and the Critics*, University of California Publications, English Studies 30 [Berkeley, 1965], 35). In *Chaucer and the English Tradition* (Cambridge: Cambridge University Press, 1972), 153, Ian Robinson takes a harsher view, saying that the depiction of the Prioress as the bearer of an ugly tale makes a mockery of her religion. However, the real irony of the tale and its teller is that the story would not be based on any genuine knowledge of Jews, since they had not been present in England since 1290. Further, it has been pointed out that the kind of ritual murder that underlies all the legends of the type from which the Prioress' tale springs would have been prohibited by the Bereshith and the Talmud. Thus the entire tale is based on an ironical and improbable situation. See John Hirsch, "Re-opening the *Prioress's Tale*," *Chaucer Review* 10 (1975): 31.

Chaucer's tale does not therefore emphasize the Virgin's role of one who, as in *Gaude Maria*, destroys heresies.

The appropriateness of the tune, both for musical and dramatic reasons, is not difficult to demonstrate. Of course the beauty and perfect structure of the melody as well as the brilliant imagery of the poem do not make the piece particularly easy. Paull F. Baum has wondered why the boy has such great difficulty learning the piece (he must go to his elder "felawe" for assistance),[43] but one will no longer question the boy's acumen once one has examined the antiphon in all of its richness and complexity. The boy, according to Chaucer's account, is only seven years old! But in spite of the difficulty of *Alma redemptoris mater* and the extreme youth of the boy, it is precisely this antiphon which he is challenged to learn out of devotion to the Blessed Mother. I submit that the heavy burden of the tune must be considered a significant motivating factor in the child's decision to learn it. Once he has mastered the opening phrase, he asks his older "felawe" to teach him the remainder of the song, and the fact that he succeeds shows that the task, while difficult, is not impossible. No other Marian antiphon rises melismatically to the octave at the beginning. The beautiful sweep of the phrase *Alma redemptoris mater* seems almost unequaled in chant. In addition, there is repetition of the musical setting of the words *quae pervia caeli* at the phrase *ac posterius*, giving unity to the antiphon. There is striking, even dramatic triple repetition of a note on the same tone at the word *surgere*, a device which is found again at the word *Gabrielis*. The musical phrases are perfectly balanced. The phrase which soars to the highest pitch is found at the center, like the capstone of an arch; from this point, the phrases gently rise and fall and then gradually subside to a final-sounding, satisfying close.

---

[43] Paull F. Baum, *Chaucer: A Critical Appreciation* (Durham: Duke University Press, 1958), 78–79.

High, Clear, and Sweet: Singing Early Music

Any singer who is concerned with creating a reasonably authentic performance of early music must begin by asking questions regarding the quality and production of the voice. We all have our criteria for what we like to hear in early music, most of us preferring a clean, "pure" tone, one which is not pushed into a heavy, overly vibratoed tone. A director of a mixed vocal and instrumental group who has stated in print his abhorrence of all vocal vibrato, and whose recordings and performances have usually seemed to be sensitive to historical performance practice, was observed on one occasion on television directing his singers in a leaden rendition of John Dowland's "Now, O Now, I Needs Must Part" with sustained legato lines and heavy vibrato. The song cried out for a delicacy which was entirely lacking in the performance in question. Why did this performance seem so anachronistic and unimaginative? We might say, "Because it was out of style," but what is meant by "out of style"? Andrea von Ramm pointed out that there is not one medieval-renaissance singing style but rather many medieval and renaissance *styles* of various countries and regions, of different centuries and periods, and of traditions of sacred and secular usage.[1] It seems obvious that Leonin and

---

[1] Andrea von Ramm, "Singing Early Music," *Early Music* 4, no. 1 (Jan. 1976): 12–15, and "Style in Early Music Singing," *Early Music* 8, no. 1 (Jan. 1980): 17–20. See also Audrey Ekdahl Davidson, "The Performance Practice of Early Vocal Music," *EDAM Newsletter*, 4, no. 1 (Nov. 1981): 3–8. On the question of authenticity, see additionally the comments of Richard Taruskin, Daniel Leech-Wilkinson, Nicholas Temperley, and Robert Winter, "The Limits of Authenticity: A Discussion," *Early Music* 12, no. 1 (Feb. 1984): 3–25. The quest for authenticity may indeed be elusive and may even be a chimera. For a different view of the quest for authenticity, see Curt Sachs's important remarks which suggest that in attempting to find historic performance practices, we have projected

Perotin, Machaut, and Dowland would not be performed alike, but perhaps at the start it is well nevertheless to underline this fact. Thus, in any discussion of early vocal practice, we cannot ignore these regional and period differences that demand a different approach in each case to such matters as vocal quality, which includes the important elements of register and vibrato as well as some other matters that can only be mentioned at this point tangentially—e.g., tuning, articulation, handling of ornaments, and treatment of melodic and rhythmic structures. Hence the present study is about vocal style but style narrowly confined to quality, vibrato, registers, and the methods used to produce the appropriate sounds.[2]

It is commonly believed that there are few practical helps for discovering vocal quality and production methods in early treatises and other writings on music of the Middle Ages and the Renaissance. Nevertheless, it will be useful to examine some of the terms that appear over and over in the works of early writers and to analyze them in the light of the vocal apparatus which itself has not changed or evolved appreciably since even the time of Isidore of Seville—in spite of the perilous vocal techniques which have been visited upon defenseless students by too zealous vocal teachers.

Among the heterogeneity of times and places by the various writers, there can be, of course, little seeming agreement except for the desire expressed by many for some ideal or standard of perfection of vocal quality. Isidore of Seville (c.600) exemplifies the search for perfection when he says that "the perfect voice is high [*alta*], sweet [*suavis*], and clear [*clara*]: high, to be sufficient to the sublime; clear, to fill the ear; sweet, to caress the spirits of the hearers. If any one of these qualities is absent, the voice is not

---

backward the practice of later music and in so doing "we overshot the mark; we took for granted that the early Middle Ages, being European, sounded like today's music" ("Primitive and Medieval Music: A Parallel," *Journal of the American Musicological Society* 13 [1960]: 49).

[2] For a fuller study of a range of voice production issues, see "Vocal Production and Early Music" in the present book, below.

High, Clear, and Sweet: Singing Early Music 77

perfect."[3] Conversely, an imperfect voice is said to be thin (*subtilissimae*), fat or breathy (*pingue*), sharp (*acuta*), or hard (*dura*), harsh (*aspera*), or to possess a choked-up quality that Isidore calls "blindness" (*caeca*) because it denotes a voice lacking in carrying quality.[4] Thus we may assume that even in the seventh century there was an ideal tone to which one should aim—one which may stem from having a naturally pleasant-sounding voice by heredity, but one which is capable of being preserved and improved through careful listening and experimenting with tones until most flaws are eradicated. It is evident that some principles of relaxation and breath support were known, because otherwise voices would have partaken of the faults listed specifically by Isidore.

Others who, following Isidore, discuss the perfect voice in terms of being high, sweet, and clear include Aurelian of Réôme (ninth century),[5] Jerome of Moravia (fl. 1272–1304),[6] and Biagio Rossetti of Verona, who was also known as Blassius Rossettus (d. after 1547). In 1529, Rossetti defined the perfect voice (*perfecta vox*) as follows:

---

[3] Isidore of Seville, *Etymologiarum*, ed. W. M. Lindsay, 2 vols. (Oxford: Clarendon Press, 1911), Book 3.20; cf. Oliver Strunk, *Source Readings in Music History* (New York: Norton, 1950), who translates *clara* as "loud" (96).

[4] *Etymologiarum*, 3.20, as translated by Strunk, *Source Readings in Music History*, 96.

[5] "Perfecta autem est vox alta, suavis et clara" (Aurelian of Réôme, *Musica Disciplina*, ed. Lawrence Gushee, Corpus Scriptorum de Musica 21 [American Institute of Musicology, 1975], 70). For a translation, see *The Discipline of Music*, trans. Joseph Ponte (Colorado Springs: Colorado Music Press, 1968), 12.

[6] Jerome of Moravia, *Tractatus de musica*, in *Scriptorum de musica medii aevi*, ed. E. de Coussemaker, 4 vols. (1874; reprint Hildesheim: Georg Olms, 1963), 1:8. "Perfecta autem vox esta alta, suavis et clara; alta, ut in sublime sufficiat; suavis ut animas audientium blandiatur; et clara, ut aures adimpleat."

high [*alta*], music [sweet, *suavis*], strong (firm) and clear; high, so that it has brilliance, clear so that it satisfies the ear, strong so that it does not waver or lose its strength (or go off pitch), musical [sweet] so that it will not grate on the ears, rather caress them and lure the hearts of the listeners and capture them.[7]

If one of these four qualities is missing, Rossetti says, perfection has not been achieved. As should be obvious, his statement, except for the addition of "strong," is almost verbatim from Isidore.

Singing in the sixteenth century as in the seventh required good breath support and a maximum of relaxation in the vocal cords and muscles used for singing. In addition, the qualification that the good voice is "high" means that a smaller, more precise aperture is needed to produce these sounds, and thus more skill is required than for the relatively easier low tones. Further, Mauro Uberti, writing in the journal *Early Music*, has demonstrated that the actual opening of the mouth in singing in *camera* in the sixteenth century was limited to the extent of the opening normally utilized in speaking. He also has shown that a particular forward thrust of the jaw was utilized, creating a brighter tone and more contrast in the enunciation of vowels. His evidence is drawn in part from musical iconography, and includes as one of his examples the marble relief of Florentine choir singers by Lucca della Robbia (1400–82).[8] A graphic illustration, not cited by Uberti, of the jaw thrust forward is found in a woodcut depicting a singing lesson in Rodericus Zamorensis' *Spiegel des menschlichen Lebens*, a book printed at Augsburg in c.1475.

---

[7] Biagio Rossetti, *Libellus de rudimentis Musices* (Verona, 1529), as cited in Bernard Ulrich, *Ueber die Grundsätze der Stimmbildung der Acappella-Periode und zur Zeit des Aufkommens der Oper—1474–1640* (Leipzig: Arno Theuerkorn, 1910), 18; trans. John W. Seale and ed. Edward Foreman, under the title *Concerning the Principles of Voice Training during the a cappella Period and until the Beginning of Opera* (Minneapolis: Pro Musica Press, 1973), 20.

[8] Mauro Uberti, "Vocal Techniques in Italy in the Second Half of the 16th Century," *Early Music* 9 (1981): 488–89, fig. 5. Such a bright tone may still be heard in Florentine churches, as I discovered upon attending services in the summer of 1983 at S. Maria Novella.

High, Clear, and Sweet: Singing Early Music

Less dependent on Isidore's prescription for the perfect voice is Camillo Maffei da Solofra (fl. 1562–73), a vocal teacher, philosopher, and medical doctor who wrote extensively about the voice. Maffei identifies the good voice as "strong and delicate, high *and* low [italics mine], lovely and elastic."[9] For the low voice he may be returning to Aristotle, who preferred the low to the high voice, finding nobility in the deep voice and, in contrast to medieval and renaissance opinion, debility in the high.[10] Of course, we have difficulty in giving Aristotle's preference in voices much credence, since we know that he thought the cause of the highness or lowness of voices is the temperature of the breath that passes through the throat: hot breath causes deep voices and cold breath causes high, thin voices.[11] This explanation is used for pitches produced by wind instruments also, and here it is true that heat and cold do affect the pitch of such instruments. However, the effect of heat and cold on voices is not that of changing them from soprano to alto, from tenor to bass, or vice versa.

One common vocal trait which appears to have been required quite universally is strength of tone. This trait again could be at least partially a natural attribute of the voice, but certainly it is one which needs good breath support and regular practice to attain and retain. And surely, when St. Bernard advised his Cistercian monks to "sing out [with] full voice," he was showing his approval of the strong voice, one produced not by "pulling back" on the tone but rather by producing a well-supported, authentic tone.[12]

---

[9] Camillo Maffei da Solofra, *Discorso*, 9–13, as cited in Ulrich, *Concerning the Principles of Voice Training*, trans. Seale, 21; see also Maffei, "Letter on Singing," trans. Carol MacClintock, *Readings in the History of Music in Performance* (Bloomington: Indiana University Press, 1979), 41.

[10] Aristotle, *The Generation of Animals*, Book 5, chap. 7; ed. and trans. A. L. Peck (Cambridge, Mass.: Harvard University Press, 1979), 545.

[11] Ibid., 553.

[12] Bernard of Clairvaux, *Institutes*, cited and trans. Chrysogonus Waddell, "A Plea for the *Institutio Sancti Bernardi quomodo cantari et psallere debeamus*," in *Saint Bernard of Clairvaux: Studies Commemorating the Eighth Centenary of his Canonization* (Kalamazoo: Cistercian Publications,

The ideal tone, according to Isidore, is commonly described as "sweet," which indeed is the term frequently found in Middle English writings to signify satisfactory singing.[13] In the anonymous *Legend of St. Anthony* in British Library MS. Royal 17.C.XVII, sweetness is linked with the voices and songs of angels which, when heard by men in the night, caused them to feel as though "thai warne in paradyse."[14] Angelic song involves surely the highest possibility for beauty in music. But whether linked with human beings or not, the word *sweet* is always used to indicate a quality highly to be desired. In the anonymous *Visions of Tundale*, the clear voice is said to be allied with sweetness and cleanness of sound:

> They song all ther with myld chere
> Aleluya with vocys soo clere
> Hym thoght they song so swete and clene
> Hyt passed all the joyes that he had seen.[15]

In Lydgate's *Pilgrimage of the Life of Man*, the voice described is said to be "mellodyus,/ Wonder soote and gracyous."[16] Each of these citations clearly refers to vocal quality as well as to intonation, since, as Andrea von Ramm noted, pleasant sensations (which one would term "sweet") in early music depend not only on quality but also on the exact tuning of unisons, octaves, and

---

1977), 195. It should be noted that in the Renaissance the full voice was used only in *cappella* and not in *camera* singing; see Uberti, "Vocal Techniques in Italy," 493.

[13] See Henry Holland Carter, *A Dictionary of Middle English Musical Terms* (Bloomington: Indiana University Press, 1961), 481–84.

[14] C. Horstmann, "Prosalegenden: V. S. Antonius (vita, inventio, translatio)," *Anglia* 4 (1881): 132.

[15] W. B. D. D. Turnbull, ed., *The Visions of Tundale* (Edinburgh: Thomas G. Stevenson, 1843), 60 (ll. 1879–82); cited by Carter, *A Dictionary of Middle English Musical Terms*, 483.

[16] Cited by Carter, *A Dictionary of Middle English Musical Terms*, 482.

fifths.[17]

Something about the handling of the voice in early music can be learned from various critical comments on voices and vocal faults. Not surprisingly, the faults of voices which are enumerated seem remarkably similar to the ones found today. To mention only a few, these include: singing too loudly, especially on high notes; forcing, shrieking, and shouting; singing through the nose; and allowing the pitch to wander. Some of these will be noted in Thomas Mace's *Musick's Monument* (1676) as characteristic of singing in rural churches: it is "*sad* to hear what *whining, toting, yelling,* or *screeking* there is in many *Country Congregations*, as if the people were *affrighted*, or *distracted*."[18]

Singing too loudly is scorned by Conrad von Zabern (d. between 1479 and 1481)—a musician, priest, and professor at Heidelberg—who especially disliked singing high notes too loudly: "A particularly striking crudity is that of singing the high notes with a loud tone, indeed with full lung power."[19] Forcing the voice is also something particularly disliked, for he compared bellowing in the choir to the sounds made by cows in the field:

> Ut boves in prates
> Sic vos in choro boatis.[20]

Similarly, we find that Jerome of Moravia advised the singer not to shout and shiek—surely the extremes to which loud singing can be carried and undoubtedly also the cause of those faults of harshness

---

[17] Von Ramm, "Singing Early Music," 12.

[18] Thomas Mace, *Musick's Monument* (1676; facs. reprint, New York: Broude, 1966), 9.

[19] Conrad von Zabern, *De Modo bene cantandi*, trans. MacClintock, *Readings in the History of Music in Performance*, 15.

[20] Ibid.

and hoarseness noted long ago by Isidore.[21]

St. Bernard in the twelfth century and Conrad in the sixteenth century both advised singers not to sing through the nose—the fault of Chaucer's Prioress and apparently a characteristic of some secular styles of the Middle Ages.[22] Bernard said that one ought to avoid singing "with weak and mincing voices effeminately stammering or sounding through the nose...."[23] Conrad was even more blunt when he said that singing through the nose makes a voice *very* unbeautiful, though his reasoning thereupon proceeds in a way that is open to question: "The nasal passages are never associated with the development of the human voice; so it is not a small sign of lack of education if one is not contented with the mouth and the ordinary natural tools, but emits the voice through the nose."[24] I think we might have little quarrel with the latter part of the statement, but it is nevertheless absurd to say that the nasal passages "are never associated with the development of the voice." A simple empirical test, involving holding the nostrils tightly pinched to close off much of the sound which would otherwise be normally emitted, would disprove the first part of Conrad's statement which seems to deny the association of voice and nasal

---

[21] Jerome of Moravia, *Tractatus de Musica*, in *Scriptorum de Musica Medii Aevi*, ed. Coussemaker, 1:94; trans. MacClintock, *Readings in the History of Music in Performance*, 7.

[22] Thurston Dart, *The Interpretation of Music* (1954; reprint, New York: Harper and Row, 1963), 50. Dart observes that the facial expressions of singers depicted in medieval and renaissance paintings and sculptures suggest that the tone quality "associated with this facial expression" would be "nasal and reedy." See also the General Prologue of Chaucer's *Canterbury Tales* for the description of Madame Eglentyne's singing: "Ful weel she soong the service dyvyne,/ Entuned in hir nose ful semely . . ." (ll. 122–23).

[23] Bernard, *Sermons on the Canticle of Canticles*, as cited by Waddell, "A Plea for the *Institutio Sancti Bernardi quomodo cantari et psallere debeamus*," 191.

[24] Conrad von Zabern, *De Modo bene cantandi*, trans. MacClintock, *Readings in the History of Music in Performance*, 14–15.

passages.

The best concise description of nasal tone perhaps comes from Lilli Lehmann, writing in 1902; she indicates that nasality comes from "raising, rounding, and spreading the pillars of the fauces (rather far back) and jamming the broad back of the tongue against them."[25] One utilizes the nasal passages correctly by singing toward them, singing into the mask of the face, and using all the resonating capabilities of the bones and cavities of nose and face. But in distinction to modern practice, these resonating capabilities can also be used to develop sounds with more *contrast* than would normally be permitted today.

Not surprisingly, wandering pitch is another bad habit that Conrad found unacceptable in singing. He provided two categories of such instances: (1) when the pitch of a long-held note "wanders and varies" while it is being sung, and (2) when the pitch of an entire song is spoiled by the "horrid wavering" of one voice "up or down."[26] The latter problem can be caused by a poor ear (irremediable, in most serious instances) or by poor breath support (remediable, fortunately, in almost all cases not connected with aging or illness). The former is surely a tremulo (a "wobblato"), which easily becomes unmanageable.

This leads us to the important question of vibrato and its role or lack of role in early music. Andrea von Ramm stated flatly that there is no such thing as a natural vibrato: "[it] is an interaction of breathing muscles and throat muscles and can be controlled."[27] The implication of her remarks seems to be that when vibrato is not under control, as in an unsupported or undisciplined voice, or is no longer able to be controlled, as in the aging process or illness, it is

---

[25] See Lilli Lehmann, *How to Sing*, trans. Richard Aldrich and Clara Willenbücher, revised ed. (1924; reprint, New York: Macmillan, 1960), 76. [The author did not intend to argue that this singer's technique is otherwise particularly applicable to singing pre-baroque music, though her book has much of value. For further discussion of nasal resonance in contrast to unpleasant nasality, see "Voice Production and Early Music," below.—Ed.]

[26] Conrad von Zabern, *De Modo bene cantandi*, trans. MacClintock, *Readings in the History of Music in Performance*, 15.

[27] Von Ramm, "Singing Early Music," 12.

not suitable for early music. Von Ramm does not, of course, assert that vibrato was never used in early music, but rather that it has its place in specific styles. Speed and floridity of songs are also factors in deciding whether vibrato is appropriate. Fast and florid works require such accuracy that uncontrolled vibrato cannot be permitted. In polyphonic music vibrato is best used as an ornament or not at all.

Some writers on early music permit the use of vibrato, to be sure. Michael Praetorius cited the classical ideal as set forth by Cicero to indicate that a singer should have "a beautiful, sweet, tremulous and vibrating voice."[28] And Georg Quitschreiber, describing singing at Jena in 1598, seems to have thought it best to sing with vibrato (*Temula voce optime canitur*).[29] However, others—e.g., Rossetti[30] and Francinus Gafurius[31]—found fault with the vibrato, especially when it is excessive. Writers on early instrumental music viewed it as an ornament to be added for special effect. As late as the seventeenth and eighteenth centuries, the vibrato was added rarely and only at specific notes in string music. For Mersenne (1621), vibrato was used for pleasure at specific points: "players sweeten [the tone] as they wish and render

---

[28] Michael Praetorius, *Syntagma Musica*, 2 vols. (1614–15; reprint, Kassel, Bärenreiter, 1959)1:195; trans. in Ulrich, *Concerning the Principles of Voice Training*, trans. Seale, 66.

[29] Thurston Dart, "How They Sang in Jena in 1598," *The Musical Times* 108 (1967): 316–17.

[30] See Ulrich, *Concerning the Principles of Voice Training*, trans. Seale, 72.

[31] Franchinus Gafurius, *The Practica Musicae*, trans. Irwin Young (Madison: University of Wisconsin Press, 1969), 160. Joseph Dyer, in a reply to Andrea von Ramm's remarks on vibrato, argues that Gafurius' denunciation of *voces tremebundas* is not a reference to "a natural vibrancy which still permits correct tuning" but rather a reference to "*excess* [italics mine] vibrato" ("The Universal Voice," *Early Music* 4, no. 4 [Oct. 1976]: 489).

it inimitable by certain tremblings which delight the mind."[32] It does not seem that singing and instrumental styles would necessarily have been so different, and indeed we can argue for the compatibility of the two styles.

Normally whenever vibrato is used in early music it must be used with great caution and restraint. Exact tuning of unisons, octaves, and fifths is made impossible by excessive vibrato, and it causes beats between the voices in long-held notes as well as unpleasant fluctuations in faster passages. Thus, if vibrato is used in polyphonic music, it can cause great disturbance of the vertical sonorities. It seems rather inappropriate for monophonic unison singing such as chant.[33] Voices with uncontrolled vibrato create unpleasant clashings of sound. Even in solo song, a voice out of control is undesirable. However, vibrato used as an ornament in such songs is often intrinsic to the style and adds to the pleasure of the listener.

One final requisite of the well-trained medieval or renaissance voice is the clear definition of differences between chest, middle, and head registers. As early as 1309, Marchetto of Padua in his *Lucidarium* treated the registers, which he identified under the terms *graves*, *acutae*, and *superacutae*, and gave specific ranges for each.[34] And Conrad describes the registers as follows: "Whoever sings well must use his voice in three degrees. The low notes are to be sung entirely from the chest, the middle ones with a moderate

---

[32] Marin Mersenne, *Harmonie Universelle: The Books on Instruments*, trans. Roger E. Chapman (The Hague: Martinus Nijhoff, 1957), 24.

[33] See Lance Brunner, "The Performance of Plainchant: Some Preliminary Observations of the New Era," *Early Music* 10, no. 3 (July 1982): 325. Brunner writes: "In chant, singing that is both appropriate and beautiful is generally based on a sound that is well supported and focused (although more subdued than in later music); clear, open vowels; and a controlled vibrato."

[34] Marchetto de Padova, *Lucidarium Musicae Planae*, 14, in *Scriptores Eccelsiastici de Musica*, ed. Martin Gerbert, 3 vols. (1784; reprint, Hildesheim: Georg Olms, 1963), 3:120. On registers, see also Franz Müller-Heuser, *Vox Humana* (Regensburg: Gustav Bosse, 1963), 124–32.

strength, the high ones with a soft voice."[35] The advantage of having three possibilities for tonal color rather than one blended, homogeneous color seems too obvious even to comment upon. The various colors, used in different parts of a song or in different types of songs, can create stunning effects and variety essential to early music performance.

References to the way singers should breathe are much fewer in early writers on music than are descriptions of the voice, but the following injunctions regarding breathing are found: (1) Inhale easily and quietly,[36] and (2) plan your breathing so that you do not need to breathe after every note or even in the middle of a word.[37] In spite of the last injunction, no less a composer than Guillaume de Machaut shows how to break a word in two in his *Notre Dame Mass.* In the *Agnus Dei*, Machaut breaks the words "Agnus," "tollis," "peccata," "miserere," and "nobis."[38]

It is difficult to pinpoint an exact date for the discovery that allowing the abdomen to relax and expand when breathing is more efficacious than breathing only from the chest, and that supporting the breath with the abdominal rectus muscles is a way of avoiding the wobble. Nevertheless, Uberti has suggested that a reference in the sixteenth century by Lodovico Zacconi to *fiancho* ("flank") means that the writer was aware of the physiological phenomenon

---

[35] Conrad von Zabern, *Tractatus de Musica*, trans. MacClintock, *Readings in the History of Music in Performance*, 15. See also Jerome of Moravia, *Tractatus de Musica*, in *Scriptorum de Musica Medii Aevi*, ed. Coussemaker, 1:93; trans. MacClintock, *Readings*, 6.

[36] Rossetti, *Libellus de rudimentis Musices*, as cited in Ulrich, *Concerning the Principles of Voice Training*, trans. Seale, 67.

[37] Bovicelli, *Regale, Passaggi di Musica* (1594), cited in Ulrich, *Concerning the Principles of Voice Training*, trans. Seale, 68. Bovicelli criticizes "beginners who often tear the notes apart while they skip over notes as they take a breath, and this indeed in such haste that one can scarcely hear their tones."

[38] *Notre Dame Mass*, in Guillaume de Machaut, *Oeuvres Complètes*, ed. Leo Schrade, Polyphonic Music of the Fourteenth Century, 2–3 (Monaco: Editions de L'Oisèau-Lyre, 1977), 24–27.

High, Clear, and Sweet: Singing Early Music

of lower abdominal support.[39] Nor can we discover how or when it was decided that relaxation of the throat muscles creates a rounder, less pinched tone. But we must assume that these discoveries were made and utilized by singers at least to a limited degree as early as Isidore of Seville's time, for from such techniques comes the tone that is at once strong, delicate, firm, clear, high, bright, and sweet.

---

[39] Uberti, "Vocal Techniques in Italy," 494.

II

Palestrina and Mannerism

Wylie Sypher in his work on interrelationships between the arts defines *mannerism* as an art which "holds everything in a state of dissonance, dissociation and doubt."[1] Applied to music, this definition could easily be adopted, for example, to describe the compositions of the Prince of Venosa, with their frequent, sudden key changes and shocking dissonances. Palestrina, however, does not in any way fit this definition of mannerism, since in his works the dissonant or jarring elements, whether melodic, rhythmic, harmonic, or structural, are all resolved and not ever left in a state of "dissociation" or "doubt."

The treatment of dissonances in Palestrina's compositions has been admirably handled by Knud Jeppesen in *The Style of Palestrina and the Dissonance.*[2] This careful scholar finds that the composer's dissonance practice is controlled rigidly by rules devised from his immediate predecessors and by his own stringent taste. His conclusion is that "Palestrina—strictly speaking—only recognizes the conjunct method of dissonance treatment. Only the passing note, the returning-note, the cambiata (in its classic form!), and the Portamento of the descending second are of general validity."[3] In other words, we can say that the dissonance practice of Palestrina is much more narrowly defined than was the case with his predecessors. It is clear that Palestrina does not introduce dissonance without careful control. No musical work could be less

---

[1] Wylie Sypher, *Four Stages of Renaissance Style* (Garden City, N.Y.: Doubleday, 1955), 117. Sypher is, of course, deriving his understanding of mannerism from an earlier generation of art critics.

[2] Knud Jeppesen, *The Style of Palestrina and the Dissonance* (1946; reprint, New York: Dover, 1970), esp. 94–276.

[3] Ibid., 221. See also Malcolm Boyd, *Palestrina's Style* (London: Oxford University Press, 1973), 23.

like the paintings of El Greco or the poetry of John Donne, whose creations have been put forward as the epitome of mannerist art.

However, as an article by James Haar suggests,[4] the question of Palestrina and mannerism may still remain. Crucial here is the fact that criticism subsequent to Sypher has questioned the definition of *mannerism* used by him and by others. The term was not applied to music or to any of the other arts in the Renaissance.[5] As John Shearman and others have insisted, in the sixteenth century *maniera* (from which *mannerism* has been derived as a modern equivalent) was the equivalent of the modern word *style*. *Maniera*, in turn, stemmed from an Old French word for correct deportment or behavior. Prior to 1550, a related Italian word, *manieroso*, had meant *polished* or *stylish*.[6] For the critic Varchi, writing in 1548, *maniera* and *artifiziosa* are closely related; for him, the work of art involves "an artificial imitation of nature."[7] Giorgio Vasari, writing in 1558, distinguished between "objective imitation of nature" (as in the works of fifteenth-century painters)

---

[4] James Haar, "Classicism and Mannerism in 16th-Century Music," *International Review of Music and Aesthetics and Aesthetics and Sociology* 1 (1970): 55–67. Haar notes that the term *maniera* had been associated with certain sixteenth-century musical styles as early as the 1930s; see Leo Schrade, "Von der 'Maniera' der Komposition in der Musik des 16. Jahrhunderts," *Zeitschrift für Musikwissenschaft* 16 (1934): 3–20, 98–117, 152–70.

[5] See Claude V. Palisca, "Ut oratoria musica: The Rhetorical Basis of Musical Mannerism," in Franklin W. Robinson and Stephen G. Nichols, eds., *The Meaning of Mannerism* (Hanover, N.H.: University Press of New England, 1972), 37– 61. Palisca's approach, which emphasizes a different approach to the problem than mine, cites Renaissance praise for Palestrina's contemporary Orlandus Lassus as the epitome of *musica reservata* and a new style of composition appearing in the sixteenth century.

[6] John Shearman, *Mannerism* (Baltimore: Penguin, 1967), 17–19.

[7] Ibid., 18.

and *maniera*, the "ideal imitation of nature."[8] Thus in its own time, *mannerism* (*maniera*) meant that which possessed artifice, grace, and polish—in short, it was the stylish style. Hence, in the light of a new understanding of the term *mannerism*, the work of Palestrina as a composer might be re-evaluated. His artificiality, his smooth texture, his well-formed structures, and his control over thematic materials are all illustrative of a technique which creates a sound supremely polished and idealized.

Four essential qualities of mannerist style in painting and related arts are identified by Shearman as "grace, complexity, variety and difficulty."[9] Standing between the so-called "classical" Renaissance artists and the baroque, such artists as Bronzino, Giulio Romano, Rosso, and Parmigianino surely share these qualities, which were understood in the sixteenth century in very precise ways. If these artists are to be understood by our revised definition of mannerism, Palestrina too might be included as an exemplar of mannerist art in music.

The remarkable grace with which Palestrina handles his materials needs little comment. He has the poise, the stylishness, the polish expected during this period.[10] His compositions consequently sound transparently simple, though indeed his resolution of dissonances and his handling of polyphonic voices demonstrate that his art hides great complexity under the apparent simplicity. The idea toward which he aspires might well be labeled *sprezzatura*, the term used by Baldesar Castiglione in *The Book of the Courtier* to describe the art of making the difficult seem effortless.

Complexity and variety are particularly in evidence in Palestrina's treatment of his thematic material, as everyone who has sung or conducted his work will know. My own approach has further been to look more closely at all of Palestrina's compositions based on a single chant, the antiphon *Alma redemptoris mater*, which has been itself discussed in its English manifestation elsewhere in the present book. Palestrina, utilizing of course the

---

[8] See Luisa Becherucci, "Mannerism," *Encylcopedia of World Art*, 16 vols. (New York: McGraw-Hill, 1959–83), 10:444.

[9] Shearman, *Mannerism*, 84.

[10] See ibid., 19.

Continental version of this antiphon, used it as the basis for his thematic material in three motets, *Alma redemptoris mater a 8* VI, *Alma redemptoris mater a 8* VII, and *Alma redemptoris mater a 4*, as well as for his *Missa Alma redemptoris*. My own modest observations in this essay are based largely on my analysis of these

USE OF CHANT NOTES 1–25 IN *MISSA ALMA REDEMPTORIS*

Section	Voices	Measures	Chant Notes
Kyrie I	All 6 voices	1–12	1–7
	Cantus only	7–10	6–9 transformed
	All 6 voices	12–30	17–25
Gloria	C, T, Q	1–8	1–16 with additions and elisions
	C, B	26–30	17–22
	Q	48–50	1–6
Credo	C, S, T, Q	1–18	1–9
	All 6 voices	1–18	17–23
	C, A, B, Q	27–33	17–22
	B, Q	156–59	1–4, 6–9
Sanctus	C, T, B, Q A.S. imit. at 4	1–17	1–10 with additions
	Q, T	24–39	Possibly 17–23
	Q, B, S, A, T (5-voice texture)	40–55	1–4
Agnus Dei	All 6 voices	1–17	1–16 with great elaborations
	All 6 voices	18–36	17–23

Palestrina and Mannerism 95

selected works.[11]

In these compositions, free use of material from the antiphon seems to be characteristic. Palestrina's method is to regard the notes of the chant only as building blocks from which he creates his own aesthetic entities. His compositions each must involve the overcoming of difficulty and the achievement of precise effects, and hence cannot follow simply the contour of the entire melody of a chant. The sixteenth-century word was *difficultà*, at that time admired in both small and large forms.[12]

The complexity with which Palestrina used his thematic material is shown by the accompanying table, which tabulates the use of the first twenty-five notes of the antiphon *Alma redemptoris mater* in the *Missa Alma redemptoris*. Such a tabulation, of course, only indicates which notes from the antiphon were utilized by Palestrina; it reveals little about the even more complex way in which he added and/or subtracted notes and built his phrase curves.

Example 1: Kyrie I, *Ms. 1-6 cantus*

---

[11] Editions used: Giovanni Pierluigi da Palestrina, *Le Opera Complete*, ed. Raffaele Casmiri et al., 24 vols. (Rome, 1939–), 11:52–57 (Motet, *Alma redemptoris mater a 4*), and 27:148–84 (*Missa Alma redemptoris*); Giovanni Pierluigi da Palestrina, *Werke*, ed. F. Espagne, F. X. Haberl, et al., 33 vols (Leipzig: Breitkopf und Härtel, 1862–1907), 6:159–64 (*Alma redemptoris mater a 8* VI); 7:73–75 (*Alma redemptoris mater a 8* VII). The roman numerals affixed to the titles of the two motets *a 8* distinguish each by the number of the volume in Palestrina's *Werke* in which it appears. The Continental version of the chant is conveniently accessible in the *Liber usualis* (Tournai: Desclee, 1961), 273–74.

[12] Shearman, *Mannerism*, 21.

In the first instance in which Palestrina uses material from the antiphon in *Kyrie I*, he appears not to be using very much of the chant (see Example 1). In this example, I have shown the composer's additions in brackets. It will be noted that the addition of the last note makes a better close for the phrase than breaking off at note 7, which is also scale step 7.

Although the first phrase seems short, there is a transformation of it at measures 7–10, which provides added emphasis:

Example 2: Kyrie I, *Ms. 7-10*

[Ky - ri - e   e - le - i - son]

Chant Notes 6   8 7   9   6   6   7 8 9

Phrase 1 is repeated and imitated through all voices, while phrase 2 is not imitated. When this exposition is completed, Palestrina picks up the *redemptoris mater* material (notes 17–25) and uses it quite literally in the cantus and quintus, but elaborates on it in the other four voices (measures 13–20).

In all there are fourteen separate entrances of the *redemptoris mater* theme in *Kyrie I*, in addition to four other entrances that are at least tangentially related to the theme. The utilization of only two themes in *Kyrie I*, each one amplified and imitated—and thus creating an A and a B section—gives this Mass movement carefully controlled coherence, a unity juxtaposed with the rich variety of the additions, interpolations, and transformations.

The opening of the *Gloria* section presents more extensive use of material from the antiphon than in the first phrase of *Kyrie I* (see Example 3). The addition of three notes and the subtraction of two others does not make the chant any the less recognizable, and these few changes show that Palestrina is using discretion in his use of the antiphon. He incorporates his material with perfect ease, neither being too tightly tied to his material nor being completely emancipated from it.

In the *Credo*, he is more brief in his quotation of the antiphon, but the result is on a higher level of artifice by the addition of a few chant notes in retrograde form (see Example 4). Both the *Sanctus*

Palestrina and Mannerism 97

and the *Agnus Dei* use extremely elaborated forms of the chant as first statement (see Examples 5–6).

Example 3: Gloria, *Ms. 1-10*

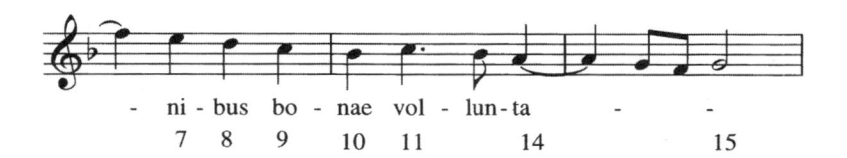

Cantus

Et in ter - ra pax ho - mi-
Chant Notes 1   1 2   3   4   5 6

- ni - bus bo - nae vol - lun - ta - -
  7   8   9   10   11   14   15

tis. Lau - da - mus te.
16   9   8   8   7

Example 4: Credo, *Ms. 1-8*

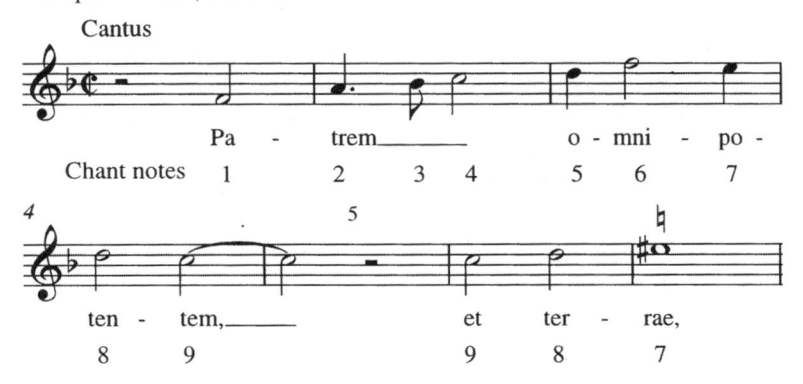

Cantus

Pa - trem_____ o - mni - po -
Chant notes 1   2   3   4   5   6   7

ten - tem,_____ et ter - rae,
 8   9   9   8   7

Example 5: Sanctus, *Ms. 1-11*

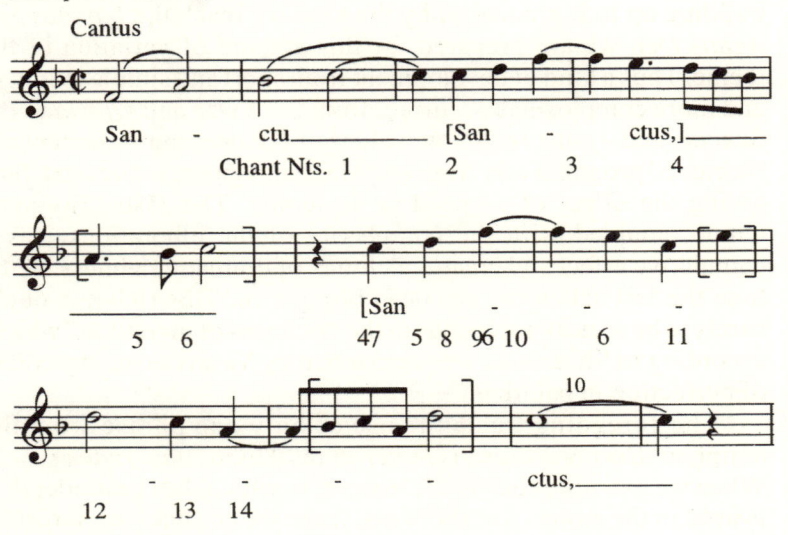

Example 6: Agnus Dei I, *Ms. 1-10*

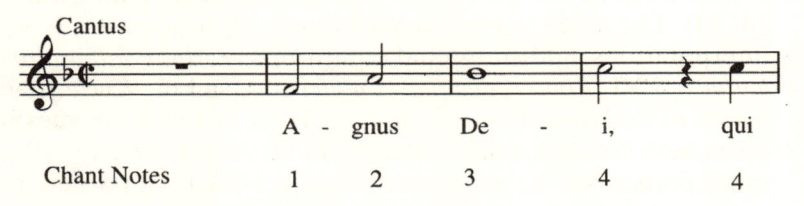

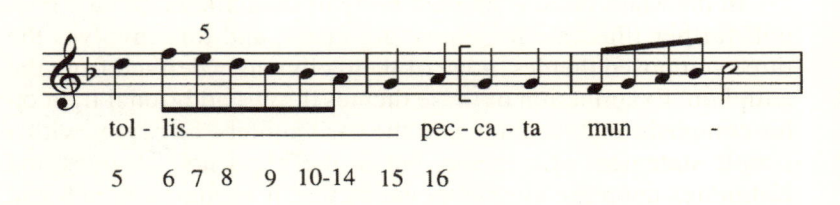

Palestrina has set the stage for this elaborate treatment by building up to it gradually; by the time we reach the *Sanctus* and *Agnus Dei*, we are prepared for this amount of variation of the theme. Thus a kind of development from short and simple to longer and more complex has occurred, from the *Kyrie* and *Gloria* to the *Sanctus* and *Agnus Dei*. Note values of the opening statement are shortened progressively from one Mass movement to the next, thus giving the effect of a speed-up in tempo. The faster rhythmic tempo, coupled with the complexity of the elborations, has a cumulative effect and creates a climax of dramatic richness by the time the last statement has been brought in. This richness ought surely to be seen as analogous to the "richness of invention" which, according to Shearman, was demanded by Vasari as an ingredient of perfection in painting.[13]

The foregoing treats the use of only one phrase from the antiphon *Alma redemptoris mater* in the *Missa Alma redemptoris*. When we examine closely the manner in which the remainder of it is used in the motets and the Mass, there are no shocking surprises but at least some interesting revelations. For example, Palestrina avoids entirely the use of the *quae pervia caeli* phrase (notes 26–34). The notes at *porta manes* (notes 35–45) are used, with interpolations, additions, and repetitions in *Alma redemptoris mater a 8* VI, *Alma redemptoris mater a 4*, and the *Kyrie II* and *Gloria* of the *Missa Alma redemptoris*. In the motets the themes are given both real and tonal imitations in all voices. This relatively small portion of the antiphon is thus provided with a new importance because of the attention which Palestrina gave to it.

In the Mass there is another body of thematic material which will further illustrate the above argument, and this involves the three composed themes, none of them obviously derived from the antiphon. Examination of these themes throws additional light on his compositional technique. In the early motets, he begins with a simple statement of a theme, but in the Mass he elongates and elaborates upon the simple theme so that it becomes as rich and complex as thematic material derived from the antiphon. We are reminded of the way Bronzino or Parmigianino are able to tease and elongate lines in their paintings, as in the latter's *Madonna*

---

[13] Ibid., 21.

with the Long Neck. Like the chant-derived themes, each of these composed themes finds an integral place in the structure of the Mass. In each Mass movement, the composed themes are skillfully worked into the composition. A composed theme may even be used as one of only two themes in a two-sectioned portion of the work. And in the *Christe eleison* section, for example, two of the three composed themes are counterpoised one against the other to make up the section's sole thematic material.

What this brief essay has set out to suggest is that Palestrina's control over his source material, the selection of thematic elements, and the richness to which each theme is subjected are properly to be understood as *mannerist*. His control and originality are expressed in the notes which he interpolates, elides, or adds at the end of the chant material—all of which is done with the highest degree of grace. His melodic contours are thus chosen with the greatest precision in each of the voices. When he seems to distort in any manner the original antiphon, the distortion is always suspended within a totality which is marked by the utmost polish and stylishness.

Five Settings of Songs Attributed to Sir Philip Sidney

The frequent allusions to music in Sir Philip Sidney's poetical and critical works take in a whole gamut of meanings. In the critical writings, music is an analogue for poetry, while in the poetry music is often found to be a symbol for the state of man's soul.[1] In addition to the analogical and symbolical meanings ascribed by him to music, his *dramatis personae* often sing songs, some of which have been found in contemporary music manuscripts. The subject of this study will be a selection of five songs, four which definitely are settings of Sidney's words and one ("O sweet woodes") which may only contain a refrain by him.[2] One of these songs, "Haue I Caught my heavenlye Jewell" from the sonnet series *Astrophil and Stella*, has been transcribed from manuscript by John P. Cutts;[3] the remaining four, "O sweet woodes," "My trewe loue hath my hart and I haue his," "My Lute, wthin thy Selfe thy tunes enclose," and "Goe my flockes, goe get you hence," are transcribed by the present writer.

---

[1] See John Hollander, *The Untuning of the Sky* (Princeton: Princeton University Press, 1961), 141.

[2] For a list of other settings, including part songs, see Sir Philip Sidney, *The Poems*, ed. William Ringler, Jr. (Oxford: Clarendon Press, 1962), 566–68. [The selection in the present study of only five songs appears to suggest a larger project by the author that was not pursued.—Ed.]

[3] John P. Cutts, "Falstaff's 'Heauenlie Iewel': Incidental Music for *The Merry Wives of Windsor*," *Shakespeare Quarterly* 11 (1960): 91. See also Sidney, *The Poems*, ed. Ringer, 202

I

The song which is the most perplexing to the scholar is "O sweet woodes," found in the Henry Lawes autograph manuscript (British Library Add. MS. 57,723, fol. 11ᵛ).[4] In this setting, some stylistic characteristics of Lawes seem to be present,[5] such as his frequent shifts from major to minor modes and his attempt "to span/ Words with just note and accent." The chromatic progression in the last measure of the song seems to be similar to other chromatic cadential formulae used by the composer—for example, in his "Hymne to God the Father."[6]

Although Willa McClung Evans accepted "O sweet woodes" as Lawes's work, she indicated that there appears to have been some borrowing, melodically and rhythmically, from an earlier setting by John Dowland. She argued that "Lawes' arrangement for 'O sweet woodes' follows Dowland's setting for the same poem in the nice adjustment of notes to syllables, the pauses between musical phrases, and particularly the stressing of the syllables of the final cadence, 'for she less seacret and as sencless is,' in which both composers fitted syllables to notes of equal values."[7] But, though Miss Evans noted general similarities between the two composers' settings, on closer examination the differences between the

---

[4] For a partial description of this manuscript, formerly identified as British Museum Loan MS. 35, see Eric Ford Hart, "An Introduction to Henry Lawes, Part I," *Music and Letters* 32 (1951): 219–22. Hart dates the manuscript to c.1630–50, but Pamela J. Willetts suggests dating it from prior to 1626, when Lawes became a member of the Chapel Royal, to 1662 when he died (*The Henry Lawes Manuscript* [London: British Museum, 1969], 2). The classic study of his career is Willa McClung Evans, *Henry Lawes, Musician and Friend of Poets* (New York: Modern Language Association, 1941).

[5] Henry Lawes's claim to be the composer of all the songs in the autograph manuscript is not reliable in every case. See Willetts, *The Henry Lawes Manuscript*.

[6] Henry Lawes, *Ayres and Dialogues, Book II* (London, 1655), 44 *alias* 52.

[7] Evans, *Henry Lawes*, 19.

Five Settings of Songs Attributed to Sir Philip Sidney 103

versions become more evident. The melodic contour is quite different, with the Lawes song beginning on G and staying within the vicinity of F, G, and A♭ (with one exception) for the first three measures:

Example 1: Lawes, *ms. 1-3*

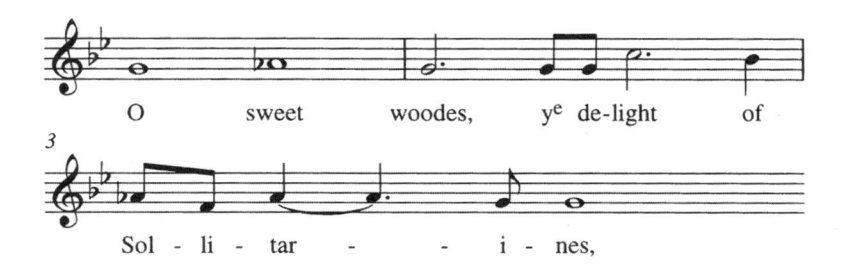

[musical notation: "O sweet woodes, y^e de-light of Sol-li-tar- -i-nes,"]

The Dowland setting,[8] on the other hand, begins in a higher register, and its progress for the first four measures is generally downward:

Example 2: Dowland, *Ms. 1-4*

[musical notation: "O Sweet woods the de-light of so-i-tar-i-nesse,"]

Nor are the rhythmic values equal, with the Lawes song showing somewhat more variety than Dowland's setting. Whatever Lawes's debt to the older composer may have been, he has created a new work, not at all a slavish imitation.

However, the text presents some variations in orthography, with the refrain in both song-setting versions offering changes from

---

[8] I have used John Dowland, *The Second Booke of Songs or Ayres of 2. 4. and 5. Parts* (London, 1600), song 10; for the modern edition, see John Dowland, *Ayres for Four Voices*, transcribed by Edmund H. Fellowes, ed. Thurston Dart and Nigel Fortune (London: Stainer and Bell, 1953), 36–37. Dowland sets three further stanzas not in the Lawes autograph manuscript.

the refrain of Sidney's poem as found in the *Old Arcadia*:[9]

> Lawes:
> O sweet woodes, ye delight of Sollitarines,
> O how I like yo^{ur} Sollitarines

> Dowland:
> O Sweet woods the delight of solitarinesse,
> O how much doe I loue your solitarinesse.

> *Old Arcadia*:
> O SWEET woods the delight of solitarines!
> O how much I do like your solitarines!

In "O how I like," Lawes alters Sidney's asclepiadean metrical pattern but adopting the word "like," as in the *Old Arcadia*. The Dowland song adopts "how much do I loue" in keeping with Sidney's metrical pattern, but alters the wording of the refrain.

Taking the text as set by Lawes, who only to be sure presents the first stanza of the song, the following provides a collation comparing it with Dowland (*D*):

> Lawes:
> O sweet woodes, ye delight of Sollitarines,
> O how I like yo^{ur} Sollitarines
> from fames desyre from Loues delight retyrde,
> in those still groues A Hermits life I led,[10]
> and those falce pleasures wch I once Admir'd,
> wth sad remembrance of my fall I dread.
> to birds, to trees, to Earth Impart I this,
> for She less Seacret and as sencless is.

> Variants in Dowland:
> 1 sweet] Sweet *R*; woodes] woods *D*; y^e] the *D*; Sollitarines] solitarinesse *D*
> 2 I like] much doe I loue *D*; yo^{ur}] your *D*; Sollitarines] solitarinesse *D*

---

[9] See Sidney, *The Poems*, ed. Ringler, 68.

[10] In Lawes's autograph manuscript, the word "find" appears crossed out and "led" substituted here.

Five Settings of Songs Attributed to Sir Philip Sidney 105

    3 from] From *D*; desyre] desire *D*; Loues] loues *D*; retyrde] retir'd *D*
    4 in] In *D*; those] these *D*; still] sad *D*; A] an *D*
    5 and] And *D*; w^{ch}] which *D*; Admir'd] admir'd *D*
    6 wth] With *D*; my fall]; my fall, ij (signifying repeat) *D*; dread.] dread, *D*
    7 to] To *D*; Earth] earth *D*; Impart] impart *D*
    8 for] For *D*; She] shee *D*; less] lesse *D*; Seacret] secret *D*; sencless] sencelesse *D*

Following the refrain, the Lawes and Dowland texts are similar except for slight verbal and orthographic variants; and, other than the refrain, neither seems to have any relationship with the poem "O Sweet Woods" as it appears in the *Old Arcadia*. It seems most likely that Lawes received the main part of his text from Dowland, and that in the refrain he excised "much doe I" and replaced it with "I like" to fit his musical idea. The substitution of "like" for "loue," however, is indicative of Lawes's probable acquaintance with the poem in the *Old Arcadia*, numerous manuscripts of which were still circulating.

Where Dowland received his text has never been satisfactorily explained. Edmund H. Fellowes made the conjecture that the refrain of "O Sweet Woods" is from a dramatic interlude in honor of Queen Elizabeth in 1561 at Wanstead House. Indeed, the last stanza of the Dowland song makes a suggestive reference: "Wansted my Mistres saith this is the doome."[11] However, Canon Fellowes's conjecture must be wrong, for Philip Sidney would have been only seven years old in 1561. There was a masque, *The Lady of May*, written by Sidney and performed at Wanstead House in 1578, but no extant version contains either the refrain or the rest of the text set by Dowland and Lawes.[12] Therefore several possi-

---

[11] See Fellowes's Introduction to Dowland, *Second Book of Ayres, 1600*, Part I.

[12] The extant songs are included in Sidney, *The Poems*, ed. Ringler, 3–5; see also Sir Philip Sidney, *The Prose Works*, ed. Albert Feuillerat, 4 vols. (1912; reprint, Cambridge: Cambridge University Press, 1963), 2:208–17. For further discussion, see Diana Poulton, *John Dowland* (London: Faber and Faber, 1982), 262–66.

bilities are open: either Dowland wrote the text himself or used a contemporary Sidney imitation, or else he knew a now-lost Sidney manuscript, which might have been included in a version of *The Lady of May.*

If the Lawes and Dowland versions are derived from a lost Sidney manuscript as has been suggested, some difficulties should be noted. First, these versions do not continue in asclepiadean meter after the refrain, but shift into iambic. The song in the *Old Arcadia* generally follows asclepiaedian meter, though differing from the classical pattern by having two unaccented syllables at the end of the line instead of the iamb.[13] It is also important to note that the Dowland and Lawes versions deal with profane matters, the confiding of a man's love to the birds and trees, since they would be more secret and as sensitive as his cold Petrarchan mistress. The song in the *Old Arcadia* is altogether different, since the narrator is celebrating the woods where man's mind is free to behold the Creator and his works. While there is reference to birds and bees, here they are part of the Creator's greater harmony, not merely things to which one might confide one's unrequited love. While there is a possibility of a lost Sidney manuscript poem, it is also not impossible that Sidney reworked an earlier, pre-existing song to fit the moral framework of the *Old Arcadia.*

II

Ginecia's song, "My Lute, within thy Selfe, thy tunes enclose," also found in the Henry Lawes autograph manuscript (fol. 3ᵛ), does not present such knotty textual problems as "O sweet woodes." The variants from William Ringler's text are mainly those of spelling, and the music is cleanly written with almost every measure having a rational number of beats, four or eight. The two exceptions are at measure 16, where a blot obscures the second half of the second beat, and at measure 20, where the bass has only two beats to the treble's four. A rational remedy, which I have adopted in my transcription, has been to add an eighth note on G, and at measure 20 to make the half note on F into a whole note. The key signature, A♭ and B♭, with D♭ irregularly added, is equivalent to our

---

[13] See Feuillerat's edition of *The Old Arcadia*, in Sidney, *The Prose Works*, 4:157.

modern F harmonic minor scale, written today as B♭, E♭, A♭, and D♭, with E♭ regularly rendered natural.

The text of the Lawes version, collated with Sidney's text as given by Ringler (*R*),[14] is as follows:

> My Lute, wthin thy Selfe, thy tunes enclose,
> thy mistris Songe is now A Sorrowes Crye,
> her hand benummde, wth fortunes dayly blowes,
> her mynde Amazd can neithers Help Applye,
> can : | :
> weare these my words as deep as weedes of woes,
> blacke Inck becomes ye state wherein I dye;
> And though my moanes be not in Musique bound
> of written greifes yet be ye Silent ground.

1 Selfe] selfe *R*
2 thy mistris Songe] Thy mistresse' song *R*; A Sorrows Crye] a sorrow's crie *R*
3 benummde wth fortunes dayly blowes] benumde with fortune's daylie blows *R*
4 her mynde Amazd] Her minde amaz'de *R*; neithers Help Applye,] neither's helpe applie *R*
5 can:] (*omit R; signifies repeat of* can neithers Help Applye)
6 weare] Weare *R*; deep as] mourning *R*
7 blacke Inck becomes thee] Blacke incke becommes the *R*
8 though] though *R*; moanes] mones *R*; Musique] musicke *R*
9 of] Of *R*; griefes] greefes *R*; ye Silent] the silent *R*

While Lawes provides a musical setting for this song, strictly speaking it is not sung in the *Old Arcadia*, but rather it is written on the belly of a lute by Ginecia and read by Philoclea, who stumbles on it by accident. The words depict the lute as Ginecia's confidante[15] and give evidence of her distracted mind ("Her mynde Amaz'de"). Sidney says that she had "made the Lute a Monument

---

[14] Sidney, *The Poems*, ed. Ringler, 81. The second stanza of Sidney's poem is not set by Lawes.

[15] See Hollander, *The Untuning of the Sky*, 139–40.

of her mynde,"[16] and as such the instrument becomes an emblem of Ginecia herself. The lute is a fitting instrument to represent her distracted mind because it is itself prone to its own kind of inconstancy, the tendency to slip out of tune easily.[17] A further motive for equating Ginecia symbolically with her lute is found in Thomas Mace's *Musicke's Monument*, in which the lute is accused of being a woman's instrument and of possessing the same feebleness and weakness that the weaker vessel, woman, allegedly displays.[18] Thus, Ginecia's lute is (1) her weak, vacillating feminine confidante and (2) the monument or emblem of her own inconstant and passion-ridden mind; in essence, she is confiding in her own self, arriving at a state of extreme self-centeredness, as the words "My Lute, within thy Selfe, thy tunes enclose" intimate, in addition to being symptomatic of the darker side of the Arcadian retreat.

At line 8 there is, for Lawes, a musical pun in the reference to "the silent ground," which may be read as a reference to a ground bass or continuous theme for variations or divisions.

III

In Book III of the *Old Arcadia*, "My trewe love hath my hart and I have his" is ironic since Dorus, lying to Miso, tells her that he has heard a shepherdess named Charitas with an "Angelike voyce" singing this song to Dametas.[19] The irony is in fact triple because neither the singer nor the song exists except in Dorus's mind, nor is there any actual affair of Dametas with such a shepherdess. Thus the words "trewe love" are completely negated. As Fellows notes,

---

[16] Sidney, *The Prose Works*, ed. Feuillerat, 4:199.

[17] See Robert Donington, *The Instruments of Music*, 2nd ed. (1951; reprint, London: Methuen, 1962), 74.

[18] Thomas Mace, *Musick's Monument* (1676; facs. reprint, Paris: CNRS, 1958), 45, 47.

[19] Sidney, *The Prose Works*, ed. Feuillerat, 179–80.

Five Settings of Songs Attributed to Sir Philip Sidney 109

there is a setting of this song by John Ward,[20] and in his view he feels that the song text "should be a favourite."[21] His discussion of the song does not take into account the ironic situation of the song's original context.

In addition to Ward's madrigal, there is an anonymous setting of the song in British Library Add. MS. 15,117, fol. 18^v.[22] I have provided the text of the song by the anonymous composer and a collation with Sidney's text as presented by Ringler.[23]

> My trewe love hath my hart and I have his,
> By Iust exchainge one for another geyven,
> I hold his deare, and myne he Cannot mysse,
> there never was a better bargaine driven
> Boath equall hurt in this Change wrought our blisse,
> my true love hath my hart and I have hys.
>
> His hart in me keepes me & hym in one
> my hart in hym his thoughtes & sences guides
> he loves my hart for once it was his owne
> I Cherish his because in me it bides.
> both etc.
>
> His hart his wounde receaved from my sight.
> my hart was wounded wth his wounded hart
> for as frō me on hym his hurt did light
> so still me thought in me his hurt did smart.
> both equall hurt etc.

---

[20] John Ward, *First Set of Madrigals to 3. 4. 5. and 6. Parts* (London, 1613); see also John Ward, *Madrigals*, ed. E. H. Fellowes (London: Stainer and Bell, 1922), 1–6.

[21] E. H. Fellowes, *The English Madrigal School* (reprint, London: Stainer and Bell, 1947), 106.

[22] Ringler has dated this manuscript to c.1616 (Sidney, *The Poems*, ed. Ringler, 566). For discussion, see Cutts, "Falstaff's 'Heauenlie Iewel'," 89–92; John P. Cutts, "A Reconsideration of the *Willow Song*," *Journal of the American Musicological Association* 10 (1957): 14–24, and Cutts's edition, *Musique de la troupe de Shakespeare* (Paris: CNRS, 1959).

[23] Sidney, *The Poems*, ed. Ringler, 75–76.

1 trewe] true *R*
2 Iust exchainge] just exchange *R*; another geyven,] the other giv'ne *R*
3 Hold] holde *R*; Cannot mysse,] cannot misse: *R*
4 there] There *R*; driven] driv'ne *R*
5–6 Boath ... hys] (*refrain omitted here, and inserted at end of poem in R*) Boath] Both *R*; wrought] sought; blisse] blisse: *R*; hys] his *R*
7 & hym] and him *R*; one] one, *R*
8 my] My *R*; & sences] and senses *R*
9 he] He *R*; owne] owne: *R*
10 Cherish] cherish *R*
11 both etc. (*See collation for lines 5–6*)
12 wounde] wound *R*; sight.] sight: *R*
13 my] My *R*; w[th]; with *R*; hart] hart, *R*
14 for] For *R*; frō] from *R*; hym] him *R*; light] light, *R*
15 so] So *R*; smart.] smart: *R*

In the *Old Arcadia*, Charitas's song is in the form of an English sonnet, but in the song manuscript, the poem is treated as three quatrains with the final couplet being used as a refrain after each.[24] Noteworthy is the use of the word "wrought" in the manuscript instead of "sought" in the version published by Ringler, while "another" appears instead of Sidney's "the other" as presented by this editor.

The musical setting presents several problems, namely, those of key signature, harmonization, and rhythm. The melody seems to be written in G, but the lute tablature is in F as if the composer had entered the melody in one key and later, in harmonizing the song, forgot the key in which he had written the melody! I have taken the liberty of transposing the melody one whole step lower to make it consistent with the harmonization, and I have changed the value of ♩ to 𝅝 in accord with modern practice. Although the basic rhythm seems to be a triple meter, with measures of three, six, and nine beats being the most frequent, there are also measures which do not conform, as would be demanded by later compositional practice. These are noted below:

---

[24] Ibid., 566.

Measure 4: Seven beats in both the melodic line and the lute tablature.
Measure 6: The notes in this measure are half, quarter, quarter, half, and whole, making a total of ten beats. Below the whole note, however, there is an indication that three quarters are to be used in the harmonization. It seems possible that the whole note stands for three beats in the song. I have, however, taken the note at its face value and have used two quarter notes and a half note to fill out the four beats of the whole note.
Measure 11: Same as Measure 6.
Measure 12: Eleven beats.
Measure 13: Seven beats in the melody; six beats in the harmonization. I have added one beat to the latter.
Measure 15: Five beats in the melody and harmonization.
Measure 16: Nine beats in the melody; ten beats in the harmonization; quarter notes into eighth notes.
Measure 17: Eight beats.

There is a discord in Measure 8 at beat 3; the B in the top space of the lute tablature, transcribed as A♭, clashes with the G in the melodic line. Changing the A♭ to G clears up the discord.

The vertical line connecting two letters in the lute tablature at Measures 7, 9, and 11 is explained by Thomas Mace; it is a direction to the lutenist to strike the upper and lower notes at exactly the same time: the bass must be struck, "*together, with the very same Letter*, at the *very same time*; with the *Thumb*; (which at the first, will seem a little troublesome, yet soon gain'd, or overcome)."[25] The rounded line under the letter in the lute tablature at Measures 5 and 8 is, as Mace explains, an ornament, either a slide or a slur.[26]

IV

In "Have I Caught my heavenlye Jewell," the second song of Sidney's *Astrophil and Stella*, a description is given of the "sugred

---

[25] Mace, *Musick's Monument*, 83.

[26] Ibid., 108. Cf. the discussion of lute tablature by Janet Dodge in *Sammelbände der internationalen Musikgesellschaft* 9 (1907–08): 318–30.

kisse" which, in the following sonnet (no. 73), Astrophil describes as stolen from Stella. The dramatic action of the poem follows the kiss from the moment when he merely contemplates the young woman sleeping to the moment when he actually kisses and awakens her. British Library Add. MS. 15,117, fol. 19, contains a musical setting, previously transcribed by Cutts.[27] The effectiveness of the setting of the words can only be shown through description and analysis of the song.

"Have I Caught my heavenlye Jewell" is not a separate entity but is linked to a chain of sonnets (nos. 73–74, 79–82 in Ringler's edition) celebrating the stolen "sugred kisse." The celebration of the kiss is made in terms of food and drink. Stella has repelled Astrophil's love with a "niggard No," signifying that she has a protective attitude toward her cupboard laden with sweets. In these sonnets Sidney uses such terminology as "Breakefast of *Love*," "frutes for new-found *Paradise*," "Cherries," and "hungrie." These underline the fact that Sidney is dealing with an appetite, albeit not for food. Already sonnet 71 had revealed the connection: "'But ah,' Desire still cries, 'give me some food'."

Nevertheless, the song itself leaps from image to image, from thought to thought in each stanza. The first contains the equation of the lady with the heavenly jewel; stanza 4 utilizes military imagery, as the lover says he intends to invade her fort. In stanza 6, there is a vivid analogy, with the beginner in love compared to a novice at reading: "who will reade must first learne spellinge"— and if Astrophil will love, he must begin with a kiss, albeit one that is disastrous to his hopes.

The anonymous composer of the song as found in British Library Add. MS. 15,117 makes no attempt to pick up the diverse images and ideas of the separate stanzas or to give each an individualized setting.[28] Instead, he sets only the first stanza and

---

[27] Cutts, "Falstaff's 'Heauelie Iewel'," 90–99, esp. 91.

[28] In his editing of this song ("Falstaff's 'Heauelie Iewel'," 90), Cutts collated the manuscript with Feuillerat's text and identified some emendations of notes, rhythmic values, and key signature. He also observes the ironic use of the first line of this poem by Falstaff in Shakespeare's *Merry Wives of Windsor*. He suggests that Falstaff, in love, may have

expects this music to fit all seven stanzas—a common practice. The music, while it may not do any real violence to the text, at times rides rough-shod over the natural rhythm of the words. For example, in stanza 3, "what no her Tonge" is set in direct opposition to the stress pattern and meaning of the words; the possessive pronoun "her" comes on an accented beat, beat 3, with the rhythmic value of a dotted quarter, while the noun "Tonge" falls on an unaccented beat, the last half of beat 4, with the rhythmic value of an eighth note. The result gives a rather amateurish impression.

V

The ninth song in *Astrophil and Stella*, "Goe my flocke goe gett you hence," is sung by Astrophil after he has been finally rejected by the lady. In the first stanza, the shepherd Astrophil warns his sheep of the rising storms in his breast and the impending showers from his eyes; therefore, he advises his flock to leave him so that they might find "a better place of feeding."

The musical setting for this stanza as found in Christ Church MS. 439, fol. 17,[29] is by Robert Taylour. Taylour was employed as a lutenist in Chapman's 1613 *Masque of the Inner Temple and Lincoln's Inn*, and was reported to be "one of Prince His Highnes Musicians" in 1618, also participating in the funeral of King James in 1625. In 1620 he was employed as a London wait, and was dead by 1637.[30] He composed settings of *Sacred Hymns, consisting of Fifti Select Psalms* (1615), texts of which were psalm paraphrases by Sir Edwin Sandys. The stanza from *Astrophil and Stella* seems rather short, only six measures, and fairly perfunctory. The key

---

started to break into song, and then, as suddenly as he started, stopped. "The first line would be sufficient indication to the knowledgeable," according to Cutts, "and would enhance their appreciation of Falstaff's not continuing any further with this song because it contained self-criticism of himself as fool and fearful coward."

[29] Some of the songs in this collection are dated 1601 and 1602.

[30] Diana Poulton, "Robert Tailour," in *The New Grove Dictionary of Music and Musicians*, 20 vols. (London: Macmillan, 1980), 18:528.

wanders from G to F and back to G with little warning to the listener, in contrast to the other songs discussed in the present study which either stay in one key or modulate to a related key.

The song appears to be in duple time, but no standard measurement seems to exist; there are three measures of eight beats, one of four beats, and two of six beats. At measure 3 in the manuscript, it is difficult to tell whether there is a rest, a flat, or simply a blot in the bass clef. A flat before the B would remove the cross-relationship at measures 3 and 4, and would help to effect the key change from G to F. For these reasons, I have chosen to add a flat before the B in the problematical measure.

The text as given in the manuscript, collated with Ringer's edition,[31] is as follows:

> Goe my flocke goe gett yo^u hence
> Seeke a better place of feeding
>   finde
> Where yo^u maie /\ haue some defence
> from the stormes in my brest breeding
> and showers from myne eies proceeding.
>
> 1 Goe] Go *R*; flocke goe gett yo^u] flocke, go get you *R*
> 2 Seeke] Seeke *R*; feeding] feeding, *R*
> 3 yo^u] you *R*; finde, *written over* haue] have *R*
> 4 from] From *R*; brest breeding] breast breeding, *R*
> 5 and] And *R*; myne eies] mine eyes *R*

Another setting, by an early anonymous composer, appears in Robert Dowland's *A Musical Banquet* (1610), no. IV. Here the text of the subsequent nine stanzas is included, but as usual only the first is provided with music, in this case with the melody written out and lute tablature.[32]

---

[31] Sidney, *The Poems*, ed. Ringler, 221

[32] [The typescript of the present study breaks off here without discussion or transcription of this song, which contains variants that differ from the text provided by Ringler. For example, Stella is described as "fayrest," not "fiercest" (ll. 16–17).—Ed.]

Five Settings of Songs Attributed to Sir Philip Sidney   115

I

O sweet woodes, y^e delight of Sollitar-i-nes, O how I like your Sol-li-tar-i-ness from fames desyre from Loues delight retyrde, in those still groues A Hermits life I led, and those falce pleasures wch I once Admir'd,

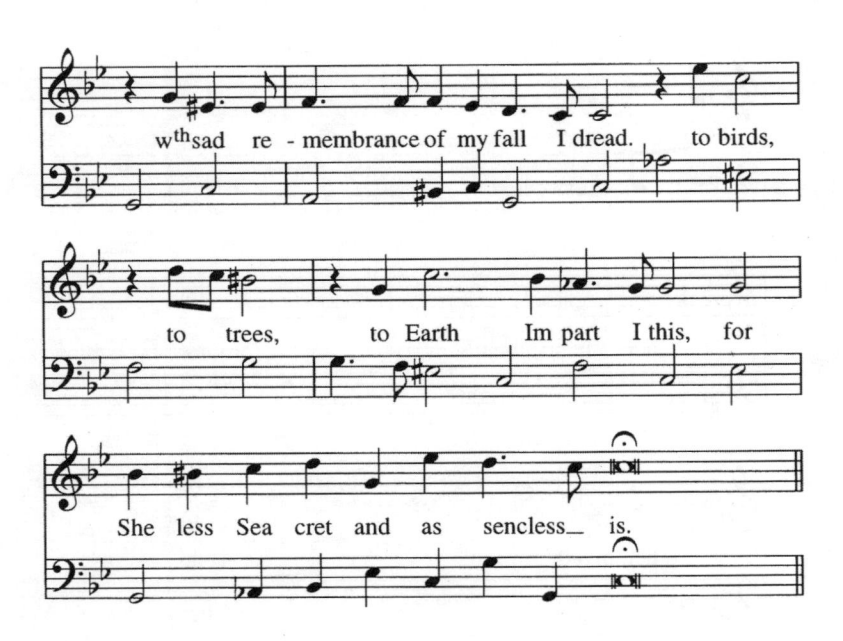

116   *Five Settings of Songs Attributed to Sir Philip Sidney*

wth sad re-membrance of my fall I dread. to birds,

to trees, to Earth Im part I this, for

She less Sea cret and as sencless is.

II

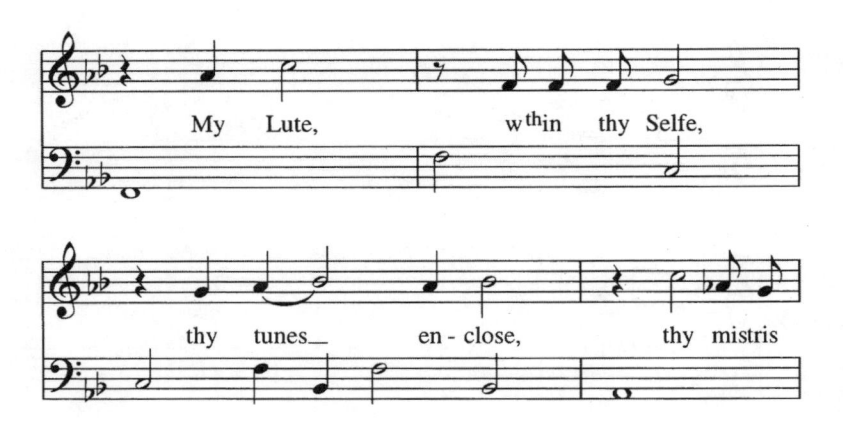

My Lute, w^thin thy Selfe,

thy tunes en-close, thy mistris

Five Settings of Songs Attributed to Sir Philip Sidney 117

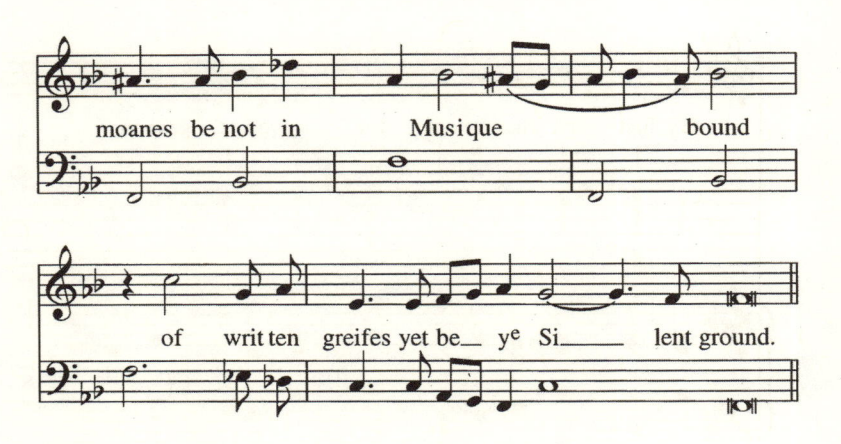

118 *Five Settings of Songs Attributed to Sir Philip Sidney*

moanes be not in Musique bound of written greifes yet be ye Si lent ground.

III

My trewe love hath my hart and I have his,

Five Settings of Songs Attributed to Sir Philip Sidney 119

120 *Five Settings of Songs Attributed to Sir Philip Sidney*

Five Settings of Songs Attributed to Sir Philip Sidney 121

122   *Five Settings of Songs Attributed to Sir Philip Sidney*

V

Goe my flocke goe gett you hence Seeke a bet-ter place of feed-ing Where you may finde haue some de-fence from the stormes in my brest breed-ing and showers from myne eies pro-ceed-ing.

Note: The notation of the lute tablature for Song III is as close to the original as the Sibelius program would allow.

Milton's Encomiastic Sonnet to Henry Lawes

Milton's encomiastic sonnet to Henry Lawes opens with the highest praise for his eminent contemporary:

> Harry, whose tuneful and well measur'd Song
> First taught our English Muse how to span
> Words with just note and accept, not to scan
> With *Midas'* Ears, committing short and long....[1]

These lines, according to Donald Tovey, reveal a Milton who has forgotten the precise and artistic word-setting achieved by the madrigal school in the previous generation. Furthermore, Tovey charges that "the composer's preoccupation with the scansion of 'just note and accent' leads him to over-punctuate the words and interrupt the flow of his music."[2] Thus in Tovey's estimation, the sonnet's claims about Lawes's primary place in the history of English music are not accurate. Eric Ford Hart, however, suggests that the poem's statements about Lawes's art have often been taken too literally when in fact Milton's intention was merely

---

[1] John Milton, *Complete Poems and Major Prose*, ed. Merritt Y. Hughes (New York: Odyssey, 1957), 144. Except for the *Comus* songs, all quotations from Milton's work are from this edition.

[2] Donald Tovey, *The Main Stream of Music and Other Essays* (1949; reprint, Cleveland: World, 1961), 210. The declamatory aspects of Lawes's style are also oversimplified by MacDonald Emslie, "Milton on Lawes: The Trinity MS Revisions," in *Music in English Renaissance Drama*, ed. John H. Long (Lexington: University of Kentucky Press, 1968), 96–102. For a balanced view of Lawes's development, see R. J. McGrady, "Henry Lawes and the Concept of 'Just Note and Accent'," *Music and Letters* 50 (1969): 86–102.

complimentary.[3]

Another approach to the poem is possible; I believe that the poem is neither inaccurate nor merely complimentary. The key to Milton's praise for Lawes as a composer and performer is to be found through a careful reading of the first line of the sonnet in which he speaks of Lawes's "tuneful and well measur'd Song." What previously has not been noticed about this line is that Milton has set forth two categories—tuneful *and* well-measured—and that Lawes is able to fulfill the requirements of each category.

Milton's sonnet demands that the words of a "well measur'd Song" be spanned "with just note and accent," and not scanned "With *Midas'* Ears, committing short and long."[4] The story of how Midas got his ears is found in Book 11 of Ovid's *Metamorphoses*, where it is related that he favored the rustic music of Pan over the artistic music of Apollo, and as a reward for his misjudgments was given asses' ears. Milton implies that someone with asses' ears would be guilty of "committing [i.e., setting in conflict] short and long." The reference is to the rhythmic values contained in the melodic line of vocal music: the length of the musical note should be determined by the quantity or length of the syllable. That music has quantity—duration—is undisputed. The use of the terms *short* and *long* is historically justifiable: in the mensural music of the Middle Ages a *long* appears to have been either twice or three times the length of a *short*.[5]

But the question of quantity as far as words are concerned—

---

[3] Eric Ford Hart, "Introduction to Henry Lawes," *Music and Letters* 32 (1951): 331n. However, it should be noted that Hart does not denigrate Lawes's work; on the contrary, he finds it to be extremely subtle in its setting of words. See also Willa McClung Evans, *Henry Lawes: Musician and Friend of Poets* (New York: MLA, 1941), 180–82.

[4] Henry J. Todd cites Richardson, who defined "committting" as "*offending against quantity and harmony*" (*The Poetical Works of John Milton*, 5th ed. [London, 1852], 4:218). Of course, the word "*harmony*" must here be taken in its aesthetic rather than its musical sense.

[5] Cf. Walter Odington, *De Speculatione Musicae, Part VI*, trans. Jay A. Huff, Musicological Studies and Documents 31 (American Institute of Musicology, 1973), 8–9.

particularly the syllables of English words—is not so clear-cut as quantity in music. Quantity clearly exists in the English language, both as a measurable objective quantity having little or no linguistic significance and as a conscious and perceived quantity having linguistic significance.[6] W. K. Wimsatt, Jr., and Monroe C. Beardsley believe that quantity is simply a variable dependent upon the individual reader; thus they hold that poetry relies for its characteristics not on quantity but on patterns of pitch and stress.[7] It seems to me, however, that if Milton could have known about the opinions of Wimsatt and Beardsley, he would not have been in agreement with them. Evidence that Milton was looking for more than stress in his poetry is found in his prefatory note to *Paradise Lost* which speaks of the "true musical delight" of poetry; this delight "consists only in apt Numbers, *fit quantity* [italics mine] of Syllables, and the sense variously drawn out from one Verse into another."[8] The first and last part of the sentence need not worry us here, but the second part, speaking of "fit quantity," should. What did Milton mean by quantity? If he thinks of quantity as weight, says G. Stanley Koehler, "he is saying nothing about English verse that requires comment."[9] But Koehler feels that Milton, having known the sweetness of sound which Latin quantitative verse possesses, would be reluctant to settle for mere weight, but would want to bring quantity into English verse. This does not mean that Milton would give up accent in favor of quantity, but that, like Sidney, he would insist that the "blessing of speech, which considers each word," should be most polished by attention not only to the "forcible qualitie" (accentual weight) of the words but

---

[6] Bertil Malmberg, *Phonetics*, trans. Lily M. Parker and Bertil Malmberg (New York: Dover, 1954), 74–79.

[7] For a survey of some prevailing notions about meter, stress, and duration in English poetry, see W. K. Wimsatt, Jr., and Monroe C. Beardsley, "The Concept of Meter," *PMLA* 74 (1959): 585–98.

[8] Hughes, ed., *Complete Poems and Major Prose of John Milton*, 210.

[9] G. Stanley Koehler, "Milton on 'Numbers,' 'Quantity,' and 'Rime'," *Studies in Philology* 55 (1958): 209.

also to their "best measured quantitie" as well.[10]

If Milton recognizes both quality and quantity in poetry, how would he want these rendered musically? Would he want every stress to be tied irrevocably to a lengthened quantity, or would he ask that stress be differentiated from quantity in some way? Judging from Lawes's music which Milton liked, the latter seems to be true. In Song I from Milton's *Comus*,[11] Lawes set the first line—"From the Heav'ns now I fly"—to a long-short-long-short-short-long rhyhmic pattern. If he were working only on a stress-quantity basis (i.e., stress equals quantity), the durations would have to be short-short-long-short-short-long. But if he is working on the assumption that meaning and function of words help to determine a quantity beyond stress, he would indicate a subtle difference in the length of the preposition "from" and the article "the"—which is, of course, what the composer does in making "from" a dotted eighth and "the" a sixteenth note.

Example 1

From the Heav'ns   now I fly,

"Heav'ns," the noun of the prepositional phrase, is rendered as a dotted half note, as befitting the word's importance. It seems to me that Lawes is doing something much more subtle than simply agreeing with Thomas Campion's principle that "in ioyning of words to harmony there is nothing more offensiue to the eare then to place a long sillable with a short note, or a short sillable with a long note,"[12] for he is showing differences within the categories of

---

[10] Sir Philip Sidney, *An Apology for Poetry*, in G. Gregory Smith, ed., *Elizabethan Critical Essays*, 2 vols. (London: Oxford University Press, 1904), 1:182; Kohler, "Milton on 'Numbers,' 'Quantity,' and Rime," 210.

[11] *The Mask of Comus*, ed. E. H. Visiak and H. J. Foss (London: Bloomsbury, 1937). In my text the first song in *Comus* is quoted from this edition.

[12] Thomas Campion, *Observations in the Art of English Poesy* (1600), chap. 1, in Smith, ed., *Elizabethan Critical Essays*, 2:329.

long and *short*.

Lawes goes further beyond the mere rendering of the quantity of poetry. In his preface to Book 2 of *Ayres and Dialogues* (1655), he says, "Yet the way of *Composition* I chiefly profess (which is to shape *Notes* to the *Words* and *Sense*) is not hit by too many." Hart thinks that shaping "*Notes* to the *Words* and *Sense*" involves not merely trying to write music in keeping with the general emotional tone of the words as the Elizabethans did, but actually capturing the meaning of the words in the musical setting.[13] Since meaning is partially conveyed through pitch in spoken language, the musical settings, to be perfectly accurate, should follow the pitch levels of the spoken phrase. Returning to Song I from *Comus*, we find that the melodic contour of "From the Heav'ns now I fly" is much the same as that of the spoken words, provided that one uses a kind of heightened declamatory speech favored for the reading of poetry in the seventeenth century. Under these circumstances, one might say:

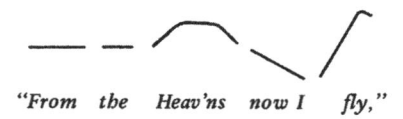

"From the Heav'ns now I fly,"

The way the voice rises in pitch on "Heav'ns" and "fly" is imitated exactly in Lawes's musical setting of the phrase. His care in matching spoken pitch levels to musical settings might almost be said to anticipate the discoveries of the twentieth-century linguists George L. Trager and Henry Lee Smith, Jr., who show that spoken English can be notated as having four different pitch levels.[14] Lawes, with the whole music gamut to choose from, does not limit himself to four pitch levels, but nevertheless, in his settings of the songs from *Comus*, he confines himself to a very small range—an octave and a fourth. In this practice, he is consistent with the insistence of the members of the Florentine Camarata upon a small

---

[13] Hart, "Introduction to Henry Lawes," 330.

[14] George L. Trager and Henry Lee Smith, Jr., *An Outline of English Structure* (Washington, D.C.: A.C.L.S., 1956), 36–45.

vocal range to make vocal music more like heightened speech.[15]

Setting the sense of the words would also include the choice of modality or tonality, which might express sadness, happiness, or, in the case of a wandering tonality, confusion; it would include imitation and repetition, word-painting (although Lawes used this device more sparingly than predecessors such as Campion and Morley), dramatic pauses or rests, and groupings of words and phrases to create either long connected thoughts or short disconnected ones. In order to show a word's importance, one might place it on a long note or a high note, or a combination of the two—a long high note. Chromatic rises and melodic leaps also would serve to make the music follow the sense more carefully.[16]

That Lawes is setting the meaning of the words is most clearly seen in "Ariadne Deserted" (see Example 2), which is the "Story" referred to in Milton's sonnet.[17] It was praised in commendatory verse not only by Milton but also by John Phillips and John Cobb, and it was sung all the way to Erith by Samuel Pepys.[18] In the song, Ariadne's distressed mind is shown in the tonality of the piece, which wanders from tonal center to tonal center. Then, the first word, "*Theseus*," is set as a descending major third (D to B♭), which is very close to the actual sound of one person calling to another at a distance. The next phrase, "*O Theseus*," descends along the intervallic distance of two minor thirds (E♭ to C to A), considered plaintive and affecting in Renaissance and baroque

---

[15] Pietro di Bardi, Letter to G. B. Doni (1634), trans. Oliver Strunk, *Source Readings in Music History* (New York: Norton, 1950), 364–65.

[16] See Hart, "Introduction to Henry Lawes," 337–38.

[17] Milton's marginal note to his sonnet as it appears affixed to *Choice Psalmes* (London, 1648), indicates that the "Story" is "The story of Ariadne set by him [Lawes] in Music." See Evans, *Henry Lawes*, 181.

[18] Diary entry for 19 November 1665; see David G. Weiss, *Samuel Pepys, Curioso* (Pittsburgh: Pittsburgh University Press, 1957), 54.

theory.[19] "Hark" is set apart by rests preceding and following it, giving the word two dramatic pauses. "Alas deserted I complain" ends with the repetition of C#, D, C#, D—an instance of the plaintive chromatic relationship.[20] "Pitty'd me" has a kind of sobbing rhythm in the figure ♪♩ ♪♩. "And beating back that false & cruell name" has the familiar chromatics coupled with a faster rhythm to indicate agitation. The end of the whole sentence and the point of it all—"did comfort and revenge my flame"—comes to a decisive cadence. Here Lawes shows himself to be a composer without peer insofar as setting the meaning of words is concerned.

Lawes's songs, well-measured and true to the sense of the words as they are, are also supremely "tuneful," as the first line of Milton's sonnet tells us. In order to verify this for ourselves, we have only to refer to Lawes's setting of Herrick's "Bid Me But Live" or to his setting of Waller's "Go Lovely Rose." Is it any wonder that Herrick and Waller also presented encomiastic sonnets to the composer of these delicate melodies?

Lawes's tuneful songs are characteristically *smooth*: "To after age thou shalt be writ the man/ That with smooth air couldst humor best our tongue." Here "smooth" is a complimentary term with none of the modern connotations of dishonesty or slickness (as in "smooth operator"), but rather it has the meaning of effortlessness and grace. "Now my Task is smoothly done," says the Attendant

---

[19] For a convenient discussion of set musical patterns which represented certain ideas or emotions (i.e., "the doctrine of the affections or *Affektenlehre*), see Manfred Bukofzer, *Music in the Baroque Era* (New York: Norton, 1947), 388–90.

[20] Henry Lawes, *Ayres and Dialogues, for One, Two, or Three Voyces, The First Booke* (London, 1653), 1. In Lawes's autograph manuscript (British Library, Add. MS. 53,723) the notes corresponding to "pitty'd me" are:

pitty'd me

For a description of the autograph manuscript, see Pamela J. Willetts, *The Henry Lawes Manuscript* (London: British Museum, 1969).

Example 2: Ariadne *sitting upon a Rock in the Island* Naxos, *deserted by* Theseus, *thus complains.*

Theseus, O Theseus, hark! but yet in vain; A-las de-ser-ted I com-plain; it was some neighb'ring Rock, more soft then he, whose hollow bowels pitty'd me, and beating back that false & cruell name, did comfort and revenge my flame,

Spirit at the end of *Comus*, and he means that his task is well done, without any embarrassing bobbles. Earlier in *Comus*, the "smooth-dittied Song" of Thyrsis has been praised, and since Lawes played the part of Thyrsis and was, like Thyrsis, a household servant, in his case tutor for the Bridgewater family, this compliment has been by extension applied to Lawes's own "smooth-dittied Song."[21] Lawes was both composer and performer in *Comus*, and thus it seems logical that "smooth air" and "smooth-dittied Song" refer both to his effortless composing[22] and his smooth countertenor voice,[23] which could handle the music and its ornaments so well.

A clear hint that Milton's sonnet is praising Lawes as a singer appears in line 10, where he is called "the Priest of *Phoebus'* Choir," and, in truth, he was a member of the Chapel Royal, the most prestigious position a professional musician could hold in those days. Lawes, a superb singer and composer, is compared in lines 12–14 to Casella, whom Dante met in the milder shades of Purgatory. Dante asks him to demonstrate whether one retains the power of song after "translation," and Casella proves that he has, by singing a *canzone* with his own melody and Dante's own words.[24] Milton, who had heard the Italian singer Leonora Baroni and had lauded her in three poems, and who had loved Italian music so much that he had shipped home from Italy a "chest or two" of music books by "Luca Marenz[i]o, [Claudio] Monte Verde, Horatio Vecci, [Antonio] Cif[r]a, the Prince of Venosa [Gesualdo],

---

[21] Hughes, ed., *Complete Poems and Major Prose of John Milton*, 92; see also ibid., 101–02.

[22] Todd, ed., *The Poetical Works of John Milton*, 4:49.

[23] Lawes is identified as a countertenor by Murray Lefkowitz, "The Longleat Papers of Bulstrode Whitelocke: New Light on Shirley's *Triumph of Peace*," *Journal of the American Musicological Society* 18 (1965): 46, 53.

[24] *Il Purgatorio*, canto 2. The song is "Amor che nella mente me ragiona" from the *Convivio*. See also Nan Cooke Carpenter, "Milton and Music: Henry Lawes, Dante, and Casella," *English Literary Renaissance* 2 (1972): 240–43.

and several others,"[25] is giving Lawes a supreme compliment by preferring him to the Italians who since the time of Casella had been avowed leaders in the world of music.

Perhaps Milton was especially pleased with Lawes' attempt to create a new music especially suited to the English language and temperament. In contrast to Nicholas Lanier and Giovanni Coprario (John Cooper), who had visited Italy and self-consciously imported the Italian baroque style, Lawes was engaged in the development of a domesticated English musical style which paved the way for the music of Henry Purcell. Some of the splendor and fire of Monteverdi is missing, but Lawes compensates for these lacks by his delicacy and extreme subtlety.

In "Ad Patrem," Milton had confessed that he loved vocal music above all other kinds of music: "What pleasure is there in the inane modulations of the voice without words and meaning and rhythmic eloquence? . . . Orpheus . . . by his song—not by his cithara—. . . stirred the ghosts of the dead to tears."[26] And it was Lawes, by his tuneful *and* well-measured song, who like Orpheus stirred the hearts of men—including the heart of John Milton—with his Apollonian music. Lawes knew best how to join words, meaning, and rhythmic eloquence with musical pitch, and thereby earned the place granted to him by Milton—above Casella's Purgatory in the heavenly choir of Phoebus. As John Berkenhead said of Lawes, he was truly "a Man to tune an Angel by!"[27]

---

[25] Edward Phillips, *The Life of Milton*, in Hughes, ed., *Complete Poetry and Major Prose of John Milton*, 1029.

[26] Translation by Hughes (ibid., 84).

[27] Henry Lawes, *The Second Book of Ayres, and Dialogues, for One, Two and Three Voyces* (London, 1655), sig. B4.

George Herbert and the Celestial Harmony

[S]o much of music as is adapted to the sound of the voice and to the sense of hearing is granted to us for the sake of harmony. And harmony, which has motions akin to the revolutions of our souls, is . . . meant to correct any discord which may have arisen in the courses of the soul, and to be our ally in bringing her into harmony and agreement with herself, and rhythm too was given by them for the same reason, on account of the irregular and graceless ways which prevail among mankind generally, and to help us against them.—Plato, *Timaeus*[1]

To the reader of George Herbert's poetry, the recurrence of musical terminology strikes the eye almost as forcefully as the recurring chime of a church bell might strike the ear of a listener. John Hollander notes that "it is as if the image of music were always running along beneath the surface of all of Herbert's poems, breaking out here and there like the eruption of some underground stream, but exercising always an informing, nourishing function."[2] Again and again Herbert brings into his poetry the lute, the consort, and song, giving to each musical reference a spiritual significance. One need not wonder about the practice; Herbert himself was a performer of no small talent—he was reported to have "had a very good hand at the Lute"[3]—and, like the other metaphysical poets, he brought to his verse a synthesis of all

---

[1] Plato, *The Collected Dialogues*, ed. Edith Hamilton and Huntington Cairns (Princeton University Press, 1961), 1175.

[2] John Hollander, *The Untuning of the Sky: Ideas of Music in English Poetry, 1500–1700* (Princeton: Princeton University Press, 1961), 294.

[3] John Aubrey, *Brief Lives*, ed. Oliver Dawson Dick (London: Secker and Warburg, 1950), 137.

his experiences. His experiences included his own performing and his understanding of music as integral to the soul's communion with God.

Of the total number of poems which Herbert produced, at least sixty utilize musical images integral to their meaning. Other poems introduce more general auditory images. Bells, for example, appear in "Prayer," "Decay," and "The Flower."[4] Even a poem entitled "Sinne (I)" invokes "The sound of glorie ringing in our eares" (10). Without any doubt whatsoever, sound was a salient part of his experience and integral to his work as a poet.

Sound enters into his relationship with the Almighty, and when he feels that he is out of touch with God his cry is "*Come, come, my God, O come,*" which he follows with the lament "But no hearing" ("Deniall," 14–15). In *The Country Parson*, he even speaks in terms of sound when he discusses the advisability of marriage for a priest. Perhaps, he thinks, it would be better not to marry, but "if he married, the choyce of his wife was made *rather by his eare, then by his eye*; his judgement, not his affection found out a fit wife for him, whose humble, and liberall disposition he preferred before beauty, riches, or honour."[5] The ear is equated with judgment, a view contradictory to the association of knowledge and of memory with seeing, regarded in the Middle Ages as a higher faculty than the auditory.[6]

For Herbert, sound would seem to be a valuable key to his personality, though in his verse he can be an "eye-man" as well as "ear-man" in establishing visually patterned verse designed specifically to be apprehended by the eye. In "Easter Wings," at the points where the lines of poetry become the shortest, the subject of the poem, man, also becomes "Most poore" and "Most thinne" (5, 15). And when the lines become longer again in imitation of spread

---

[4] References to Herbert's poems in the present study are to George Herbert, *The Works*, ed. F. E. Hutchinson (Oxford: Clarendon Press, 1941); for poems cited, line numbers appear in parentheses following quotations in my text.

[5] Herbert, *The Works*, 238.

[6] See, for example, Francis Yates, *The Art of Memory* (Chicago: University of Chicago Press, 1966), 87.

wings, the poem then speaks of man's rising as a lark and sharing Christ's victory over the grave. Since in this pattern poem Herbert wants to "sing this day thy victories" (9), there is not only fusion of content with visual form but also the introduction of an auditory reference. Herbert does not neglect sound even when he is concentrating most on sight.

Hence too sight and sound are combined in "Christmas":

> Then we will sing, and shine all our own day,
>   And one another pay:
> His beams shall cheer my breast, and both so twine,
> Till ev'n his beams sing, and my musick shine. (31–34)

"Love (II)" reiterates the idea:

> And there in hymnes send back thy [i.e., God's] fire again. (8)

Since music shines, beams sing, and hymns send back fire, Herbert reinforces the auditory with the sense of sight and vice versa.

We may look for an explanation for Herbert's exploitation of orderly visual form, religious truth, highly competent verse forms, and auditory image in his temperament and training. From his mother, Magdalen Herbert, an unusual person from all accounts,[7] he would have imbibed a strong and pervading sense of order. As F. E. Hutchinson reports, "George Herbert describes the orderliness of her life in which everything had its place and its due attention—the family household, the garden, her neighbours, her care for the needy and sick, the offices of religion."[8] In *The Country Parson*, he cites Corinthians 14 regarding the affairs of the church: "*Let all things be done decently* [and in good order]."[9] And in preserving decency, Herbert follows neither the Roman Church which he says is like a gaudily painted woman, nor Calvinist

---

[7] See especially Izaak Walton, *The Life of Mr. George Herbert* (London, 1652), 20–30. For Herbert's life, see the modern biography by Amy M. Charles, *A Life of George Herbert* (Ithaca: Cornell University Press, 1977).

[8] Hutchinson, ed., *The Works of George Herbert*, xxiii.

[9] Herbert, *The Works*, 246.

Geneva, which, being like a lady undressed, lacks the decorum and orderly beauty of the English Church—a church which is, liturgically and musically speaking, decked in "fit aray" ("The British Church," 7). For Herbert, such orderliness and decorousness involved the observation of the daily canonical hours as his friends the Ferrars did—a practice to which, he suggested to them, night vigils might be added.[10]

Such a penchant for formalism and for keeping set forms is evidenced in Herbert's poetry and also is entirely consistent with his interest in music. Music, according to theorists, consists almost exclusively of form and elements of organization. To purists there is no separation between form and content; the chosen form, in effect, decides what the content will be. A large number of Herbert's poems in fact stress music as a principle opposed to disorder, but at the same time he was nevertheless very much aware of the expressive qualities of music and capitalized on them in his poems of praise. Not by accident were the mathematicians and scientists of the time concerned with a similar connection between music and orderliness. Many scientists were musicians, and, as Manfred Bukofzer has noted, Johannes Kepler's "discovery of the laws of planetary motions grew out of his sincere belief in the actual existence of mundane harmony."[11] Kepler, writing in his *Harmonices Mundi*, was technically competent as a theorist. Like the scientists for whom music consisted of inexorable mathematical and geometrical laws,[12] Herbert, who in "Artillerie" says that he has himself "heard of musick in the spheres" (9), also sees art as form ruled by law. The greatest artist of all is God, who has created the earth and all the forms in it. And Herbert, the poet (like the musician), must bend to God the Artist's laws:

O, tame my heart:

---

[10] Austin Warren, *Richard Crashaw: A Study in Baroque Sensibility* (1939; reprint, Ann Arbor: University of Michigan Press 1957), 37

[11] Manfred F. Bukofzer, *Music in the Baroque Era* (New York: Norton, 1947), 392.

[12] See D. P. Walker, "Kepler's Celestrial Music," *Journal of the Warburg and Courtauld Institutes* 30 (1967): 228–50.

> It is thy highest art
> To captivate strong holds to thee. ("Nature," 4–6)

Yet, being human, the taming of Herbert's heart is difficult for him, but he sees that this is necessary if God's artistic and spiritual plan for his life is to be realized.

In the music of Herbert's poetry, the theme of God as the greatest artist is again played by the poet in "Man." There the poet lauds God's creation, man, for this creature "is all symmetrie,/ Full of proportions/ . . . And all to all the world besides" (13–15). Man is himself a microcosm, a miniature reflection of the universe, the great cosmos. And in the universe ordained by God, "Musick and light attend our head" (33)—a demonstration that music is an intrinsic part of God's careful and orderly arrangement of things.

God created music as intrinsic to his universe and made the spheres to tune together, but, more than that, God is himself a performer. As Herbert says in "Providence," "If we could heare / Thy skill and art, what musick would it be!" (39–40). God's music is perfectly harmonious, not cacophonous. Ideally, "all together may accord in thee, / And prove one God, one harmonie" ("The Thanksgiving," 41–42). This view is not inconsistent with the musical thinking that would later appear in Richard Crashaw's "Musick's Duell," which assigns only a melodic line to nature but adds harmony, a symbol of heavenly grace.[13] And John Dryden says in other words what Herbert and Crashaw imply: "From Harmony, from heav'nly Harmony/ This universal Frame began."[14]

God is also the Divine Conductor, the Musical Director of the cosmic ensemble. Herbert begs, "Lord, place me in thy consort; give one strain/ To my poore reed" ("Employment (I)," 23–24). God, also ultimately the Composer as well as Conductor, is claimed by Herbert in the poem "Gratefulnesse" to have "Much better tunes then [human] grones can make," while his love nevertheless can take these "countrey-aires" (22–23) and transform

---

[13] See W. G. Madsen, "A Reading of Musicks Duell," in *Studies in Honor of John Wilcox*, ed. A. Dayle Wallace and Woodburn O. Ross (Detroit: Wayne State University Press, 1958), 39–50.

[14] "A Song for St. Cecilia's Day," in John Dryden, *The Poems and Fables*, ed. James Kinsley (London: Oxford University Press, 1962), 422.

them into something truly worthy. In this poem, even the pulse praises God. Pulse, the beating of the heart, is the precursor of the modern metronome; Barnabas Oley, in *Herbert's Remains* (1652), calls it a *"native watch."*[15]

As God the Father is a musician, so also is the Son. Herbert, in "Aaron," speaks of "My doctrine tun'd by Christ" (23). Christ brings nature into harmony with grace, for he is the very principle of harmony. The theorist Johannes Tinctoris, in his *Proportionale musices* (1476), had noted: "But, after a fullness of time had passed, in which that greatest musician, Jesus Christ, our peace made both one [i.e., by combining two natures, divine and human] in duple proportion."[16] The divine and the human are joined in him, both harmonically and rhythmically. Christ is, for Herbert, "my onely head, . . . My onely musick." On the other hand, nature's sound, without assistance from grace, is unmusical, "a noise of passions ringing me for dead" ("Aaron," 16, 18, 8). The word "noise" signifies a band of musicians,[17] and therefore the picture given is that of the world's ragged hurdy-gurdy players in opposition to the fine symphony of God's orchestra.

God supplies perfect tuning for the soul to bring him up to pitch. In "Justice (II)," however, God is an instrument on which a human may play:

> For where before thou still didst call on me,
>   Now I still touch
>   And harp on thee. (19–21)

This is unusual, however, for God is normally too transcendent for Herbert to treat him as accessible to human touch. More often, man is the instrument which needs tempering by God. In all the poems which use the term "temper," the literal meaning of tuning (as of bringing an instrument into tune) was actually in Herbert's mind,

---

[15] Quoted by Hutchinson, *The Works of George Herbert*, 521. "Pulse" had a specific musical meaning.

[16] Johannes Tinctoris, *Proportions in Music*, trans. Albert Seay (Colorado Springs: Colorado College Press, 1979), 1–2.

[17] See *OED*, *s.v.* noise 5b.

but at the same time there is wordplay on "temper" as applicable to the poet himself. His brother, Lord Herbert of Cherbury, has left a testament pointing out that George was not always so balanced and saintly in temperament as Izaak Walton makes him out to be.[18] The poet was at times choleric. So Herbert's statement in "Providence" "And be dispos'd, and dress'd, and tun'd by thee, / Who sweetly temper'st all" (38–39) probably reflects his awareness that he, of all men, needs God's tempering to bring him back into harmony with himself and the deity.

The poet, who was a viola da gamba player as well a lutenist, describes the tuning of the human soul by God in "The Temper (I)":

> Stretch or contract me, Thy poore debter;
> This is but tuning of my breast,
> To make the musick better. (22–24)

The concept of the breast as the strings and the body as the instrument is a commonplace that derives from antiquity. Gustave Reese cites a saying by Eusebius of Caesaria (c.260–340): "Our cithara is the whole body, by whose movement and action the soul sings a fitting hymn to God."[19] In a commentary on the psalms formerly attributed to Origen (c.185–c.265), "The many strings brought together in harmony, each ordered musically in its proper place, are the many commandments and the doctrines concerning many things, which exhibit no discord among themselves. The instrument embracing all this is the soul of man wise in Christ."[20]

Being brought into tune by God is the subject of "The Temper (II)" as well as of "The Temper (I)." In these two poems the poet sets up a deliberate contrast, with the first being exultant, though hinting a lack of security—perhaps like a musician with an

---

[18] Charles, *A Life of George Herbert*, 39.

[19] Gustave Reese, *Music in the Middle Ages* (New York: Norton, 1940), 62, citing Eusebius, *In Psalmum* 91.4.

[20] Pseudo-Origin, *Selecta in psalmos*, 90.5, as quoted in translation in James McKinnon, ed., *Music in Early Christian Literature* (Cambridge: Cambridge University Press, 1987), 39.

instrument in tune who hopes the strings will stay that way:

> How should I praise thee, Lord! how should my rymes
> Gladly engrave thy love in steel,
> If what my soul doth feel sometimes,
>   My soul might ever feel! (1–4)

Yet this poem is tuned tightly and brightly, as if in a sharp key. The second poem, "The Temper II," is melancholy and is filled with self-doubt:

> It cannot be. Where is that mightie joy,
> Which just now took up all my heart?
> Lord, if thou must needs use thy dart,
> Save that and me; or sin for both destroy. (1–4)

In this poem, obviously in a flatter tone or key than the first, it is also as if the strings also have not retained their temperament.

Then, in "Deniall," Herbert says, "my soul lay out of sight/ Untun'd, unstrung" (21–22). Tuning was in fact a serious difficulty in the early seventeenth century. With keyed instruments such as harpsichords or virginals, temperament was particularly problematic, for the tones of one key would be in agreement with one another but not in other keys. Lacking the modern well-tempered scale, modulation to other keys was a difficulty. However attractive for performing early music, these kinds of tuning systems were not always a blessing. Frequent re-tuning the instrument may have been necessary. Then, those who played the lute had the problem of making the instrument stay in tune, for its gut strings sometimes stretched or contracted during playing. In "Easter," Herbert bids his lute to awaken and struggle for its part.[21] In addition to the considerable challenge involved in playing this difficult instrument, the poem invokes its instability as an analogue for the need to keep the human instrument in tune with God. One may be reminded of Robert Fludd's cosmic monochord, with the hand of the deity tuning an instrument that obviously required

---

[21] On this poem, see also Hollander, *The Untuning of the Sky*, 293.

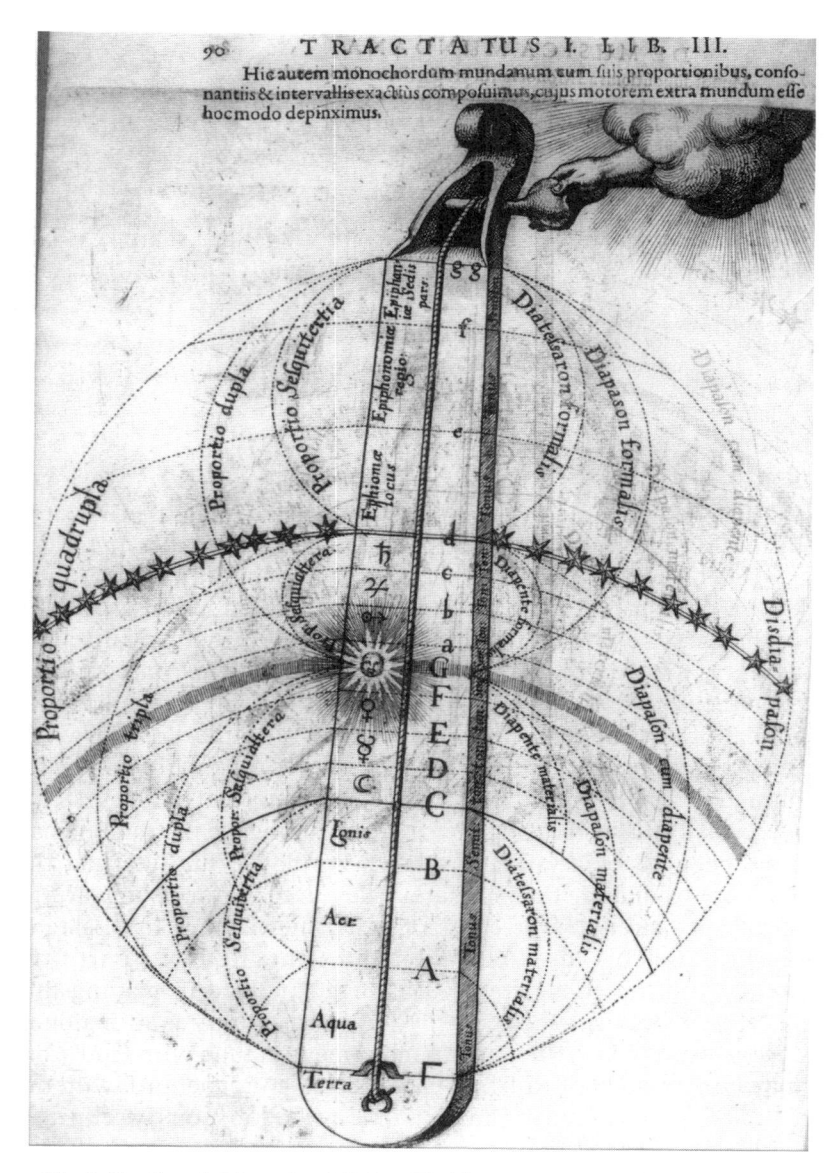

Fig. 3. The Cosmic Monochord. Robert Fludd, *Utriusque Cosmi maioris scilicet et minoris Metaphysica, Physica, atque Technica Istoria* (1617–18).

regular attention to maintain harmony (see fig. 3).²²

The lute also lacks sustaining power. In "Grieve Not the Holy Spirit," when Herbert writes of taking up his "lute, and tun[ing] it to a strain" with God in order to "complain," he concludes: "There can be no discord but in ceasing be." Discord, then, comes not in straining but "in ceasing" (19–22). Perfect and sustained tuning between human and divine is not possible because humans are not capable of it. Yet truly irremediable discordance occurs only when the song is discontinued, when the attempt to bring the imperfect instrument into concord is halted.²³ Yet, even though the lute is not able to achieve perfect tuning, its sound has a powerful emotive quality. The lute's gut strings are unusually sensitive. Marble weeps, Herbert says, but "surely strings / More bowels have, then such hard things" (23–24). The bowels were, in Herbert's day, considered the seat of the affections.

Written at a time when, with the coming into fashion of the early baroque style, the affections were being unusually emphasized in music, Herbert's poems are directly opposed to cold or formal religiosity. His expression of feelings in his poetry is akin to the practice of the early baroque composers who began to favor the expressive representation of the passions—e.g., love, rage, sadness, and especially excitement—in their music.²⁴ Something like such excitement is perceivable in "Easter," in which Herbert writes, "Rise, heart; thy Lord is risen. Sing his praise/ Without delays" (1–2). In "Easter Wings," there is a note of exultant triumph when the poet urges "And sing this day thy victorie" (9). Again, in "Repentance," exultation is emphasized:

>   And tune together in a well-set song,

---

²² See S. K. Heninger, Jr., *Touches of Sweet Harmony: Pythagorean Cosmology and Renaissance Poetics* (San Marino, California: Huntington Library, 1974), 185 and passim.

²³ Cf. Joseph H. Summers, *George Herbert: His Religion and Art* (London: Chatto and Windus, 1954), 158.

²⁴ The introduction of the new Italianate early baroque style to England has sometimes been credited to Giovanni Coprario (John Cooper); the style strongly influenced William and Henry Lawes and others.

Full of his praises,
    Who dead men raises. (33–35)

Sometimes the expressive uses of music lead one directly "to heavens doore," as in "Church-Musick" (12). Here Herbert is evincing no Puritan's view of religious music. As is well known, the Puritans, following Calvin, had an innate distrust of sacred music and in church services tried to limit its use to unaccompanied metrical settings of the psalms for congregational singing.[25] Herbert, who was known to assist with the instrumental accompaniment of the choir at Salisbury Cathedral where he felt the music connected him with heaven,[26] was not one to prescribe that religious music must be vocal only rather than performed with instruments, and one suspects that he understood celestial music, which inheres in the order of things, also to include polyphonic music—an opinion shared by Kepler.[27] He certainly did not distrust the sensuous qualities of music as performed in God's "house of pleasure" ("Church-Musick," 3). He clearly had no qualms like those expressed by St. Augustine in Book 10 of his *Confessions*:

> I fluctuate between peril of pleasure and approved wholesomeness; inclined the rather (though not as pronouncing an irrevocable opinion) to approve of the usage of singing in the

---

[25] [See the attack on cathedral music in Peter Smart, *The Vanity and Downfall of Superstitious Popish Ceremonies* (Edinburgh, 1628), as excerpted in Paul Elmer More and Frank Leslie Cross, *Anglicanism* (London: SPCK, 1935), 552. Smart objected in particular to practices under John Cosin at Durham Cathedral: "he hath turned most of the Service into piping and singing, so that the people understand it not, no more than they do Greek or Hebrew. He hath brought mere ballads and jigs into the Church, and commanded them to be sung for anthems. . . . He will not suffer so much as the Holy Communion to be administered without an hideous noise of vocal and instrumental music. . . ."—Ed.]

[26] See Summers, *George Herbert*, 156–57; Charles, *A Life of George Herbert*, 163–68; and, for Salisbury Cathedral music, see Dora Robertson, *Sarum Close*, 2nd ed. (Bath: Firecrest, 1969), esp. 159–99.

[27] See Walker, "Kepler's Celestial Music," 228.

church; that so by the delight of the ears the weaker minds may rise to the feeling of devotion. Yet when it befalls me to be more moved with the voice than the words sung, I confess to have sinned penally, and then had rather not hear music.[28]

Herbert's more balanced view of music has closer affinities to the high Protestantism of Richard Hooker and Martin Luther. Luther's view is interesting in this regard:

> I am not satisfied with him who despises music, as all fanatics do; for music is an endowment and a gift of God, not a gift of men. It also drives away the devil and makes people cheerful; one forgets all anger, unchasteness, pride, and other vices. I place music next to theology and give it the highest praise.[29]

Hooker adds a point that suggests the quotation from *Timaeus* at the head of the present essay:

> So pleasing effects it hath in that very part of man which is most divine, that some have been thereby induced to think that the soul itself by nature is or hath in it harmony.[30]

Of course, as Plato understood, there is nothing inevitably divine about man's music. It can even be put to silly or perverse uses. The writer of a poem labeled "doubtful" (but possibly by Herbert) confesses in "The Convert":

> My *voice*, that oft with foolish Lays,
> With Vows and Rants, and sensless Praise,
> Frail Beauty's Charms to Heav'n did raise,
>   Henceforth shall only pierce the Skies

---

[28] *The Confessions of St. Augustine*, trans. E. B. Pusey (London: Dent, 1907), 235.

[29] *Tischreden*, no. 7034, as quoted in *What Luther Says*, ed. Ewald M. Plass, 3 vols. (St. Louis: Concordia, 1959), 2:980.

[30] Richard Hooker, *The Works*, ed. William Molesworth, 3 vols. (reprint, New York: Burt Franklin, 1970), 2:159, referencing (in a note) Plato, *Phaedo* 85e.

>In Penitential Cryes. (11–15)

All things need to be understood in their proper perspective. Since this world is a space of mutability, "foolish Lays" may laud what is impermanent and neglect the permanent and eternal.

But many humans do prefer praising a mistress to praising God, as shown in "Love (I)":

> Who sings thy praise? onely a skarf or glove
> Doth warm our hands, and make them write of love. (13–14)

Henry Vaughan, Herbert's disciple, reiterates the theme of the toys and trifles which make us write or sing of earthly love:

> The doting Lover in his queinest strain
>   Did their Complain,
> Neer him, his Lute, his fancy, and his flights
> Wits sour delights. ("The World," 8–11)[31]

Such persons who have only "Wits sour delights" are contrasted in the poem with the saints, who "weep and sing,/ And sing, and weep," and who soar "up into the *Ring*" prepared for the Bride by the "*Bride-groome*," Christ (46–47, 59).

Herbert too weeps and sings as he emphasizes another aspect of the doctrine of the affections—sadness, melancholy. Sadness seems to have been Herbert's daily lot, for he was followed by ill health throughout his days; also, his hopes for a vocation in the Church were not fully realized until three years before his death. Thus, sighs and groans must have been his only music on many occasions. He attests to such melancholy too when he says that the "Countrey Parson is generally sad, because hee knows nothing but the Crosse of Christ, . . . or if he have any leisure to look off from thence, he meets continually with two most sad spectacles, Sin, and Misery; God dishonoured every day, and man afflicted. . . . Wherefore he . . . intermingles some mirth in his discourses

---

[31] Henry Vaughan, *The Complete Poetry*, ed. French Fogle (Garden City, N.Y.: Doubleday, 1964), 231.

occasionally, according to the pulse of the hearer."³² The poetry of the actual country parson, Herbert, intermingles sad and joyful imagery, as he advises:

> But grones are quick, and full of wings,
> And all their motions upward be;
> And ever as they mount like larks they sing;
> The note is sad, yet musick for a King. ("Sion," 21–24)

Sometimes, however, his grief is too deep for mirth and music:

> And keep your measures for some lovers lute,
> Whose grief allows him musick and a ryme:
> For mine excludes both measure, tune, and time.
> ("Grief," 16–18)

God, whose Son has gone through the tragicomedy of the Crucifixion and Resurrection, is able to make a joyful paradox out of sorrow:

> I live to shew his power, who once did bring
> My *joyes* to *weep*, and now my *griefs* to *sing*.
> ("Joseph's Coat," 13–14)

Music is able to express gladness, it can accommodate itself to a sad mood, and it can heal illnesses. In "Dooms-day," the power of "peculiar notes and strains" to "Cure Tarantulas raging pains" is noted (11–12).³³ Tarantism, an illness which manifested itself in a hysterical kind of dance, was erroneously thought in the sixteenth and seventeenth centuries to be caused by the bite of the tarantula. The "cure" for the disease was a dance, the tarantella, in rapid 6/8 rhythm. It is not only in reference to the power to cure tarantism

---

[32] Herbert, *The Works*, 267–68.

[33] Concerning the healing power of music, Herbert realistically quotes an "outlandish proverb": "Musick helps not the tooth-ache" (*The Works*, 339). The idea that music has healing powers has often been traced to Pythagoras on the testimony of Iamblichus' life of the philosopher; cited by Heninger, *Touches of Sweet Harmony*, 103.

that Herbert is referring, for he also has in mind the power of God's music to repair broken lives, which come together here as a "broken consort." When Herbert says, "Lord, thy broken consort raise" (29), however, we need to recognize that he is using a term that denotes a mixed group of instruments, including both winds and strings. Such a "broken consort" was likely to be used in domestic situations where it was not always possible to find a homogeneous group of instruments. These are social settings that Herbert knew well from childhood.[34] But the implication here is that God can use any music offered to him for his glory, no matter how aesthetically limited it might be.

The healing of broken spirits through the therapeutic power of music was a commonplace among ancient and medieval writers. Clement of Alexandria made reference to David and his cithara who was able to "put to flight by his music" the demons afflicting "Saul, who was plagued by them."[35] Music therapy of this kind is also famously noted in Boethius' *De institutione musica*, which recounts the tale of Terpander and Arion of Methymna who "saved the citizens of Lesbos and Ionia from very serious illness through the assistance of song." Boethius continues:

> Moreover, by the means of modes Ismenias the Theban is said to have driven away all the distresses of many Boeotians suffering from the torments of sciatica. Similarly, it is said that Empedocles altered the mode of music-making when an infuriated youth attacked one of his guests with a sword because this guest had condemned the youth's father by bringing an accusation. Thereby Empedocles tempered the wrath of the youth.[36]

Hooker too speaks of tempering the spirits:

---

[34] Charles, *A Life of George Herbert*, 42–43.

[35] Clement of Alexandria, *Protrepticus*, as quoted by McKinnon, ed., *Music in Early Christian Literature*, 30.

[36] Boethius, Introduction to *Fundamentals of Music* (*De Institutione Musica*), trans. Calvin Bower, ed. Claude V. Palisca (New Haven: Yale University Press, 1989), 6.

> The very harmony of sounds being framed in due sort and carried from the ear to the spiritual faculties of our souls, is by a native puissance and efficacy greatly available to bring to a perfect temper whatsoever is there troubled, apt as well to quicken the spirits as to allay that which is too eager, sovereign against melancholy and despair, forcible to draw forth tears of devotion if the mind be such as can yield them, able both to move and to moderate all affections.[37]

Besides being medicine for the soul, music is associated with good works. St. Jerome had famously said that even if "one might be, as they are wont to say, *kakophonos*, if he has performed good works, he is a sweet singer before God."[38] An anecdote from Izaak Walton's *Life* provides an example of Herbert's agreement with this view. Herbert, after having put off his "Canonical Coat" to help a poor man whose horse had fallen and who was mired in mud, arrived at his appointment; his musical friends marveled at the mud-stained clothing of one noted for his careful dress. Herbert's explanation was that his good deed, which may have wrought him some hardship, would be to him "Musick at Midnight."[39]

But to someone who lacks God's grace, "Musick . . . doth howl" ("Conscience," 4). "As dirtie hands foul all they touch," so do people with "clay hearts" negate the goodness of music ("Miserie," 37, 39).

> His house still burns, and yet he still doth sing,
> > Man is but grasse,
> > He knows it, fill the glasse. ("Miserie," 4–6)

Another singer, sweet but diabolical, is the allegorical figure of human Love, through whose enchanting voice the world has destroyed thousands of souls. Delight, another pleasure of this

---

[37] Hooker, *The Works*, 2:160.

[38] Jerome, *Commentarium in Epistulam ad Ephesios*, 3.5.19, as quoted by McKinnon, ed., *Music in Early Christian Literature*, 144.

[39] Walton, *The Life of Mr. George Herbert*, 92.

world, also purports to come bringing comforting music to Herbert's soul, but she stays only for half an hour. Because of Delight's inconstancy, he is justified in reproaching her and advising that she should have "More skill in musick, and [to] keep better time" ("The Glimpse," 6–7). Using an analogy with music, his point is that the delights of this world are transient and not to be depended upon.

But music can also warn of our nearness to the next world, eternity:

> When youth is frank and free
> And calls for musick . . .
> That musick summons to the knell
> Which shall befriend him at the houre of Death.
> ("Mortification," 13–14, 17–18)

Then, the approach of Death and the Last Things is not necessarily to be feared. Though Death "wast once an uncouth hideous thing,/ . . . / Thy mouth was open, but thou couldst not sing" ("Death," 2–4), now he has become lovely on account of Christ's death on the cross. Death has changed dramatically and has become "fair and full of grace" (15): Now he has been taught the skill of music and is able to sing. The dead, however, neither sing nor hear; they are, in effect, tone-deaf to all but one sound at a single moment in history: "Dust, alas, no musick feels,/ But thy trumpet" ("Doomsday," 9–10). It is a deafness that will be remedied through the working out of God's plan of salvation.

All earthly things must eventually depart from this life, as Herbert notes in "Vertue": "My musick shows ye have your closes,/ And all must die" (11–12). The word "closes" is a musical term, referring to cadences, the last notes of phrases—a term which appeared as early as the fourteenth century when the first ending of a song was called *ouvert* (open) and the second ending was called *clos* (closed).[40] The mention of the musical cadence in "Vertue" comes toward the end of the third stanza, which does not have musical imagery; instead, it opens with "Sweet spring," a kind of "box where sweets compacted lie" (9–10). These are "sweets" that,

---

[40] Willi Apel, *The Notation of Polyphonic Music, 900–1600* (Cambridge: Harvard University Press, 1945), 349.

when compared to the permanence of that otherwise seemingly ephemeral art, music, are in fact impermanent.

"The Familie," on the other hand, is rich in musical imagery, on which he rings changes, piling image on image. He opens with "What doth this noise of thoughts within my heart,/ As if they had a part?" (1–2). Noise, says Hutchinson, offends Herbert's ear,[41] and well it might, for the term "noise," as indicated above, signifies a band of street musicians like the one called "Sneak's noise" that appears in Shakespeare's *2 Henry IV*, act 2, scene 4. But idea of noise shifts in meaning as Herbert invokes griefs without noise, fears distempered, and nothing "so shrill as silent tears" (20). Thereafter:

> . . . Order *plaies* the soul;
> And giving all things their set forms and houres,
> Makes of wilde woods sweet walks and bowres.
> (ll. 10–12; italics mine)

A further resonance appears at "set forms and houres," for here he seems to invoke the canonical hours at which psalms, hymns, and antiphons are to be sung.[42]

In "The Pearl," however, no antiphon or hymn is sung by Pleasure, who is known for his singing of "strains" (portions of a melody), "lullings" (soothing passages), "propositions" (introduction of musical utterances, probably indicative of embellishments), and "relishes." An example of the relish, a highly florid embellishment, from Giulio Caccini's *Le Nuove Musicae* follows:[43]

---

[41] Hutchinson, ed., *The Works of George Herbert*, 524.

[42] Herbert understood the antiphon differently from the usual Roman form, which can be observed in the *Liber usualis*. His "Antiphon (I)" and "Antiphon (II)" present a refrain sung by a chorus, and vericles, perhaps based on psalms, sung by a soloist.

[43] Giulio Caccini, *Le Nuove Musicae*, ed. H. Wiley Hitchcock (Madison, Wisconsin: A–R Editions, 1970), 50.

While attention has been called to some of these musical terms by Joseph Summers,[44] it should be added that there is also a religious connotation in "lullings"; the ways of Pleasure are not conducive to devotions, and hence the term suggests not only a soothing passage but also a narcotic effect of lulling to sleep spiritually.

Herbert's preparation for his last sleep is described in "The Forerunners." Even when death threatens to transform him into a clod, he praises God: *"Thou art still my God"* (32). And he says that God "will be pleased with that ditty" (11), i.e., meaning the "theme" or "burden of a song." Herein lies the clue to the poet's intent in creating praises to God. But written language is also invoked: "if I please him, I write fine and wittie" (12). What Herbert has written or sung consists not only of his original theme—*"Thou art still my God"*—but also of embellishments on it by metaphors and phrases from the brothel. Of these "sweet phrases, lovely metaphors" (13), the poet says:

> Then did I wash you with my tears, and more,
>   Brought you to Church well-drest and clad:
> My God must have my best, ev'n all I had. (16–18)

The profane is transformed into sacred meaning in the poem.

"A Parodie" uses a similar practice of transformation, which is so much like a secular poem attributed to the second earl of Pembroke that some critics suspect Herbert used the "Pembroke" poem for a model. Rosemond Tuve, however, argued that he did not draw on the form of the "Pembroke" poem so much as he followed a musical setting for it, a setting which is, unfortunately, now lost. If this had been the case, the process would have provided a delicate interrelationship to verse and music, an interrelationship we have seen Herbert exploit in the sung metaphors of "The Forerunners."

The relationship between verse and song is noted again in "The Quidditie," in which a verse is said to be "nor yet a lute," and it "cannot vault, or dance, or play" (4–5). Verse comes off second best in this comparison, for in Herbert's view it is by itself more limited than music. When speech and song are contrasted in his poetry, the former often imitates the irregularity of speech rhythms,

---

[44] Summers, *George Herbert*, 158–59.

while text that seems as if designed for a musical setting will comprise the best lines.

Yet Herbert was not writing music but poetry, with language as his medium of expression. If he loved music most, his greatest gift was for verse. The harmony that his verse makes of the two arts, however, has been often noticed, though sometimes in misleading ways. Albert M. Hayes long ago in an article "Counterpoint in Herbert"[45] emphasized the poet's love of form, but his adoption of the term "counterpoint" to describe the clash of rhythm and rhyme in many of his poems is unfortunate. The analogy is a false one, since "counterpoint" implies contrapuntal music in which at least two voices must be heard simultaneously. The thought makes me imagine, perhaps unfairly, a clashing of voice and song ending in chaos, which would be an absurdity.

And chaotic is anything but the effect achieved by Herbert in his poetry. His careful contrivances operate to produce a powerful emotional effect, an effect felt fully in the sixty "musical" poems and in the sixty-seven poems not directly concerned with music. In the expressive use of musical imagery in his verse and in his concern for achieving harmony between humans and the higher order of things, he can perhaps be seen as aspiring to be the minister of music to those who love music and poetry alike. This is not mere formalism, and perhaps for Herbert the image of God in man, as for Kepler, resides in music properly in tune, perhaps even in just intonation.[46]

---

[45] Albert McHarg Hayes, "Counterpoint in Herbert," *Studies in Philology* 35 (1938): 43–60.

[46] See Walker, "Kepler's Celestial Music," 228.

III

The Origin and Development of Quasi-Dramatic Passion Music

The roots of the quasi-dramatic Passion, including examples from Scandinavia, go back as far as some of the earliest recorded devotional and liturgical practices, although the musical practice may be traced no further than the Carolingian reforms of the eighth and ninth centuries. Devotion to the Passion of Christ was evident as early as the writings of St. Ignatius, bishop of Antioch, who lived c.35–107 and whose euphoric words read: "Him I desire who rose again for us. . . . Permit me to imitate the Passion of my God."[1] Devotion to the Passion has also been noted in the words of second-century Melito of Sardis (d. c.190) and of the somewhat later St. Ephraem of Syria (c.306–73).[2] St. Melito says in one of his homilies: "Listen while you tremble! He that suspended the earth was hanged up; He that fixed the heavens was fixed with nails; He that supported the earth was supported on a tree; the Lord was exposed to ignominy with a naked body; God put to death!"[3] It is said of St. Ephraem that he "used to interrupt his own sermons from time to time to exclaim, 'Glory be to Him, how much He suffered!' "[4]

Devotion to the Passion of Christ is, of course, directly related

---

[1] *An Epistle of St. Ignatius to the Romans*, 6, in *The Apostolic Fathers*, trans. W. Burton, 2 vols. (London: Griffith Farran, n.d.), 2:99. See also J. Mead, "Devotion to Passion of Christ," *New Catholic Encyclopedia* (New York: McGraw Hill, 1967), 10:1059.

[2] Mead, "Devotion to Passion of Christ," 1059.

[3] W. Cureton, *Spicilegium Syriacum* (London, 1861), 55, as quoted in Mead, "Devotion to Passion of Christ," 1059.

[4] Mead, "Devotion to Passion of Christ," 1059.

to passages in the four Gospels dealing with the suffering and death of Christ (Matthew 26:1–75, 27:1–66; Mark 14:1–72, 15:46; Luke 22:1–71, 23:1–53; John 18:1–40, 19:1–42). The earliest record of the usage of these passages in the liturgy of Holy Week has been provided in the writings of the Gallican nun Etheria, who gives an eyewitness account of the services, the readings, and the congregational participation in Christian worship at Jerusalem in c.380 A.D. For Wednesday of Holy Week, she chronicles the fact that the priest reads the passage which recounts the betrayal of Christ by Judas, and when he has finished "there is such a moaning of all the people that no one can help being moved to tears at that hour."[5] On Holy Thursday, the Gospel reading at Gethsemane deals with Christ's being taken captive, and again there is a strong emotional outburst—"so great a moaning and groaning of all the people, together with weeping, that their lamentation may be heard perhaps as far as the city."[6]

On Good Friday, Etheria reports a service at daybreak which includes the Adoration of the Cross (a carefully guarded relic since, as she reports, a piece of the sacred wood had been bitten off by a worshipper during a previous service) as well as readings from the psalms, the Acts of the Apostles, the prophets, and "the Gospels where He mentions His Passion." The effect of the Old Testament and New Testament foreshadowings and descriptions of the Passion, read at the very place on Golgotha where Christ was crucified, was again reported by the pilgrim Etheria to be impressive; "the emotion shown and the mourning by all the people at every lesson and prayer is wonderful; for there is none, either great or small, who, on that day during those three hours, does not lament more than can be conceived, that the Lord suffered those things for us." Finally, there is read "that passage from the Gospel according to John where He gave up the ghost," and, after a prayer,

---

[5] *Peregrinatio Etheriae*, trans. L. Duchesne in his *Christian Worship: Its Origin and Evolution*, 5th ed. (London: SPCK, 1919), 555. For the Latin text, see *Itinera Hierosolymitana, Saeculi VI–VIII*, ed. Paul Geyer, Corpus Christianorum Ecclesiasticum Latinorum 39 (Prague, 1898), 89.

[6] Duchesne, *Christian Worship*, 557.

the people are dismissed.[7]

As is evident from Etheria's account, the exclusive use of the St. John's Gospel passages for Good Friday was not yet the practice for the Gospel lesson in the late fourth century, but rather a syncretic compilation of the four gospels was the general rule.[8] But that the Gospels telling the Passion history were inextricably tied to Holy Week, especially to the Good Friday service, not only in Jerusalem but elsewhere in the Western Church, is evidenced by St. Augustine's Sermon for Good Friday, which also quotes or makes references to a number of verses from the Gospel Passion passages (e.g., John 19:17, Matthew 16:24, etc.). The sermon begins:

> The Passion of Him by whose blood our sins were wiped out is being read solemnly and is being honored with due respect, so that by this yearly devotion our memory may be more readily refreshed, and our faith more brightly illuminated by the great gathering of people. Hence, this solemn celebration obliges me to give you a sermon on the Passion of the Lord, such as He Himself gives [in the words of sacred Scripture].[9]

The sermon itself proves that again the Gospel of St. John was not exclusively used on Good Friday, but rather was included among the accounts in the other three Gospels. It was therefore later than St. Augustine's time that the four Gospels became associated with different days in Holy Week, with St. Matthew's account being read on Palm Sunday, St. Mark's on Tuesday, St. Luke's on Wednesday, and, of course, St. John's on Good Friday. This latter practice was established by the sixth century.

Regarding the actual presentation or performance of the Gospel lesson for Good Friday in the early Christian centuries, we have

---

[7] Ibid., 558–60.

[8] *The Oxford Dictionary of the Christian Church*, 2nd ed., ed. F. L. Cross and E. A. Livingstone (Oxford: Oxford University Press, 1974), 583.

[9] St. Augustine, *Sermons on the Liturgical Seasons*, trans. Mary Sarah Muldowney, Fathers of the Church 38 (New York, 1959), 164 (Sermon 218); Latin text in Migne, *Patrologia latina*, 38:1084.

small knowledge of the musical practice that was involved. One thing about which we can be certain is that the Gospel was not merely read aloud, but was rather *chanted*. Eric Werner's attempt to trace back Christian liturgical practice to Jewish traditions reveals that neither Jewish nor Christian lessons would have been read or recited without intonation. He quotes an ancient Jewish source which prescribes the manner in which Scriptures were to be presented in public worship: "Whosoever reads Scripture without chant and the Mishna without intonation, to him the word of Scripture is not applicable: 'I gave them laws that were not beautiful'."[10] In the Eastern Church, the evidence for scriptural chant is displayed in the "numerous lectionaries with ecphonetic notation,"[11] while in the Western Church the evidence appears in the distinction frequently made between the more florid rendering of the psalms and the moderate recitation of the lessons.[12]

Though precise information regarding the chanting of the Gospel lesson before the ninth century is lacking, we may, however, feel certain that the medieval and post-medieval form of the liturgy and its music depends greatly on what occurred in the Frankish Empire under Pepin and Charlemagne and in this region during the succeeding centuries. Helmut Hucke even asserts strongly that "none of the forms of Gregorian Chant can be traced back to early Christian times" and that "the version [of the so-called Gregorian chant] which has come down to us originated in

---

[10] *B. Meg.* 32a, Ezekiel 20:25, as quoted in Eric Werner, *The Sacred Bridge: The Interdependence of Liturgy and Music in Synagogue and Church during the First Millenium* (New York: Columbia University Press, 1959), 103.

[11] Ibid., 117.

[12] Ibid., 121; see especially St. Augustine's comment about St. Athanasius, who is said to have "made the lector render the psalms in so moderate an inflexion, that it came nearer recitation than singing" (*Confessions* 9:33, as quoted by Werner, *The Sacred Bridge*, 121).

the Frankish Empire in the 8th and 9th centuries."[13]

The story of the Carolingian liturgical reforms which attempted to impose the Roman rite and its music is well known. Pepin and Charlemagne, whether religiously or politically motivated or both, suppressed the rich, even extravagant Gallican rite in favor of the plainer liturgy and chant used in Rome. Walafrid Strabo in 840 writes of Pepin's rôle:

> That superior knowledge of plainsong which almost the whole of Gaul now cherishes, was introduced by Pope Stephen, when he came into France to Pippin, father of Emperor Charles the Great, seeking justice for St. Peter from the Lombards. At Pippin's request the papal clerics introduced the chant, and thence its use spread far and wide.[14]

Needless to say, there was a great deal of popular resistance to the austere Roman rite, which very quickly became enriched through creative additions in the region that had previously used the Gallican rite.[15] Charlemagne, however, was loyal to the Roman forms, which he felt were directly derived from the teaching of the apostolic Church, and his loyalty is attested to in the *Libri Carolini*:

> For whereas the [Gallican] Church since its very conversion to the faith has always stood in loyal and close union with the holy Church of Rome, and differed from it but little—not to be sure as touching the faith—but in the celebration of divine worship, it is

---

[13] Helmut Hucke, "New Historical Light on Old Gregorian Chant," paper read at the Fourteenth International Congress on Medieval Studies, Kalamazoo, Michigan, 3–6 May 1979; I quote from the *Abstracts* of the Congress.

[14] *Walafridi Strabonis liber de exordiis et incrementis quarundam in observationibus ecclessiasticis rerum*, ed. Aloysius Knoepfler, 84, as quoted in translation by Gerald Ellard, *Master Alcuin, Liturgist* (Chicago: Loyola University Press, 1956), 19.

[15] Theodor Klauser, *A Short History of the Western Liturgy* (London: Oxford University Press, 1969), 78, 84.

now, thanks the zeal and solicitude of our most excellent father of happy memory, King Pippin, and in consequence of the journey into Gaul of the blessed and most Reverend Stephen, Bishop of Rome, entirely at one with you even in this matter of psalmody. No difference in chanting should divide those who share a common faith, and united by the reading of one holy law, they should also be linked in the venerable tradition of a common song, nor should the differing celebration of the offices separate those linked by the holy tie of the true belief.[16]

And Charlemagne's personal interest in liturgical reform is further chronicled by Einhard, his biographer, who states that he "was at great pains to improve the church reading and psalmody, for he was well skilled in both, although he neither read in public nor sang, except in a low tone and with others."[17] Undoubtedly the adoption of Roman forms and the concomitant "plainness" in liturgy owes much to the tastes of Charlemagne's tutor and trusted advisor, Alcuin, whose preferences are expressed in a letter to his former pupil, Eanbald II, newly installed as Archbishop of York in 796. Alcuin advises the archbishop: "Let the clergy be in the habit of honesty and in the likeness of constancy, and let their singing be in a *restrained tone* [italics mine], as being more anxious to please God than men."[18]

The qualities in the Gallican rite which seemed most in need of reform must therefore have been the richness, extravagance, prolixity, and especially the dramatic quality that it possessed.[19]

---

[16] *Monumenta Germaniae Historica, Leges III, Concilia aevi Karolini II, Supplementum*, 21–22, as quoted in translation by Ellard, *Master Alcuin*, 49.

[17] Einhard, *The Life of Charlemagne*, trans. Samuel E. Turner (Ann Arbor: University of Michigan Press, 1960), 55.

[18] Epist. 4, in *Monumenta Germaniae*, as quoted in translation by Ellard, *Master Alcuin*, 55–56.

[19] For a description of the Gallican rite in all its effulgence, see A. Archdale King, *Liturgies of the Past* (London: Longmans, 1959), 77–185. But see also *The Bobbio Missal*, ed. E. A. Loew (London; Harrison, 1920).

Josef Jungmann, surveying the Gallican liturgy in his important study, *The Mass of the Roman Rite*, notes the heavy reliance on ceremony and "splendor" as well as its essentially dramatic nature; indeed, he finds that "the *dramatic* build-up of the Mass-liturgy" is central to its structure.[20] This ritual had been much more satisfying in a cultic way than Charlemagne's reformed rite, and it is no surprise therefore that elements of the older Gallican forms kept creeping back into the practice of the Church of the Frankish Empire.[21] In fact, a great deal of the ceremonial and much that is emotionally satisfying in the liturgy of the Mass can be traced back to Gallican practice.[22]

It is significant that, just at the time that the liturgy supposedly was to have been cleansed from the dramatic elements which characterized the Gallican rite, new and important non-Roman features such as sequences, tropes, and even liturgical drama developed.[23] These innovations emerged in the area where the Gallican rite had been practiced because, as C. Clifford Flanigan has noted, they were considered ways of attempting "to reassert the cultic nature of liturgical celebration which was lacking in the

---

[20] Josef Jungmann, *The Mass of the Roman Rite*, trans. Francis A. Brunner, 2 vols. (New York: Benziger, 1951), 1:77.

[21] But there was confusion even among those who sought purity of ritual. In 831 or 832, Amalarius of Metz became concerned about the purity of service books and went to Rome to find out what the true practice should be. He was directed to the monastery at Corbie which possessed one of the few antiphoners available. When he saw the Corbie volumes, he found that numerous revisions to the liturgy had been made at Rome and that his copy at Metz was no more "faulty" than those at Rome and Corbie. See Peter Wagner, *Introduction to the Gregorian Melodies*, 2nd ed., Part I, trans. Agnes Orme and E. G. P. Wyatt (London: Plainsong and Mediaeval Music Society, n.d.), 1:211–13.

[22] See W. S. Porter, *The Gallican Rite* (London: A. R. Mowbray, 1958), 28, as cited in C. Clifford Flanigan, "The Roman Rite and the Origins of the Liturgical Drama," *University of Toronto Quarterly* 43 (1974): 277.

[23] See ibid., 263–84, and Richard Crocker, *The Early Medieval Sequence* (Berkeley: University of California Press, 1977).

Roman rite," and indeed these "cultic elements" are ones "which the history of religions has suggested fulfill basic human needs."[24] From this time also would have come a more dramatic presentation of the Gospel lesson for Good Friday.

In the Gallican rite, it is especially true that the Gospel lesson was read as if Christ were ritually present. The Gospel procession leading up to the reading symbolized or even actualized Christ's presence, and, as Jungmann comments, it "became Christ's triumphal march; to Christ resounds the *Gloria tibi Domine*, of which until then the Roman Mass knew nothing."[25] Flanigan, extending Jungmann's comments, marks especially the use of incense at the Gospel reading and the extended ceremonial as significant:

> If I understand Jungmann correctly, he is suggesting that the ritual coming of Christ through the reading of the Gospel is given heightened prominence by a proliferation of ceremonies. That Christ is coming ritually among his people at this point in the mass is emphasized by the censing of all the worshippers. That it is God himself who is made present through the cult—and here we are touching on one of the chief concerns of the Gallican rite—is expressed by the dramatic gesture of censing the altar at the very beginning of the mass. These censings are not arbitrary; as Eliade has taught us to expect, they have an archetype, the censings which according to several scriptural passages take place before the heavenly throne. Such a ritual gesture suggests that the boundaries of time and space are rolled back for the duration of this event. Both the past historical coming of Christ recounted in the Gospel, and the future worship of God by the faithful in heaven, have become present in the timelessness of the ritual.[26]

---

[24] Flanigan, "The Roman Rite and the Origins of the Liturgical Drama," 280–81.

[25] Jungmann, *The Mass of the Roman Rite*, 1:77; see also King, *Liturgies of the Past*, 160.

[26] Flanigan, "The Roman Rite and the Origins of the Liturgical Drama," 274–75. The apparent use of the *Trisagion* at the Gospel procession also suggests that Christ is present in the chanting of the lesson; see Duchesne,

Quasi-Dramatic Passion Music 163

The above argues especially for *dramatic* presentation in the chanting of the long lesson from St. John's Gospel on Good Friday.

In about the ninth century, the missals containing the Gospel lessons began to show letters before the words of Christ, of the Evangelist, and of the other personages which indicate that the cleric who was chanting the text would attempt to portray some rôle changes by means of variations in vocal quality, tempo, or other means of interpretation.[27] These letters, called Romanus or Romanian letters after a legendary man said to have brought the Roman rite to St. Gall,[28] are interpreted by Notker Balbulus (840–912), who is known as the father of the sequence, in an epistle to his fellow monk Lambert.[29] The letters, which are indicative of the kind of dramatic expressiveness that Aelred of Rievaulx later found offensive, are here given according to Notker's explanations of their meaning:[30]

Christian Worship, 197.

[27] Bruno Stäblein, "Die einstimmige lateinische Passion," *Die Musik in Geschichte und Gegenwart*, 17 vols. (1949–86), 10:888.

[28] Romanus, said to have been one of two persons sent to Charlemagne with an authentic antiphoner in 790 but sidetracked at St. Gall at first because of illness, was believed to be the founder of the song school at St. Gall. See Wagner, *Introduction to Gregorian Melodies*, 1:219. The source of this story is Ekkehard IV, *Casus Sancti Galli* (eleventh century), whose account is printed in Rombaut van Doren, *Étude sur l'influence de Saint-Gall (VIIIe au XIe siècle)* (Brussels: Maurice Lamertin, 1925), 128.

[29] St. Gall 259, cited in Willi Apel, *Gregorian Chant* (London: Burns and Oates, n.d.), 117. The symbols and their meaning are more fully set forth in Peter Wagner, *Einführung in die Gregorischen Melodien*, 3 vols. (Leipzig: Breitkopf und Härtel, 1911–21), 2:237, 241, and they are, of course, widely used in indicating performance practice of Gregorian chant generally.

[30] Ibid., 2:235.

Terms having to do with the elevation of pitch:
    a = *altius*
    l = *levatur*
    s = *sursum*
    g = *gradation*

Terms having to do with the lowering of pitch:
    i = *iusum* or *inferius*
    d = *deponatur*

Term signifying the unison:
    e = *equaliter*

Terms having to do with rhythm:
    (1) Signifying quicker movement:
        c = *celeriter*
    (2) Signifying slower movement:
        t = *trahere* or *tenere*
        x = *expectare* (to await, to retard)
    (3) Signifying moderate movement:
        m = *mediocriter*[31]

Terms having to do with intensity:
    p = *pressio* (pressing)
    f = *cum fragore* (with breaking—ornament?), often associated with *fortiter* (strong)
    k = *clange* (an energetic emphasis)

Grouped terms:
    b l = *bene levatur* (well or much lifted)
    t b = *bene teneatur* (much held back)
    I v = *iusum valde* (extremely below—i.e., descending a fourth or fifth)
    a m = *altius mediocriter*
    c m = *celeriter mediocriter*
    i m = *inferius mediocriter*
    t m = *teneatur mediocriter*[32]

---

[31] Apel, *Gregorian Chant*, 117, wonders if this term might mean "retard."

[32] A thirteenth-century explanation from Paris, Bibliothèque Nationale, MS. nouv. acquis. lat. 229, is as follows:
        A monet alta peti; B tolli sive teneri.

Not all of the Romanian letters are used in extant manuscripts, and only a limited number are, of course, used to indicate the chanting of the Passion Gospel. Presented in the accompanying chart is a list of the terms used in the Passion Gospel and associated with each of the three personages or groups of personages.

Generally speaking, the earliest manuscripts use the terms *celeriter* for the Evangelist's words, *tenere* or *trahere* for Christ's speech, and *alt(i)us* or *sursum* for the others. However, it would be impossible without making an exhaustive search of extant manuscripts and their provenance to separate early from late practice—e.g., the Linköping Missal (Cod. Holm A 97) probably from the parish of Skönberga in Östergötland and dated c.1400, in which the same letters (c, s, and t) appear that are characteristic of the earlier manuscripts. And we cannot tell whether a letter such as c means *celeriter* or *cronista*; therefore a certain amount of ambiguity is present in the interpretation and dating of the so-called Romanian letters, otherwise known as *litterae significativae*, inserted in the Gospel texts. The t, which in earlier manuscripts signified *tenere* or *trahere*, as noted above, from the fourteenth century began to take the form of a capital T and to be associated with Christ's cross. In certain missals, the words "*Te igitur* . . ." which begin the Canon of the Mass, the capital T was rendered as an historiated initial with a painting of the cross holding the body of Christ. One such pictorial rendition of the T is found in the *Missale Lundense* printed in 1514: below the crucified Christ which comprises the letter T is shown Ecclesia under Christ's right hand, and under his left is Synagoga who is weeping and should

---

C celera sursum; D dicit deprimo uisum.
E iubet equari; docet F cantando feriri.
G moderare gradum; H rarum pandit hiatum.
I trahit inferius; levat L si quando subimus.
M mediocriter sonat; O cantus ordine donat.
Pressio Fit per P; facit V nos recta videre.
Sibilat S susum; T tractus continet usum.
X habit expecta; litteris sic exprime verba.

Quoted by Wagner, *Einfürung in die Gregorischen Melodien*, 2:235.

LETTERS AND TERMS FOUND IN PASSION GOSPEL TEXTS
and associated with words of the Evangelist, Christ, and the others

1. EVANGELIST	2. CHRIST	3. CROWD, OTHER PERSONS
c = *celeriter*	t = *tenere* or *trahere*	s = *sursum*
c = *cronista* or *cantar*	t = *cross* (symbolic)	s = *synagoga* or *succentor*
m = *mediocriter*	b = *bassa voce*	a = *altius*
d = *directe* (= *tonus directaneus*, direct psalmody)	i = *isum or inferius*	l = *levare*
l = *lector*	h = *humiliter* (humble)	f = *cum fragore*
	d = *dulce* (sweet)	f = *fortiter* (strong)
	d = *deprimatur* (heavy, depressed)	p = *pressio*
	l = *leniter, lente* (gentle)	
	g = *graviter, gravandum*	
	e = *euangelium*[33]	
	p = *plane* (rarely)	

---

[33] This might seem unusual. See H. M. Bannister, *Monumenti Vaticani de Paleografia Musicale Latina* (Leipzig, 1913), nos. 913ff.

be turning away though she is inaccurately depicted by the artist.[34] The T as a cross used to note Christ's words in the Good Friday Gospel lesson is found in English manuscripts, and is sometimes also found in the shape of a four- or eight-sided object turned on its axis to indicate the words of his antagonists.[35] In a manuscript at Munich (Clm 3005), the l indicating Christ has been later turned into a cross, and "a yet lighter and later hand has written a 'p' over it."[36]

In some cases, the various letters indicate not simple pitch but voice range, as in *bassa voce* for Christ and i v (*iusum valde*) which indicates that Christ's words are to be sung at a pitch which drops a fourth or fifth below the reciting tone. Thus Christ's words are associated with a bass range, the Evangelist's words with the tenor range, and the crowd and other personages' words, since they are indicated by a or s, with the countertenor range. This does not need to mean that in the early centuries three separate voices were used, but rather, as is consistent with medieval practice, that the deacon would be able to modulate his voice in high, low, and medium ranges.[37]

In regard to the interpretation of the Gospel Passion and the manner in which the voice is changed to indicate rôles in the presentation of the lesson on Good Friday, the statements of Durandus of Mende (c.1230–96) have sometimes been misconstrued.[38] Durandus asserts that the Passion should not be chanted

---

[34] The Lund Missal has been edited in facsimile by Bengt Strömberg, Laurentius Petri Sällskapets Urkundsserie 4 (Malmö: John Kroon, 1946).

[35] See the example in *Die Musik in Geschichte und Gegenwart*, 10, pl. 61.

[36] Stäblein, "Die einstimmige lateinische Passion," 10:890.

[37] Otto Kade, *Die ältere Passionskomposition* (Gütersloh: C. Bertelsmann, 1893), 2.

[38] Durandus, *Rationale divinorum officiorum*, ed. John Beletho (Naples, 1859), 506: "Non legitur etiam tota sub tono Evangelii, sed cantus verborum Christi dulcius moderantur, ad notandum quod dulcius verba Christi in ipsius ore resonabant, quam in ore cujuslibet Evangelistae referentis, cuijus verba in tono Evangelii proferunter. Verba vero. impiissimorum Judaeorum clamose et cum asperitate vocis, ad designandum quod ipsi Christo aspere loquebantur. In fine tamen, in quibusdam Ecclesiis,

entirely in the usual Gospel tone. The words of Christ should be sung sweetly and with moderation, and while the Evangelist's words should be in the solemn Gospel tone, the hostile words of his enemies should be presented clamorously and with harsh voices "to show how harshly they spoke to Christ." Earlier scholars understood these comments to mean that, already by the thirteenth century, the Passion Gospel for Good Friday was commonly sung in an even more dramatic form by three persons; however, more recently the tendency has been to view this development in which rôle division is assigned among three clerics as not occurring until the end of the medieval period.[39] The Sarum Missal (Burtisland edition) thus notes that the St. John Passion "ought to be sung or recited in a three-fold-pitch, namely high, low, and intermediate pitch" (*triplici voce debet cantari aut pronunciari, scilicit voce alta, bassa et media*), with the Romanian letters thereupon assigned to the parts.[40]

The chanting of the Gospel lesson at Mass—a practice which merges with the chanting of the Passion from St. John's Gospel on Good Friday—during the early and later Middle Ages has been described by C.-A. Moberg, who explains that the earliest practice involved chanting everything in the Gospel lesson with the exception of Christ.[41] Christ's words, however, are presented in a particular way which involves intonation and/or a specific vocal

---

benedicto petitur, incensum portatur et sub Evangelii tono legitur, quia finita est jam narratio Passionis, et ex tunc omnia verba sunt Evangelistae narrantis quae post Christi mortem usque ad resurrectionem contingerunt" (Book 6.68.68).

[39] Kade, *Die ältere Passionskoposition*, 1; C. S. Terry and William Smoldon, "Passion Music," *Grove's Dictionary of Music and Musicians*, 5th ed., ed. Eric Blom (1954), 6:572.

[40] *Missale ad usum insignis et praeclarae Sarum*, ed. F. H. Dickinson (Oxford, 1861–63), 264.

[41] C.-A. Moberg, *En Svensk Johannespassion från Stormakstiden*, Uppsala Universitets Årsskrift 7 (Uppsala, 1941), 6.

Quasi-Dramatic Passion Music 169

quality of inflection. Moberg's explanation of what happens after the early period is as follows:

> In the later Middle Ages, the Gospel tone was as a rule subsemitonal, that is to say, the recitation was sung on a tone (the *tuba* or *tenor*) which moved to the scale step a half tone below to assist in building the cadence. The *tuba*-tone, in other words, would be c or f (which in combination with b ♮ or e creates the *flex*). The subsemitonal *tuba* . . . for various reasons became the style around the thirteenth century and was disseminated by means of the Dominican choral reform, which had adopted its use.[42]

The practice described above is well known to liturgists and musicologists; what Moberg adds to our knowledge is the fact that this ancient formula was given new impetus by the Dominicans and was disseminated widely by them through their program of liturgical reforms.[43] A piece which instructs one in the proper way to sing the Gospel tone is found in a fourteenth-century manuscript from Basel (Basel Univ. Bibl. Cod. B.V.29).[44] This item is particularly useful in shedding light on music for the Gospel lesson since it shows, by means of an explanatory text, what the notes should be for various syntactic patterns—e.g., the statement followed by a period, and the interrogation followed by a question mark. Each of these linguistic formulas has its own pattern of notes: there are not only clearly defined musical patterns for the statement and the question, but also for the half-closes governed by commas and colons. Below are presented examples of the statement using the period and the interrogation using the question mark:

---

[42] Ibid., 3–4.

[43] See W. R. Bonniwell, *A History of the Dominican Liturgy* (New York: J. F. Wagner, 1944).

[44] Edited by Wagner, *Einführung in die Gregorischen Melodien*, 3:47. See also the Dominican manuscript (Basel Cod. A.IX.2), also of the fourteenth century, which presents formulae with the instructional text. This item is also edited by Wagner.

Example 1

A. STATEMENT

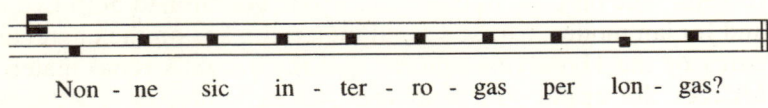

Sic flecte longas. Sic que le-va. Sic con-clu-de.

B. INTERROGATION

Non-ne sic in-ter-ro-gas per lon-gas?

By the fifteenth century it was fairly common practice to have the Gospel on Good Friday sung not by the deacon alone as had been his privilege since at least the time of Gregory the Great,[45] but rather by three clergy when sufficient clergy were available; hence the York Missal printed in 1509 indicates that the deacon should begin the Gospel on this day, or it should be read by three clergy (*vel legatur a tribus presbiteris*) if that happens to be the local custom. This flexibility as to the numbers of the clergy involved in the quasi-dramatic presentation of the Gospel lesson Good Friday pertains also to Swedish churches, where the larger and more affluent congregations would be likely to have several clergy available.[46]

The additionally dramatic singing of the Gospel according to St. John with three clergymen cast the deacon as the Evangelist, the priest as Christ, and the subdeacon as the crowd and remaining characters.[47] As noted above, the early medieval practice utilized some range changes by the deacon (i.e., lower for Christ, middle

---

[45] Michel Andrieu, *Les Ordines Romani du haut moyen age*, 2 vols. (Louvain, 1960), 2:40–41.

[46] Moberg, *En Svensk Johannespassion*, 6.

[47] Kade suggests that "only out of the mouth of the sacred priest must the words of Christ be announced," though he does not give a source for this idea (*Die ältere Passionskomposition*, 2).

Quasi-Dramatic Passion Music

range for Evangelist, and upper or countertenor range for the crowd and other personages), but now the ranges for each of the three singers became codified, with the Evangelist's words being set to a reciting tone on C, but utilizing F, g, a, b, and C; Christ's words being set to a reciting tone on F, but utilizing C, D, E, and F; and the crowd's words being set to a reciting tone on f, but utilizing C, d, e, and f. Glareanus, in his *Dodecachordon* (1547), shows that these ranges have true modal characteristics. The Evangelist's reciting tone on C is, in this case, a tone common to both Lydian and Ionian modes. Christ's tonal material takes on the characteristics of the Hypolydian mode, and the crowd's tonal material utilizes the upper fourth of the Lydian mode, in Glareanus' system.[48] To be sure, Glareanus was familiar with the somewhat earlier way (although not the earliest way) of chanting the Gospel, as the following example demonstrates:

Example 2

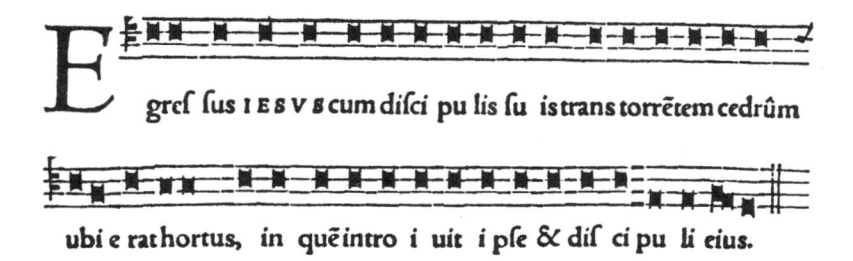

Egref fus I E S V S cum difci pu lis fu is trans torrētem cedrûm ubi e rat hortus, in quē intro i uit i pfe & dif ci pu li eius.

Glareanus contrasts the above passage of the Evangelist's narration, showing what he considers to be the earlier, more "simple" practice, with the same passage in the style of "our time"—i.e., the sixteenth century. Both examples illustrate the use of the comma as well as the musical *formulae* which are used to accompany this punctuation.[49]

---

[48] Heinrich Glarean, *Dodecachordon*, trans. Clement A. Miller, 2 vols., Musicological Studies and Documents 6 (American Institute of Musicology, 1965), 1:180–83.

[49] Ibid., 1:181.

Example 3

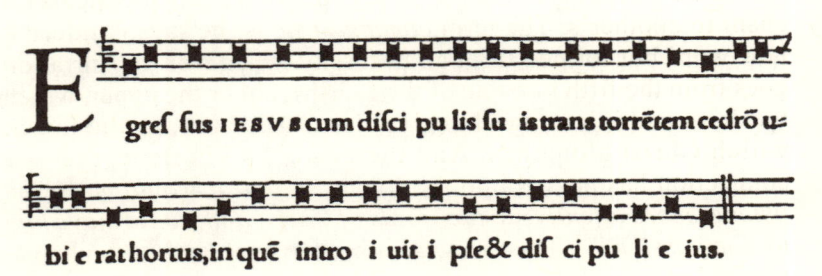

Egressus IESVS cum discipulis suis trans torrentem cedron ubi erat hortus, in quẽ introiuit ipse & discipuli eius.

Christ's words are set in the Hypolydian mode and what Glareanus calls the use of the "lower fourth":[50]

Example 4

Si male locutus sũ, testimoniũ perhibe de malo, Sin bene, qd me cędis.

Si male locutus sũ, testimoniũ phibe de malo, Sin bene, qd me cædis.

Si male locutus sũ, testimoniũ phibe de malo, Sin bene, qd me cædis.

The *formulae* for the crowd are presented below:[51]

Example 5

Aue Rex Iudæorum. Aue Rex Iudæorum. Aue Rex Iudæ orum.

---

[50] Ibid., 1:182.

[51] Ibid.

Glareanus also treats the question of connections or *commissurae* which serve the purpose of leading from one speaker's chant to another's. The term *commissurae* is, he says, "indeed a new word but formed through necessity, whenever the narration goes from the fifth into one of the fourths, either the upper, which the Jews and others speaking besides Christ have, or the lower, which Christ alone has. And therefore, as I believe, the one connection has passed into the Ionian *so that it would make the listener more attentive to the words of Christ and would move him to compassion."*[52] This passage not only explains the technical musical matter of the *commissurae* but also gives insight into the devotional intent of the musical and quasi-dramatic practice of the St. John Passion throughout Europe.

The fifteenth century also sometimes saw the use of a three-voice choir for the crowd and other portions (e.g., the rôles of St. Peter, Pilate, etc.) to augment the quasi-dramatic Passions for Holy Week.[53] The motet Passion, a different development of the early sixteenth century, cannot be discussed here.[54]

Since the chanting of the St. John Passion developed as described above into a very elaborate quasi-dramatic presentation using three separate rôle differentiations and even in some cases choral sections, why then did it not ever evolve into a fully dramatized performance with costumes and stage directions as in the case of the Easter drama which introduced the three Marys at the tomb (e.g., the elaborate *Visitatio* contained in the Fleury Playbook)? There was, of course, also a Passion play such as the one with music in St. Gall neumes in the Benediktbeuern Manuscript.[55] It is unlikely, however, that the Passion play was

---

[52] Ibid., 1:181 (italics mine).

[53] See Bertram Schofield, "A Newly Discovered 15th-Century Manuscript of the English Chapel Royal—Part I," *Musical Quarterly* 32 (1946): 512ff.

[54] See especially Kurt von Fischer, "Die mehrstimmige und katholische Passion," *Die Musik in Geschichte und Gegenwart*, 10:898–911.

[55] Text in Karl Young, *The Drama of the Medieval Church*, 2 vols. (Oxford: Clarendon Press, 1933), 1:518–32. An earlier Passion play is the Montecassino Passion, for which see Sandro Sticca, *The Latin Passion Play*

ever associated with Good Friday services, and a study has indeed suggested that the Benediktbeuern play was designed to be presented on Palm Sunday, the day when the Passion according to St. Matthew was normally read.[56] David Bevington has correctly noted: "The events of Good Friday, the day of the Crucifixion, proved especially resistant to dramatic treatment, perhaps because the liturgical ceremonies for that day—the darkening of the church, the intoning of Christ's reproaches to the people, the burial of the cross or the host in a sepulchre—were deeply moving without dramatic amplification."[57] We might add, however, a qualification: the Passion Gospel did indeed receive *limited dramatic presentation*. But the Gospel reading has always been regarded as one of the most holy parts of the Mass, and the Passion Gospel for Good Friday has long been seen as worthy of the deepest veneration. While the choral Passions as well as the quasi-dramatic Passions as discussed above would have been permissible and the latter even the preferred practice with regard to presentation, tampering with or changing the text of the Gospel in any way in order to create a play would have been forbidden. The most that would have been allowed, most likely, would be a simple textual change—e.g., the insertion into the St. John Gospel of a passage from St. Matthew reporting Christ's words "Eli, Eli, lama sabachthani."

Curiously, however, a seventeenth-century Danish Passion text (*Passio Vor* HERRIS *Jesu Christi Pinis oc Døds Historie Efter De*

(Albany: State University of New York Press, 1970), esp. 66–78, and Robert Edwards, *The Montecassino Passion* (Berkeley: University of California Press, 1977), esp. 10–21.

[56] Michael Rudick, "Theme, Structure, and Sacred Context in the Benediktbeuern 'Passion Play'," *Speculum* 49 (1974): 267–86.

[57] David Bevington, *Medieval Drama* (Boston: Houghton Mifflin, 1975), 202. But see the unusual *Burial of Christ* from Bodleian MS. e Museo 160 which is described as a play for "Gud Friday after-none" [*The Late Medieval Religious Plays of Bodleian MSS Digby 133 and e Museo 160*, ed. Donald C. Baker, John L. Murphy, and Louis B. Hall, Jr., EETS, 283 (Oxford: Oxford University Press, 1982), 141–68. For the *Planctus Mariae*, as a Passion drama for Good Friday, see the article on the Cividale play in the present volume.—Ed.].

fire Evangelisters Beskrivelse) without music and bound with the Danish *Alterbogen* (c.1681), contains a compilation from the four Gospels, divided according to a four-act structure. Actus Primus begins with John 18:1, the passage which opens with the description of Christ crossing over the brook Cedron into the place where he was to be betrayed. It ends with a passage from Mark 14: "A certain young man followed him, having a linen cloth cast about his naked body. And the young man laid hold on him, and he dropped the linen cloth and fled naked." Actus Secundus begins with the account of Christ being taken before the high priests, and concludes with the taunting of Christ by the crowd ("Est du da Guds Søn?"—"Are you truly God's Son?") and their statement that they need no further witness against him because of his own admission (Luke 22:70). Actus Tertius involves Christ's being bound and led before Pilate, and ends with the release of Barabas instead of Christ. The final act introduces the soldiers placing a purple robe on Christ and leading him away to be crucified ("Da toge Stridsmændene Jesum / oc førde hannem Purpuret / . . . oc førde hannem bort / at de skulde kaarszfeste hannem / oc hand bar sit Kaars"); its conclusion is with a passage based on Matthew 27:62–66, which recounts the coming of the chief priests and Pharisees to Pilate asking that the sepulcher might be sealed to prevent the potential theft of the body ("paa det hans Disciple skulle icke komme oc stiele hannem") and the claim that he has risen. This unusual four-act Passion, derived from the harmony of the Gospels, shows that the Passion material itself was looked on as inherently dramatic.

But the inherent dramatic quality in the Passion material is further evidenced in a more basic way in the traditional rubrics for the Good Friday service especially as these have bearing on the reading of the Passion Gospel for the day. For example, the *Missale Lundense* of 1514 contains directions for the clergy, who are told to enter in vestments but without using candles or other lights. They are to cense the Gospel book which is placed in the middle of the altar upon the altar cloths, whereupon the preparation is made for the subdeacon to read the lesson from the prophets. Then, during the chanting of the Passion from the Gospel book which has been removed from the altar, at the point of the words "They parted my vestments among them" ("Partiti sunt vestimenta mea"), two acolytes already positioned at the altar are to take from it the cloths as if stealing and disappear with them (*in modom furantis rapte abscondantur*). Similar rubrics occur in the Sarum Missal.⁵⁸

This little ceremony at the altar during the Passion on Good Friday looks back to the early Roman Ordo (*Ordo I*, though it is probably not the earliest), a liturgical work which probably played a part in the Carolingian reforms chronicled above.⁵⁹ In this Ordo, which dates back to the eighth century, we find the post-Gospel direction that "statim duo diaconi nudant altare sindone, quae prius fuerat sub Evangelio posita, in modum furantis . . ." ("two deacons remove the cloth from the altar which had earlier been placed under the Gospel book. They should do this in a furtive manner").⁶⁰ In the pseudo-Alcuin *De divinis officiis*, the ceremony of the altar cloths takes place more appropriately at the words in the Gospel Passion "paritia sunt vestimenta mea sibi" ("they parted my vestments among them"), when they show them and then abscond with them in imitation of the soldiers at the Crucifixion.⁶¹ Amalarius, like the compiler of the *De divinis officiis*, understands the nature of the action as symbolic of the way in which the apostles fled from Christ during his time of suffering: "When the Gospel is removed, that which is under it is snatched away, because when our Lord was given over into the hands of evil men, the apostles fled and hid like thieves."⁶²

---

⁵⁸ Burntisland ed., ed. Dickinson, 323.

⁵⁹ Andrieu, *Les Ordines Romani*, 2:54.

⁶⁰ Migne, *Patrologia latina*, 78:953, as quoted in translation by O. B. Hardison, Jr., *Christian Rite and Christian Drama in the Middle Ages* (Baltimore: Johns Hopkins Press, 1965), 130.

⁶¹ *Patrologia Latina*, 101:1208

⁶² Ibid., 105:1026, as quoted in translation by Hardison, *Christian Rite and Christian Drama*, 130.

The Roskilde St. John Passion and Its Suppression

Until 1736, a vernacular Danish St. John Passion had been sung at Roskilde Cathedral on Good Friday with interpolations that included chorales, sinfonias, and arias—additions in line with developments characteristic of the previous century but the result of a long tradition of church music. In that year the quasi-dramatic Roskilde Passion was at the center of a controversy with the Danish Crown, at that time deeply committed to the Pietist movement within the state Church of the country. Fortunately, the manuscript of this Passion survives in the Danish National Archives (Copenhagen, Rigsarkivet MS. DK D 21 Indlæg og koncepter til Sjællandske Tegnelser 1736 13/4, nr. 179).[1] It is dated 1673, but has some later additions, and is an unbound folio consisting of 8 leaves (see fig. 4). Corrections were entered in 1713 by I. C. Ringe, whose signature appears along with the date of his work. This manuscript represents the copy forwarded to the king in the controversy of its performance at Roskilde, but clearly had been used for performances at Good Friday services. It has the passages to be sung by the Evangelist marked with an x.

While Luther had originally objected to the elaborateness that had been introduced into the singing of the Passion prior to the Reformation in Germany—early in his career he had condemned

---

[1] [Transcribed in Audrey Ekdahl Davidson, *The Quasi-Dramatic St. John Passions from Scandinavia and Their Medieval Background* (Kalamazoo: Medieval Institute Publications, 1981), 83–133; this Passion, along with the Swedish St. John Passion, is discussed in more detail in ibid., 46–65. The present essay, which was largely incorporated in the first chapter of this book, appears here in so far as possible in the form presented at a meeting of the American Musicological Society at Denver in 1980.—Ed.]

Fig. 4. The Roskilde Passion. Manuscript in the Danish National Archives (Copenhagen, Rigsarkivet, MS. Dk D 21 Indlæg og koncepter til Sjællandske Tegnelser 1736 13/4, nr. 179), which was the subject of controversy leading to its suppression.

this development as *gyckelwerk*—he had not prohibited it[2] and even may have collaborated with Johann Walter in the composition of the first German Passion, the St. Matthew Passion of 1530, as well as the later St. John Passion sometimes attributed to Walter.[3] But with the rise of Pietism in Germany and Scandinavia, the dramatic quality of such Passions with their responsorial singing, use of instruments, and interpolations was considered by puritanical churchmen to be threatening.

Like the Swedish St. John Passion which exists in ten manuscripts from the late sixteenth and seventeenth centuries,[4] the Roskilde Passion is directly influenced by the German Passions of Walter and his successors. These Passion settings form a connection between medieval Latin practice and the Passions of Heinrich Schütz and Johann Sebastian Bach. There may actually have been contact between Schütz and not only the German but also the Scandinavian practice of Passion music, since he had, after all, been in the employ of a Danish monarch upon three occasions—in 1633–35, 1637–38, and 1642–44.

The personally unattractive Danish king, Christian VI, however, had different ideas about religious music than the monarch of the time of Schütz. His attitude arose from the Pietist

---

[2] Martin Luther, Introduction, *Deutsche Messe*, as cited by C.-A. Moberg, *En Svensk Johannespassion från Stormaktstiden*, Uppsala Universitets Årsskrift 7, no. 13 (Uppsala: 1941), 8; Walter Blankenburg, "Die protestantische Passion," *Die Musik in Geschichte und Gegenwart*, 17 vols. (1947–86), 10:911–12; cf. Friedrich Blume et al., *Protestant Church Music* (New York: Norton, 1974), 178.

[3] Some controversy surrounds the attribution of the extant Passions to Walter as well as other aspects of collaboration between Luther and Walter. See Konrad Ameln and Carl Gerhardt, *Johann Walter und die ältesten deutschen Passionshistorien* (Göttingen: Vandenhoeck und Ruprecht, 1939), 1–15. Otto Kade's term for these Passions is "dramatic Passion"; see his *Die ältere Passionskomposition bis zum Jahr 1631* (Gütersloh: C. Bertelsmann, 1893), passim.

[4] See Moberg, *En Svensk Johannespassion*, passim; Lennart Reimers, ed., *Johannespassion*, Monumenta Svecicae 3 (1962); and my *Quasi-Dramatic St. John Passions*, passim.

movement, founded by Philipp Jacob Spener (1635–1707) in Germany. Pietism was well known for its hostility toward pure aesthetics in worship, and instead it encouraged warm devotional hymn texts and settings.[5] As Albert Schweitzer noted in his study of J. S. Bach,

> pietism was fundamentally inimical to art of any kind in worship, and was especially set against the concert style of the church music. The musical performances of the Passion were a particular abomination to it; it wished the service to be adorned only with simple congregational hymns.[6]

In Denmark, the Pietists could thus claim victory in a significant battle in their war against aesthetics when they were able to suppress the St. John Passion at Roskilde Cathedral, one of the most richly endowed cathedrals of Northern Europe and a perfect visual and acoustical setting for this type of performance. Inside the building the center of attention then as now was the altarpiece of Flemish design of about 1550 which features the Crucifixion in its central and most prominent panel.[7] On the south side of the nave is the ornate pulpit, a gift of Christian IV in 1610, which served as a symbol of the preaching so much desired by the Pietists.

The conflict between art and Pietism can be followed through a series of letters concerning the Roskilde Passion written in 1736 and now filed with the manuscript containing the music in the Danish National Archives. The letters are from Pastor H. Buch, incumbent priest at the cathedral; from Pastor Bernhard Schnabel, rector of the cathedral school; from C. W. Worm, bishop of the Zealand diocese; and from the king of Denmark.

The trouble apparently begins with Pastor Buch's letter of March 1, 1736, to the king's chief secretary, J. L. Holstein, in which the clergyman describes the present practice at Roskilde

---

[5] See Blume, *Protestant Church Music*, 258–62.

[6] Albert Schweitzer, *J. S. Bach*, trans. Ernest Newman, 2 vols. (1911; reprint, Boston: Bruce Humphries, 1962), 1:169.

[7] Eric Moltke and Elna Møller, *Danmarks Kirker: Københavns Amt*, 3, pt. 3 (Copenhagen: G. E. C. Gads, 1951), 376–89, fig. 309.

Cathedral of performing the St. John Passion at Evensong on Good Friday with certain personages portrayed: the Evangelist, Herod (sic!), Pilate, Judas, and Peter (no mention is made of Christ) are represented in a "ceremony which seems to be a relic of former Carnival performances [*Forrettninger*—literally, "business"] and which strives against devotion, quietude, and seriousness." He finds it to be a "comedy" and a "theater-play" entirely unfitting to the gravity of the Good Friday service, and asks therefore that this "misuse" of the church be abolished and in its place substituted a Passion sermon chronicling the history of Christ's suffering and death.[8]

On March 8, the king, the Pietist Christian VI, through his chief secretary sent the letter of Pastor Buch on to Bishop Worm for his assessment of the situation—a necessary step before the king could make a decision.

A further letter, written on March 21, 1726, by Schnabel is clearly a response to the bishop's request for more information. This letter is accompanied by a copy of the controversial work. Schnabel apologizes for not having the manuscript recopied before sending it on. But his main point in writing is to take the side of the musicians and cantors in this battle of art *vs.* piety and to defend the work as a fitting and serious presentation for Good Friday. He says that it is true that the work has been performed with the important personages taken by the best singers and the chorus singing the words of the crowd, but he notes that it is not true that Herod is portrayed, here noting a slip in Pastor Buch's biblical

---

[8] The letters, which I have examined at the Danish National Archives, are transcribed by Joseph Hammermüller, "Passionen i Roskilde Domkirke," *Aarbog for Musik, 1924* (Copenhagen, 1926), 50–56. Schnabel (1691–1754) had been appointed to his post at Roskilde in 1726 (*Dansk Biografisk Leksikon* [Copenhagen: J. H. Schultz, 1941], 21: 278–79). The orthodox Bishop Worm (1672–1737) was actually antagonistic to some crucial points of Pietist theology (ibid., 26:267–72). For Holstein (1674–1763), see ibid., 10:518–23. See also ibid., 3:314–15, for the character of the king, Christian VI, described as personally "unimpressive, fragile, clumsy, shy of manner, and with a high piping voice. . . ." His religious bigotry was joined with a high level of personal anxiety which made him less effective in public affairs. He was also antagonistic to the public theater.

knowledge since the appearance of Jesus before Herod does not occur in St. John's gospel. He goes on to point out that the organ accompanies the music with a "sweet and low tone," thus denoting the organ's unobtrusive role. Additionally, Schnabel points out that hymns such as "O Herre Gud benaade mig" ("O Lord God, forgive me") and "O, Guds Lam unskyldig" ("O, Lamb of God unspotted") are inserted into the fabric of the work. He clearly hopes that the mention of the hymns will make the work seem more pious. Further, he offers a compromise: because of the period of mourning for the king's aunt, the arias and sinfonias could be dropped from the Passion.

Schnabel's impassioned plea seems to have been heard by the bishop, for when the latter wrote to the king on March 31 he also suggested compromise. While he agrees with Pastor Buch that preaching should be added to the Good Friday service, he also strongly agrees with his adversary, Schnabel, that there really is nothing wrong with the performance of the St. John Passion. One section of Bishop Worm's letter shows the nature of his approval of the Passion:

> When the preaching is over, it is recommended . . . that the present custom of Roskilde Cathedral, which is to have the Passion of disciples performed musically, might be continued, though without instrumentalists. Regarding its continuation, your majesty can learn about it from the letter to myself from the rector of the school in Roskilde dated March 21 which accompanies a copy of the traditional music, although it is a somewhat untidy copy. I cannot consider such to be a relic of carnival business, but rather a rite which can awaken devotion in the hearers' hearts, which it assuredly and actually does; and beyond this, the custom is practiced in various Protestant churches, including some here in this kingdom.[9]

The letter closes here with the usual overly polite but necessary phrases of humility and undying loyalty to the Crown. The bishop obviously wants to placate the Pietists' wish for more sermonizing, but does not want to give up the important tradition of the St. John

---

[9] Hammermüller, "Passionen i Roskilde Domkirke," 54; Rector Schnabel's letter is transcribed on 52–55.

Passion at Roskilde Cathedral.

The attempted compromise failed, however. Holstein's memorandum of April 6, 1736, records the doom of the Roskilde Passion. The king's letter allowing the Passion to be abolished was written on April 13, 1736, and addressed to Bishop Worm. As Joseph Hammermüller notes, by this suppression of ancient and also Protestant tradition, there was an irreparable loss with regard to liturgics, music, religion, and culture.[10]

The Pietist objections to what seemed theatrical in the church service are very reminiscent of earlier strictures against the alleged intrusion of the modes of worldly amusement. Roger Loomis cites three useful examples from the twelfth century. St. Bernard of Clairvaux, in a letter written in c.1126, wrote: "The religious game has nothing of the childish, nothing of the *theatre*, which excites lust. . . ."[11] Hugh of St. Victor, who died in 1141, warned against "those who enjoy the pleasures of this world, pomps, and *theatrical* delights [*theatricalibus voluptatibus*], corrupted by tragedies and comedies, lulled as it were into a deep sleep."[12] Even more interesting is the view of Aelred of Rievaulx, who in his *Speculum Charitatis* (c.1141) railed against singers' abuses of unchurchly decorum through their overdramatizing of liturgical music:

> His whole body meanwhile is in histrionic agitation; his lips twist and turn, his shoulders play, his fingers bend in response to every changing note. . . . Meanwhile, the common folk stand in trembling awe; . . . it is not without grinning laughter that they watch the singers' wanton gesticulations, the meretricious alternations and irregularities of the voice, so that you would think they had come together, not to a house of prayer, but to a

---

[10] Ibid., 52.

[11] Roger S. Loomis, "Some Evidence for Secular Theatres in the Twelfth and Thirteenth Centuries, *Theatre Annual* (1945): 34; see also, by the same author, "Were There Theatres in the Twelfth and Thirteenth Centuries?" *Speculum* 20 (1945): 93.

[12] Loomis, "Some Evidence for Secular Theatres," 34, and "Were There Theatres in the Twelfth and Thirteenth Centuries?" 93.

playhouse [*ad theatrum*].[13]

Even more extreme, of course, were the later anti-theatrical and anti-musical attitudes of the Calvinists, especially the Puritans in England and America. Indeed, the Puritan emphasis on preaching and the congregational singing of psalms looked forward to similar emphases by the Pietists in their modification of Lutheran theology. The Pietists, however, were not as restrictive as the Puritans with regard to the texts and performance practice in congregational singing, and they fostered numerous masterful hymn writers like Johann Crüger, whose melodies and harmonizations are still heard. The suppression of the Roskilde Passion, which is hard to imagine as a controversial work, is in line with these earlier attacks on allegedly theatrical elements in the liturgy.

---

[13] Loomis, "Some Evidence for Secular Theatres," 34–35, and "Were There Theatres in the Twelfth and Thirteenth Centuries?" 93; Karl Young, *The Drama of the Medieval Church*, 2 vols. (Oxford: Clarendon Press, 1933), 1:548. Loomis's translation is from G. G. Coulton, *Five Centuries of Religion*, 4 vols. (Cambridge: Cambridge University Press, 1923–50), 1:530.

IV

Vocal Production and Early Music

> I myself have seen with indignation excellent singers become debased and deformed, with distorted and gaping mouths, with head tossed back, and with bleating and barbaric cries, which (with preconceived opinion) they hold bellowing and singing to be one and the same thing, they ruin and deform the most beautiful music. What a deplorable sight![1]

Because singing early music demands more flexibility, more accuracy, and thus a more complete understanding of the vocal mechanism than is usual, I have undertaken here to describe some techniques that are requirements for early music performance, including necessarily some aspects that are commonly taught or noted by modern voice teachers. Since vocal production derives from a process involving the human body, it has been necessary to look closely at the physical processes of singing. For the modern performer, this examination extends to anatomy.

The anatomical elements that need to be understood include the lungs, the rib cage, the muscles of the thorax area, and more: the intercostal muscles and the diaphragm, the muscles of the abdomen, back, and buttocks areas, the delicate larynx with the vocal folds (commonly known as vocal cords) and the throat and neck muscles, the naso-pharyngeal cavity which includes the sinuses and bones of the face (the latter known familiarly as the "mask"), and the lips, teeth, and tongue as instruments of resonance, articulation, and enunciation. The body itself can be regarded as an instrument which makes the production of sound possible, but it needs the mind to control and make intelligent this

---

[1] Hermann Finck, *Practica musica*, as quoted by Carol MacClintock, trans. and ed., *Readings in the History of Music in Performance* (Bloomington: Indiana University Press, 1979), 62 (hereafter cited as MacClintock).

activity just as the mind controls and makes intelligent all other human activity. The anatomical elements that I have mentioned need to be considered in conjunction with the main aspects of vocal technique: (I) stance; (II) relaxation; (III) breathing; (IV) phonation; (V) resonance; and (VI) diction.

I

Stance and Body Position. In discussing the vocal apparatus, it may not be the conventional approach to start with the lowest part of the body—that is, with the feet and legs. However, without an adequate stance, which also implies good body alignment, one cannot breathe well, and, needless to say, breathing is the basis for singing just as it is for life and health generally. Thus a good vocal technique begins with body alignment, entailing the feet placed firmly on the ground, well apart, and it continues by having the vertebrae and spinal cord properly aligned.

A test for the adequacy of one's stance is to line one's body up against a wall, trying to get the back as straight as possible and attempting to have as many areas of the back as possible to touch the wall without slipping into an exaggerated or uncomfortable position. If there is too large a space between wall and body at mid-back, the singer is standing incorrectly and realignment is necessary. The singer should stand with one of his/her feet positioned a little ahead of the other one, the knees slightly bent and relaxed, and the entire body positioned so that the knees can be flexed almost in the way a runner flexes his/her knees just before taking off from the starting line.

Good body alignment also involves having the rib cage slightly raised so that the lungs are not cramped and the chin neither raised nor lowered. A good test for the correctness of the rib position is to hold one's fingers below the lowest pair of ribs in front, ascertaining that these are in evidence and perceptible to the touch rather than so far receded as to be imperceptible. The reason for the raised rib cage is to allow more breath to flow into the lungs and to prevent cramping of them. The position of the head is important also, for a chin raised too high will pull up the larynx and vocal cords, while a chin lowered too far can press down on the vocal cords. Both raising and lowering the chin thus can tighten or cramp the cords, thus impeding their action and harming the sound. (More technical information will be provided below when I discuss phonation.)

The reader can try some simple experiments by singing with raised and lowered chin to demonstrate the value of keeping the chin on an even level. But on the whole the achievement of a good bodily position cannot be overemphasized, especially for someone with an interest in early music who is just beginning to sing. An experienced singer can adapt so that he/she can sit, stand, lie, or even jump while singing, but the young or inexperienced person needs to avoid unusual or odd positions at first.

The foregoing observations are corroborated by early writers on vocal practice. Conrad von Zabern (fl. c.1470), for example, advised one against "raising the head too high,"[2] and Hermann Finck (1527–58) warned that "the bending of the head backward spoils the song."[3] Blasius Rosettus in the early sixteenth century said that attention should be paid by the teacher so that boys stand erect, and Girolamo Diruta (b. c.1550) said that the singer's position should be "erect and gracious" ("Ma star dritto, e gratioso").[4] And, in the light of my warning above not to lock the knees, what is to be made of the statement by Adriano Banchieri (1568–1634) that the singer should stand like a statue?[5] But most likely he is referring to the avoidance of unnecessary movements or grimaces which would detract from the performance. Yet it will be noted that statues do usually stand in a relaxed posture, with one foot ahead of the other and in perfect balance.

---

[2] Conrad von Zabern, *De modo bene cantandi*, as quoted in translation by MacClintock, 16.

[3] Bernhard Ulrich, *Concerning the Principles of Voice Training during the a cappella Period and until the Beginning of Opera*, trans. John W. Seale, ed. Edward Foreman (Minneapolis: Pro Musica Press, 1973), 37. The German text of Ulrich's work (*Über die Grundsätze der Stimmbildung während der Acappella-Periode und zur Zeit des Aufkommens der Oper—1474–1640* [Liepzig: Arno Theuerkorn, 1910]) has also been consulted.

[4] Ulrich, *Concerning the Principles of Voice Training*, 37, 198.

[5] Ibid., 37, 198.

II

Relaxation. In conjunction with the above, one needs to know which muscles must be relaxed and which require a "good" kind of tension to be placed on them. This aspect will need to be discussed below in connection with breathing, but at this point it would be well to say that the muscles which benefit most from relaxation are those in the throat and neck area as well as the abdomen, the latter especially during the act of inhaling. However, the abdominal muscles need to be activated with a certain amount of tension as the act of exhaling occurs. Nevertheless, it cannot be overemphasized that the more relaxed an individual is overall, the more likely he or she will be able to call upon the mental and physical qualities necessary for singing well. Meditation techniques and exercises are not precisely within my scope, but as an antidote to the frantic pace of the modern world whatever one can do to replicate the calmer atmosphere of earlier times will be beneficial. There might even be no harm in visualizing oneself as a medieval monk or nun to bring oneself into a proper state of mind.

The larynx area (fig. 5) should be as completely relaxed as possible. This is the area that becomes most tense when a physical blow is anticipated. The neck and shoulder area also collects all the tension which an individual gathers throughout the day; thus, after a day of even mildly stressful events, one's neck, shoulder, and throat areas are liable to be extremely tight and tense. Frequent exercises should be done, even at one's desk if that is his or her workplace, in order to relieve tension throughout a day. And particularly before singing, tension should be dissipated by yawning and by revolving the head on the neck, though the latter movement should only be done if medically safe. Revolving each arm separately in its socket in the same manner is also a good relaxant of the shoulder area. Another good exercise involves shrugging the shoulders and allowing them to fall into place naturally.

Probably the most useful vocal exercise for gaining relaxation and also for discovering higher head tones involves making a siren-like sound that can be coupled with the revolving of the head on the neck. Beginning with the head sunken onto the chest and the mouth nearly closed, the singer makes a sound like a siren. As the head

Vocal Production and Early Music 191

revolves around and upward, the jaw is dropped open gently and the sound is allowed to go higher in pitch. The jaw drops open, the head revolves and stretches a little higher until it falls to rest on the topmost vertebra, and the sound ascends and gets louder just as the wail of a siren does. Coming back down and around, the jaw falls gently closed, and the sound becomes lower in pitch. This exercise is guaranteed to bring relaxation and also to bring both higher and lower tones into the singer's range. However, for many experienced singers a favorite technique for warming up is to sing long scales with careful attention to removing all traces of tension.

One of the most unfortunate, if not *the* most unfortunate place to have tension is at the base of the tongue in the back of the nasopharyngeal cavity. If the tongue is "muscle-bound," the tone will likely be tinged with a gagging sound. This is not only unpleasant but also involves a habit that one will find difficult to master.

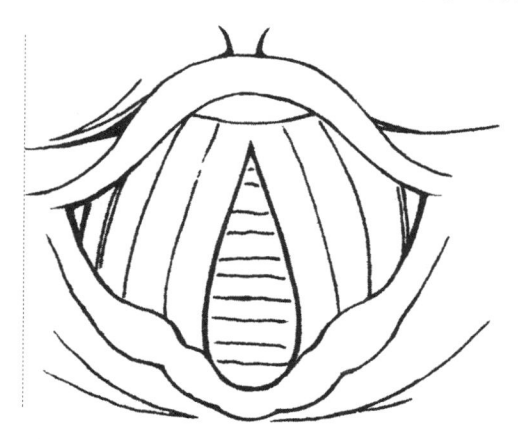

Fig. 5. The larynx. Vocal folds are on each side of the trachea (center, teardrop-shaped in this drawing); beside them are the ventricular folds; below, the corniculate cartilage; at top, the epiglottis. Drawing by Marianne Cappelletti Lutes.

Constant attention to relaxation of the tongue is necessary for a person who has a tendency toward such constriction. Resting the tongue just behind the lower teeth usually helps to keep it relaxed and low enough in the mouth to keep it from interfering with the free expression of sound.

The best way to think of the whole passageway comprising the laryngeal and naso-pharyngeal cavities is to visualize a thoroughfare through which air and sound can pass freely, without obstruction. In phonation, an amount of friction is of course required to create the sound, but the mental concept of an unimpeded channel through those areas is absolutely necessary in order to gain as much freedom and ease of production as possible. Thus it is possible to assert that the person who has attained relaxation is in a much more solid position to achieve good vocal technique than someone who is a "bundle of nerves."

III

Breathing. For most people, the act of breathing is an involuntary, unconscious activity. However, the singer cannot afford to allow his or her breathing to remain thus. It is necessary to gain a considerable amount of voluntary control over the activity, making it into a semi-voluntary process, and this is particularly true of much early music though perhaps no more urgent than when, for example, one is performing early baroque arias or solo cantatas by composers such as Monteverdi or Carissimi which take immense precision. As Bénigne de Bacilly noted in his *Remarques curieuses sur l'art de bien chanter* (1668) with regard to the practice of singing the music of his time, good breathing practice "is essential to good vocal performance so as to avoid cutting a word short or cleaving a syllable in two," and this, he says, requires good lungs and training.[6]

The main organs of respiration, the lungs, not only facilitate breathing, but they also cleanse the blood, which is important for maintaining the alertness of the singer. The lungs consist of a light, porous, and spongy substance, which is elastic and capable of

---

[6] Bénigne de Bacilly, *A Commentary upon the Art of Proper Singing*, trans. Austin B. Caswell (New York: Institute of Mediaeval Music, 1968), 25. Not a matter under consideration in this present essay but nevertheless important for early vocal practice is the matter introduced in ibid., 11–13 (chap. 4: "The Necessity of Instrumental Accompaniment in Vocal Music").

expansion.⁷ The average male's vital capacity is 3700 cc., but the amount that may be taken in at a quiet respiration is only around 500 cc.⁸ Capacity can—and needs—to be increased for singers by breathing exercises.⁹ Some find meditational techniques to be useful in this regard. These train one to retain the breath for long periods of time. But, as Arnold Rose indicates, the ordinary individual can increase breath capacity instantaneously through slow inhalation.¹⁰

The breathing process is activated by means of the autonomic nervous system, which sets off impulses that cause the diaphragm to rise and fall. Ordinarily there are eighteen of these per minute, but control over the pattern of one's breathing is necessary in singing. It is the motion of the diaphragm, a muscle dividing the lungs from the visceral area, that permits the breathing process to occur. As the diaphragm moves downward, air flows into the lungs as it would into a vacuum. When the diaphragm contracts upward, air flows out of the lungs. But breathing from the diaphragm alone, as some voice teachers advise, is a simplistic and unsatisfactory technique guaranteed to produce a harsh and unpleasant tone.

The process of breathing also must include the rib cage, made up of twelve pairs of ribs, seven of which are attached to the sternum, three to themselves, and three only to the backbone. Around and below the rib cage are muscles, which include: (1) the intercostal muscles between the ribs; (2) the abdominus rectus muscle, the long muscle which originates under the sixth and seventh pairs of ribs and extends down to the pubic bone; (3) the

---

[7] For a description of the lungs, see Henry Gray, *Anatomy of the Human Body*, 13th American ed., ed. Carmine D. Clemente (Philadelphia: Lea and Febriger, 1985), 1385–98.

[8] For this information I am indebted to Marshall MacDonald, M.D.

[9] An excellent source, because the author is a singer, is Nancy Zi, *The Art of Breathing: Thirty Simple Exercises for Improving Your Performance and Well-Being* (New York: Bantam Books, 1986). Unfortunately, because issued only as a cheap paperback, this book may be hard to find.

[10] Arnold Rose, *The Singer and the Voice: Vocal Physiology and Technique for Singers*, 2nd ed. (1971; reprint, London: Scolar Press, n.d.), 83.

external oblique muscle, the muscle above and below the waist; (4) the transversus abdominus, the muscle just at the waist; (5) the latissimus dorsi, the long muscle of the back; and (6) the muscles of the buttocks, especially the gluteus maximus.

In order to utilize these muscles effectively in the act of breathing, the abdomen must be relaxed, allowing the diaphragm to expand downward in order to give the lungs maximum space for expansion. At the same time, the lower rib cage is raised and the bottom ribs of the non-floating type—that is, those attached only to other ribs—are permitted to protrude. Then a long, slow, quiet breath is taken in, allowing the bottom of the lungs to fill first, then the middle, and finally the upper part. This should not be done in a convulsive, jerky manner but rather as a smooth, continuous process. This again may seem to have something in common with the type of breathing recommended by some practitioners of meditation. Long, slow breaths, with or without the singing of long scales, are by themselves very good relaxation techniques for the singer.

Relaxing the abdomen to expand in order to accommodate the downward thrust of the diaphragm has been found to be the most satisfactory way of handling the inhalation of the breath. There are those who would think the abdomen should remain taut as the breath is inhaled in order to control the sound, but this again will not result in the desired freedom of tone. Lilli Lehmann, who is extremely reliable on this point, advocates the involvement of the relaxed abdomen as the most efficacious method of breathing.[11]

It is often argued as to whether nasal breathing alone or a combination of nose and mouth is better. The nasal method alone may be slightly superior since there is less drying of the back of the throat; however, the singer's quick breath may only be taken through both mouth and nose.

In exhaling, the abdominal muscles, particularly the long abdominis rectus muscle, will move back toward the backbone,

---

[11] Lilli Lehmann, *How to Sing*, rev. ed., trans. Richard Aldrich and Clara Willenbücher (1924; reprint, New York: Macmillan, 1964), 14ff. [The author would have been the first, however, to remind readers that Lehmann represented a very different style of singing from early music—that is, the nineteenth-century operatic style—in spite of the usefulness of her work.— Ed.]

thus aiding the diaphragm in its contraction and supporting the breath as it is exhaled. Some writers speak of a continuous expansion of the abdominal muscles, or of their expansion to gain more space to expand downward.[12] The downward expansion gives the singer some additional breath once all the breath seemingly has been squeezed out of the lungs. It has been suggested also that in exhaling one might benefit from bearing down with the abdominal muscles, at the same time tightening the gluteus maximus. Through such long, slow, supported inhalation and exhalation one can slow down the movement of the diaphragm itself and thus achieve control over the breathing mechanism.

Some of the points made above are consistent with what Eastern writers on breath have to say about breathing and breath control, particularly for singers of early music. This therefore is a plea for attention to such Eastern practitioners, though of course insights gained from them must be accepted selectively. But in studying early music vocal production, we need to accept that some insight into vocal technique may be as old as antiquity since the ancients of Greece and Rome may have known a great deal that has been lost in the crevices of history. As Jérôme Carcopino reports, the actors in the theater of Pompey were able to cast their voices out into a theater seating 27,000 people. The theater of Balbus held 7,700 and the theater of Marcellus 14,000.[13] Though from personal experience in visiting the theater at Viterbo I can affirm that the acoustics of Roman theaters were remarkable, the ones I have noted above are much larger than the largest modern halls, regarded as difficult for singers, in which the seating holds two thousand or more—sometimes up to four thousand—people. Many of these modern halls are even surreptitiously equipped with electronic sound enhancement.

How did the ancient singer or actor train for the strenuous activity of performing in these huge theaters? Quintilian encouraged the practice of gymnastics,[14] and actors were reported

---

[12] See Rose, *The Singer and the Voice*, 139–40.

[13] See Jérôme Carcopino, *Daily Life in Ancient Rome*, trans E. O. Lorimer (New Haven: Yale University Press, 1964), 222.

[14] Quintilian, *Institutio Oratoria* 1.11.15.

to have used lead plates on their chests for breath exercises! The weight of the lead plates and the stress placed on the muscles allegedly gave the actors/singers the strength to project their voices very great distances. As is well known, the use of masks by actors in Greek and Roman theaters also was a factor, though one must be extremely skeptical, especially with regard to singers. But it is hard to be convinced about the usefulness of weights in preparing for the stage. Modern teachers have been known to have students place books on their chests or abdomens in the attempt to strengthen the muscles. However, this perhaps unconscious replication of an ancient exercise must be used with care to avoid injury. One wonders how many ancient Romans injured their diaphragms using lead plates.[15]

IV

Phonation. Earlier writers give no indication that the mechanism which produces sound was fully understood. Singers, however, undoubtedly had far more intuitive knowledge of the vocal apparatus that would has been passed down over the centuries.

The ancient Greeks apparently had made only a beginning in understanding the vocal mechanism. Galen observed the dissection of the larynx of an ox, and also provided a description of the muscles and bones surrounding the human larynx. The vocal cords, or folds, seem to have been unknown to him, however.[16] But much anatomical knowledge was uncovered by early Arabic writers, chiefly Avicenna (980–1037), Hali Abbas (d. 994), and Rhazes (d.

---

[15] [Drew Minter, in reviewing the present essay, commented to the editor that a principal distinction between singing early music and, say, modern opera, is the pressure of the breath, with early music requiring less pressure in order to achieve the appropriate effect. The author of course was fully in agreement with this, and would have referred by analogy to her preference also for low-pressure pipe organs over most (higher-pressure) twentieth-century instruments.—Ed.]

[16] Charles Singer, *A Short History of Anatomy and Physiology from the Greeks to Harvey*, 2nd ed. (New York: Dover, 1957), 53; cf. Galen, *On Anatomical Procedures*, trans. Charles Singer (London: Oxford University Press, 1956), 118, 172.

932). This would be passed on to the medieval West. Dissection, though forbidden, was practiced, and would be added to the understanding of the vocal instrument. Yet Vesalius (1514–64), who is usually given credit for founding the modern study of anatomy, has a generally unsatisfactory description of the larynx, perhaps based on inadequate opportunity to observe human subjects.[17]

For their time, two of the most illuminating drawings of the larynx are exhibited by Giulio Casserio in his *De vocis auditusque organis historia anatomica*, published in Ferrara in 1601.[18] One of the drawings shows a subject, with eyes open but with throat and chest cut open in the course of dissection, exposing the cartilages and muscles governing the larynx. The second drawing shows the tongue and its connection to the laryngeal-pharyngeal mechanism.[19] The first of thse illustrations would be virtually copied, with only slight modifications, in Athanasius Kircher's monumental *Musurgia universalis* (fig. 6). The various areas of the throat and chest are marked with small letters. The lungs, labeled Y, are shown as two stylized entities possessing cubed areas perhaps representing bronchioles or alveolar sacs. The diaphragm, labeled X, is represented as two shapeless masses flowing into one another—an indication of no real understanding of this elastic muscle.

Oddly enough, Kircher indicates in his list of the structures in the throat area that he considers the epiglottis (D) to be somehow related to phonation, since he notes that the vocal folds are inserted into its fissure ("Epigottis, cuius superior pars fissuram refert, quae voci formandae inseruit"). F marks the trachea, and a supplementary drawing, not shown in my fig. 6, shows what is represented as the muscles and cartilage which control the movement of the larynx. None of this bears any resemblance to what is seen in modern anatomy texts, but there is still value here. Kircher tries to relate these parts of the body to the act of singing, and appears

---

[17] Singer, *A Short History of Anatomy*, 125.

[18] Ibid., fig. 95.

[19] Ibid., fig. 94.

to be presenting the first such application.[20]

Singers of early music, however, will benefit from having a clearer view of the physiological basis of sound as understood today.[21] The delicate mechanism that is necessary to the production of sound is the larynx, a cartilaginous and muscular "cage." Within the larynx are delicate folds, commonly, as noted above, called vocal cords. These are variously described as "elastic" bands or as infoldings of the mucous membranes lining the larynx and surrounding the glottis, the opening from the lungs. Above the true folds are "false" folds which come into action whenever there is over-pressure of air supplied to the cartilages from the lungs. The folds are attached to the cartilages which create the above-mentioned cage. These cartilages then move by means of muscles, thus opening the folds for breathing and closing them partially for speaking and singing.[22] What is important to observe about these parts of the vocal apparatus is that they should be in as relaxed a condition as possible in order to avoid a gripping sensation. Uncontrolled gripping of the muscles causes the throat to constrict and undue tension to be placed on the vocal folds.

There are various perspectives on the working of the vocal folds—for example, that the pitch is "a direct result of a corresponding number of impulses transmitted along the recurrent nerve."[23] Accordingly, the singer hears the pitch internally and then

---

[20] Athanasius Kircher, *Musurgia universalis*, 2 vols. (Rome, 1650; facsimile reprint, Hildesheim: Georg Olms, 1970), 1:21–22 and accompanying plate.

[21] For a description from a medical point of view, see Gray, *Anatomy*, 1366–76.

[22] See Johan Lundberg, "The Acoustics of the Singing Voice," *Scientific American* 236, no. 3 (March 1977): 82–91. For high-speed photographs showing the vocal cords sounding at around C below middle C, see Joseph J. Klein and Ole A. Schjeide, *Singing Technique: How to Avoid Vocal Trouble* (Princeton: D. Van Nostrand, 1967), fig. 1.

[23] Victor Fields, *Foundations of the Singer's Art* (New York, 1977), 88–89, as quoted by Russell Hammar, *Singing—An Extension of Speech* (Metuchen, N.J.: Scarecrow Press, 1978), 32.

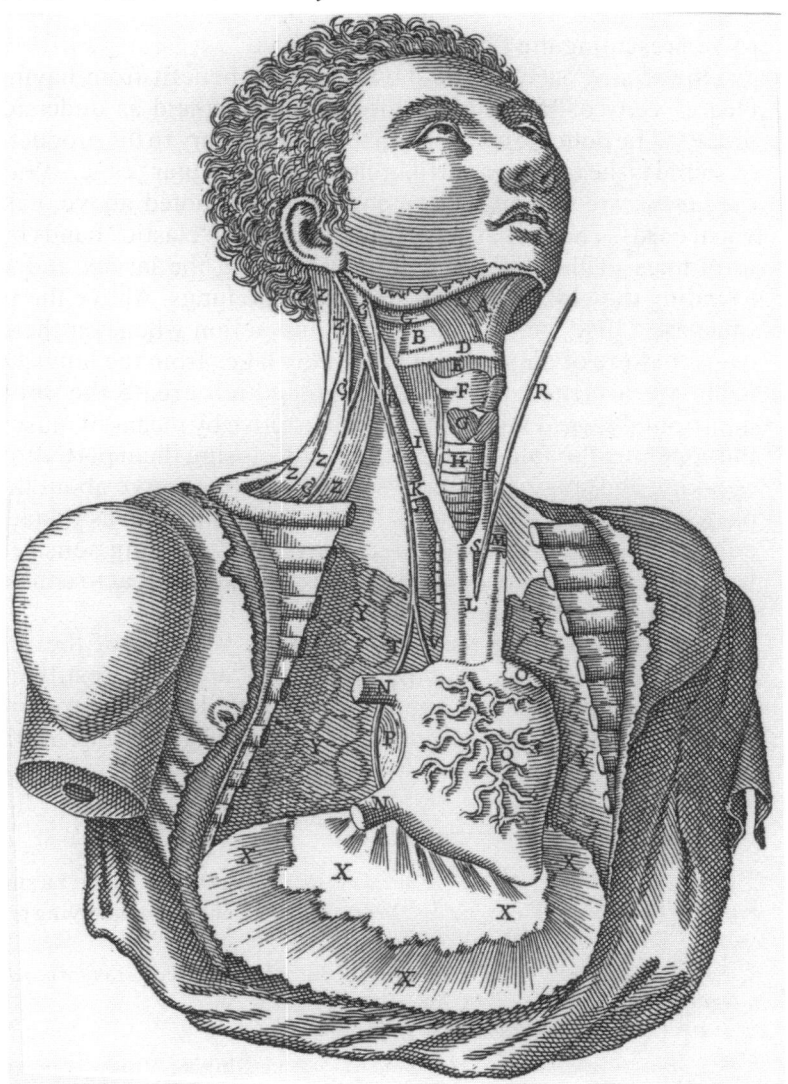

Fig. 6. The lower respiratory system and larynx. Athanasius Kircher, *Musurgia Universalis* (1650).

creates the conditions for the imitation of that pitch. This suggests a genetic basis for musicality or tone-deafness. Analysis of the dynamics of air passing through the larynx indicates that when the air pressure increases it is forced through the folds. The science here invokes the Bernoulli Effect, which comes from the study of aerodynamics. Suction is created, as in wind instruments. When the vocal folds become "fairly close to each other, there is a narrowing of the air passage sufficient for the Bernoulli Effect to draw them together, if the breath is flowing at the same time."[24] Yet another way of describing the operation of the vocal folds suggests a zipper-like effect, with the lowest tones being produced by keeping them open at their anterior. As the singer moves up the scale, the middle notes are created by vibration along more of the length of the vocal folds.[25] Finally, with the zipper partially closed, the highest notes are produced by the smallest opening at the anterior of the folds. Higher notes, however, do not require the application of more tension, simply more precision on the part of the singer. In fact, more relaxation and more support are needed to produce the highest notes reliably.

When the breath is sent to the vocal cords, they vibrate—that is, they open and close rapidly and virtually involuntarily—and sound is produced. This is similar to the way that sound is produced when a bow strikes a string on a viola da gamba, or when lips vibrate on the mouthpiece of a cornetto or sackbutt when air is blown into it, or when air is blown between a single or double reed into the mouthpiece of a clarinet or crumhorn. The loudness, softness, harshness, or sweetness of the tone can be changed by means of the type of "blow" that is sent to the vocal folds just as the skilled instrumentalist can vary tone quality and dynamics at will. It is well that the singer does not "shock" the folds with too sudden a movement of air or with too much force, since not only are unpleasant sounds created but also there is the possibility of doing damage to them. The development of vocal nodes is one of the most serious ailments that can befall a singer, and it is avoid-

---

[24] William Vennard, *Singing: The Mechanism and the Technic*, rev. ed. (New York: Carl Fischer, 1967), 39.

[25] Cornelius L. Reid, *Voice: Psyche and Soma* (New York: Joseph Patelson Music House, 1975), 42; Hammar, *Singing*, 34.

able. Especially when practicing, singers should try to begin tones with gentle attacks or, actually, non-attacks. It is not always possible or feasible to sing gently in actual performance, but having practiced carefully and being warmed up thoroughly before

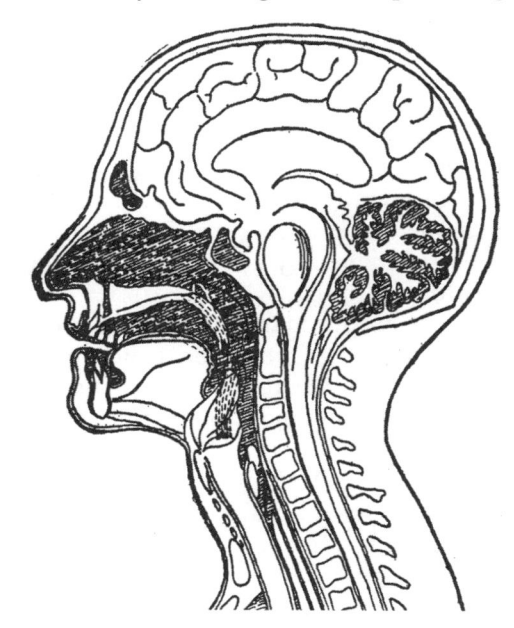

Fig. 7. The sinuses. Diagram showing (1) the forehead cavity; (2) the nasal cavity; (3) the palate involved in resonance, and (4) the soft palate.

singing will mean much less likelihood of harm.

The sound, created as described above, is sent from the vocal folds toward the naso-pharyngeal area. The soft palate (*velum*) is raised as it is in the formation of vowels, closing the passageway to the nose and allowing the sound to pass through and out of the open mouth. This process will be described more fully below.

V

Resonance. In singing, resonance comes from the utilization of the bones and cavities of the face and head, particularly those found in the front part of the face that is familiarly called the "mask." The principal cavities are: (1) the sinuses (maxillary, ethmoidal, sphenoidal, and frontal); (2) the naso-pharyngeal cavity; (3) the mouth with its appurtenances, the lips, teeth, and tongue; and (4) the throat. Important bones and membranes onto which sound is bounced include the hard and soft palates, the cheek bones and the orbits of the eyes, the bones of the nose, and even the skull. In addition, the muscles surveyed in connection with phonation move in ways that aid the resonating process. As is well known, none of these functions in isolation but rather in collaboration with one another, though it will be necessary here to take up each element separately and thereafter to explain how they may interact.

The largest facial cavities are the maxillary sinuses (fig. 7), one on each side of the nose, enclosed within the cheekbones and bounded by the orbits of the eyes above. Encroaching on them are the ethmoidal sinuses, positioned beside the nasal septum. The sphenoidal sinuses are closer to the ears, within a wing-shaped bone encasing the outer limits of the face, while the frontal sinuses are in the forehead, one on each side above the nose.[26] These are not symmetrical, and open into the meatus of the nasal cavity.

The importance of the sinuses to the singing voice was corroborated by my own experience after they were crushed in an automobile accident in 1962. I had to argue with the plastic surgeons at Henry Ford Hospital in Detroit to make them rebuild—rather than repair by means of bone grafts—my maxillary sinuses so that I could regain both resonance and my previous range. I insisted that they must examine the drawings of the resonating chambers depicted in Lilli Lehmann's *How to Sing*, and fortunately I was able to convince them of the importance of reconstructing the sinuses to a state as close as possible to their original condition. When this was done, my voice regained its vibrancy.

The cavity also between the skull and the durum mater is likewise an essential contributor to resonance, and one can feel sensations all the way around the head when singing full force. Rose refers to these head cavities as part of the "untunable

---

[26] See Gray, *Anatomy*, fig. 4–109.

resonance system."[27]

Otherwise, the soft and hard palate seem to be the most significant. It is off the hard palate particularly that sound is bounced, but the soft palate (*velum*), when raised in the formation of vowels, becomes taut and becomes a prime area from which to project the sound. In order to obtain the best usage of both of these it is necessary to raise them and then to attempt to "cup" the sound up into the mouth before sending it out; the mental concept of "hooking" the sound around the spaces of the mouth may be a useful way of thinking of this. When one is working for resonance, both lifting the corners of the mouth in a smile and wrinkling the nose, thus creating more lift and more space, are useful techniques.

But the nasal bones too are crucial, and in order to make the best use of them one may practice on a "hum." Keeping the lips very loosely together in a relaxed position, the singer should hum until a good vibration is started in the bridge of the nose. He or she can hold a finger on the nose to check what is occurring in that area. Relaxation of the throat and facial areas will be essential to this exercise.

As a resonator, the throat needs to be relaxed and open to ensure that it is utilized in the most efficient way. Even the larynx, often called the voice-box, vibrates with the application of sound. But more also needs to be said about the mouth cavity as a resonating space. Both the tongue and the teeth as well as the outer structure—the lips and the muscles surrounding them—play their part in resonation. Yet the tongue, as a large muscle attached to the floor of the mouth, can cause a blockage of the throat if it is too tense or raised too high. It should lie as low as possible in the mouth, but it must be positioned so that it also is capable of acting to aid in the creation of vowel and consonantal sounds. Having the tongue just up behind the back of the bottom teeth is a good starting position. Some singers are able to "furrow" the tongue, which gives better tone and resonance, but not all are able to do this.[28]

The teeth are a kind of extension of the hard palate, for sound bounces off them as well. In the creation of consonants, the teeth

---

[27] Rose, *The Singer and the Voice*, 169.

[28] Lehmann, *How to Sing*, 150; Rose, *The Singer and the Voice*, 125–36.

can produce small percussive sounds that are essential. It is important to preserve one's own natural teeth and to work with one's dentist on both preventive and corrective dentistry—and the preservation of one's teeth is also an argument for maintaining a good diet. As for the lips, their role is related to the matter of facial muscles, which include: (1) the masseter, an important muscle used in chewing and also generally in opening and closing the mouth; (2) the buccinator, the muscle with which air can be expelled from the cheeks; and (3) the orbicularis oris, the set of muscular fibers surrounding the orifice itself. Shaping the mouth in various ways can create different types of resonances. Bell-shaped lips can make a very stentorian sound, which would be useful for operatic singing but ordinarily not appropriate for early music.

Now we can see how vibrated sound, sent from the vocal folds toward the naso-pharyngeal region, becomes amplified and resonant sound that emits from the mouth. The soft palate is raised (as it is especially in the creation of vowel sounds), closing the passageway to the nose and allowing for the sound to pass through and out of the mouth. Resonance is increased by "bouncing" the sound off the soft and hard palates; lifting the pharynx widens the opening and makes possible more utilization of the area. To refer back to the section on relaxation above, one must continually remember to keep the jaws relaxed. Tight, tense jaws interfere with the resonance of the voice.

VI

Diction. An aspect of early music performance is the mastering of the sounds needed in pre-modern languages such as Latin, Old French, the Gallician dialect of Spanish, Provençal, renaissance Italian, Middle High German, Middle English, and so forth.[29] These present unusual challenges to the singer in order to achieve clear enunciation and articulation of vowels, which nevertheless demand a technique that is seemingly opposed to the relaxed jaw and open throat that have been described above. The moment that consonants

---

[29] [See especially the guide prepared by Timothy J. McGee and his colleagues, *Singing Early Music: The Pronunciation of European Languages in the Late Middle Ages and Renaissance* (Bloomington: Indiana University Press, 1996).—Ed.]

Vocal Production and Early Music 205

are added to the singer's task, a certain amount of friction, tension, and even constriction has to occur. And without clear consonants, the sense of the words in a vocal work is lost. Audiences expect neither a mediocre sound nor unclear diction, though realistically one or the other often must be compromised to some extent. Audiences do, however, deserve to hear the words clearly and to have the singer make sense of them. One might argue that diction is less important in texts that are well known to the audience (or congregation) such as the Ordinary of the Mass, but even here a kind of crispness and clarity is appreciated.

The beauty of the sound that is created depends to a considerable degree on the color of vowels. If Italian is being sung, vowels will be quite open, but in other languages this is not always the case. Whatever tongue one is singing, it is well to try to produce vowel sounds as far forward in the mouth as possible. This is a mental concept, since thinking that one can keep the sound forward is useful in maintaining a bright and clear, not "swallowed," sound. Also, those vowels that are normally produced farther forward can be a model for keeping the tone focused in the front part of the mouth. Empirical tests seem to indicate that practicing on the vowels "ee" and "oo" is efficacious in bringing sounds forward.

The diphthongs "ah-ee," "ah-oo," and "oo-ee" should be pronounced with the pure vowel in mind; they constitute combined, blended sounds, but they should still retain the purity of the original vowels. The schwa, for example, should not creep into the pure vowels, though this is a temptation among inexperienced singers of early music. In forming a vowel, a useful technique is to speak the vowel and then to sing it. This practice aids one in producing a good, open sound that is pleasant to the ear.

The consonants are, if anything, more troublesome than vowels, but, while interrupting the vowel sounds, they are important in that they make the words intelligible. They are divided into categories according to the manner in which they are produced, and are further subdivided into voiced and voiceless types. One difference here is in the amount of breath needed to produce them, with the voiceless ones requiring more force of exhalation. The accompanying chart is a rudimentary listing of categories of consonants.

	Voiced	Voiceless
Plosives	b, d, hard g	p, t, k
Affricates	j (as in *jest*)	ch (as in *check*)
Fricatives	th (as in *this*), z, j (zh), v, Engl. r	th (as in *thing*), s, sh, f
Nasals	m, n, ng, gn (Fr.)	
Rolled Consonants	foreign r	
Lateral Consonants	l, ll (Sp.), gl. (It.)	

In the production of consonants, it is necessary to get past them quickly and to move on to the vowel. Lingering on them creates a very sloppy sound. Hamlet's advice to the players is appropriate here: "Speak the speech, I pray you, . . . trippingly on the tongue" (Act 3.2.1–2). The vocal apparatus, in this case lips, teeth, and tongue, must be relaxed but definitely not lazy, capable of springing into action quickly and creating a good strong consonant sound which goes directly to the vowel without disrupting the melodic line, the flow of tone.

Good plosives, affricates, and fricatives depend on having enough breath to make an effect loud enough to be heard in the hall in which one is singing. Obviously, the larger hall will require a larger expenditure of breath; this means that one must have enough reserve even though some of the precious breath must be "wasted" on the consonants. Energy, breath supply, as discussed above, and good dental equipment are requirements for creating good consonants. For nasals, it is well to sing them with very relaxed lips, since a more plosive technique makes these sound harsh. Prolonging them very slightly—but not so long as to go into a hum, which is tasteless—gives a good effect. The rolled "r" brings the sound forward, and for that reason is to be preferred to the American "arrr" sound, which has a tendency to slip back into the throat. People who for some reason cannot roll an "r" may experiment with saying "d" in place of it. "Meddy," in place of "merry," may sound quite acceptable, especially in English madrigals. The "l" ("el") sound must never be sung at the back of the throat.

Two useful exercises for creating better consonants are (1) buzzing the lips, and (2) singing "Lips, teeth, tip of the tongue" on one tone. The latter makes one aware of the location of the consonant sounds as well as strengthening muscles around the lips.

Diction, the pronouncing of words so that they can be understood by the audience, is part of the process of imparting the meaning of the text, its sentences, phrases, and the individual words.

Two important matters which relate to diction in early music are (1) registers and (2) vibrato. These have been noted above in my essay "High, Clear, and Sweet: Singing Early Music." It is a matter of concern that modern vocal teachers have often denied the existence of register or else have attempted to achieve with their students a totally blended voice, with no evident breaks between them.[30] The break is usually "healed" by means of bringing a higher register down into the lower, and conversely by bringing the lower register up. Lilli Lehmann's means of ridding the singer of the break was *gradually* to change the position of the larynx in response to the change in pitch, and at the same time to keep the soft palate elastic and in harmony with the other parts of the vocal apparatus. In doing this, the breath pressure must also be kept steady throughout the entire compass of the voice.[31]

But neither denying the fact of registers nor attempting to blend them out of existence is consistent with early music theory or practice. Those who wrote on the subject, including Johannes de Muris, Jerome of Moravia, and Marchettus of Padua, have invariably noted a three-part division of the vocal range. According to Johannes de Muris,

---

[30] See Rose, *The Singer and the Voice*, 206; Hammar, *Singing*, 111–13.

[31] Lehman, *How to Sing*, 115, 117.

The inventor of song and the first learned ones came to the conclusion that the windpipe had three divisions and that thus the art of song [i.e., singing] likewise had three divisions; when it [the windpipe] was spread, deep tones were produced; and when it was narrowed, high tones were produced; and when it was in a moderate condition, middle tones were produced.[32]

Jerome of Moravia listed the "vox pectoris, the "vox gutturis," and the "vox capitus"—that is, the chest, throat, and head voices. Of these, the voice formed in the chest is strong in the low notes, and in the throat strong in the middle notes; those formed into the head are strong in the high notes. But the importance of the chest, and therefore the lungs, is implied in his statement that "all voices gain their vigor from the chest."[33] But there also may be the implication that all voices have potential for producing chest tones. The clearest statement regarding the existence and desirability of clearly distinguished registers was presented in 1309 by Marchettus of Padua in his *Lucidarium*. He, like Jerome, distinguished the deep voice or "vox gravis" formed in the chest ("in voce pectoris"); the middle or sharp voice ("acute"), which is formed in the throat ("voce gutturis"); and the high or very sharp voice ("superacute"), which is formed in the head ("voce capitis").[34]

Actually, the advantage of using three colors rather than a single blended one in early music should be obvious upon a little consideration. For example, the legendary Barbara Thornton provided an example that I feel is convincing in this regard, for she

---

[32] Johannes de Muris, *Summa Musicae*, chap. 5, in Martin Gerbert, ed., *Scriptores ecclesiastici de musica*, 3 vols. (reprint, Hildesheim: Georg Ohms, 1963), 3:200–01; trans. in Franz Müller-Heuser, *Vox Humana: Ein Beitrag zur Untersuchung der Stimmästhetik des Mittelalters* (Regensburg: Bosse, 1963), 125–26.

[33] Jerome of Moravia, *Tractatus de Musica*, in E. de Coussemaker, ed., *Scriptorum de musica medii aevi*, 4 vols. (reprint, Hildesheim: Georg Ohms, 1963), 1:93; translation from MacClintock, 7.

[34] Marchettus of Padua, *Lucidarium*, ed. Jan Herlinger (Chicago: University of Chicago Press, 1985), 540–42.

was able to move smoothly from low to high notes at will but with the display of all three colors. Others have been less successful in blend, but in making use of Middle Eastern techniques have produced interesting experiments, at their best maintaining smooth movement between registers.[35] But it is also clear that there must be consistency between the registers so that the result does not sound like two or three different people singing. Tuning of the registers also requires such consistency.[36]

Tuning is also impossible with a voice replete with vibrato, and it is important to see that fifths, fourths, octaves, and thirds are perfectly in tune. A huge wobbling voice can never be sufficiently flexible in rapid passages such as those demanded in much early music. Of course, as used sparingly for ornamentation, as suggested by Jerome of Moravia in the thirteenth century,[37] or for other special effects, as in the case of the French throat-vibrato, useful in the fifteenth-century chanson, there is a place for the vibrato though never for the uncontrolled variety or the out-of-control wobble. At the same time, "white" sound needs to be avoided as lacking in tonal color, but rather, as Andrea von Ramm has said, the voice should be "transparent in its expression, and flexible," so that it "can *dominate* [italics mine] the vibrato. . . . One has to have a certain kind of throat activity and flexibility for

---

[35] For the validity of studying Arabic influences, see, for example, Alexander Ringer, "Eastern Elements in Medieval Polyphony," *Studies in Medieval Culture* 2 (1966): 75–83.

[36] It should be kept in mind that pitch was not set until relatively recent times; see the overview by Mark Lindley et al., "Pitch," in *The New Grove Dictionary of Music and Musicians*, 20 vols. (London: Macmillan, 1980), 14:778–85. [Another aspect to be kept in mind is the matter of temperament; the author had a preference for baroque tuning for harpsichord and organ, especially Werkmeister II.—Ed.]

[37] Jerome of Moravia, *Tractatus de Musica*, in Coussemaker, ed. *Scriptorum de Musica medii aevi*, 1:91; trans. MacClintock, 4–5. Of particular interest is his description of the "harmonic flower" or *flos harmonicus*, which is "a very swift and stormlike vibration." But this and other ornaments should be added sparingly.

the *messe di voce* as well as for the control of vibrato."[38]

There is corroboration for the dislike of the uncontrolled vibrato, especially the noticeable tremolo, in writers of the Middle Ages and Renaissance. Biagio Rossetti, in a work published in 1529, preferred to have "the breath flow out with the voice in an even, steady stream."[39] He condemned the tremolo, as did Franchinus Gaforius, who advised the singer to "spurn excessive vibrato and voices which are too loud, for they are not compatible with other voices similarly pitched. In short, because of their own continual instability they cannot maintain harmonious proportions with the other voices."[40] And with regard to the instrumental tremula, Silvestro Ganassi wrote in his work on playing the viola da gamba in 1529 that it should be used only to add expression to slow music with sad emotional content.[41] But even as early as Charlemagne's time the educator Einhard had noted that the tremula and vinnola were used as ornaments by Gauls with Roman training, but he remarked that because they were barbarians they sang roughly in their throats.[42]

All too often contemporary singers sing with constricted throats, and they fail to support their tones adequately with the breath. Often they do not even recognize the wobble in their voices. They also fail to recognize that one who sings well with a

---

[38] William Zukof, "An Interview with Andrea von Ramm," *The American Recorder* 21 (1980): 5. In this interview von Ramm clarified earlier remarks that had appeared in her earlier article, "Singing Early Music," *Early Music* 4, no. 1 (Jan. 1976): 12–15.

[39] Biagio Rossetti, *Libellus de rudimentis musices*, chap. 3, as quoted by Ulrich, *Concerning the Principles of Voice Training*, 72, and 213: "emitte aequaliter vocem et anhiletem."

[40] Franchinus Gafurius, *The Practica musicae*, trans. and ed. Irwin Young (Madison: University of Wisconsin Press, 1969), 160.

[41] Sylvestro Ganassi, *Regola Rubertina*, [German] trans. by Hildemarie Peter (Berlin and Lichterfelde: Robert Lienau, 1974), 9.

[42] Einhard, *Annales*, in *Monumenta Germaniae Historica* (1876–1920; reprint, New York: Kraus, 1963–79), 1:170.

minimum of vibrato will sing longer and maintain his or her voice beyond the short career of the person who sings in an undisciplined and careless way. In performing early music, it is best, therefore, to keep in mind the ideal, described in an earlier essay in the present book, as "high, sweet, and clear."

Index

Adam of St. Victor 10
Adams, Henry 36
Aelred of Rievaulx 163, 183
Alcuin 160
Alexiou, Margaret 35
Alma redemptoris mater 61–73, 93–99
Alterbogen, Danish 175
Amalarius of Metz 161
Anglicanus, *English composer* 70–71
Anselm, St. 35
Aristotle 79
Astrophil and Stella 101, 111–14
Athanasius 143–44, 157–58
Aurelian of Réôme 51, 77
Ave regina caelorum 71
Avicenna 196
Axton, Richard 4, 18

Bach, Johann Sebastian 179
Bacilly, Bénigne de 192
Banchieri, Adriano 189
Barth, Sr. Pudentiana 5–7
Basel, University Library, Cod. B.V.29 169
Baum, Paull F. 73
Beardsley, Monroe C. 125
Bel and the Dragon 50
Benediktbeuern Manuscript 173–74
Bent, Ian 10–11
Berkenhead, John 132

Bernard of Clairvaux, St. 35–36, 79, 82, 183
Bevington, David 174
Bielitz, Mathias 56
Böckeler, Maura 5, 7–8
Boethius 147
Bonaventure, St. 35–36
Bourgeault, Cynthia 46
Bovicelli, Giovanni Battista 86
Boyd, Beverly 63, 70, 72
breath, *in singing* 192–96
British Library
  MS. Add. 15,102 8, 19
  MS. Add. 15,117 109, 112
  MS. 57,723 102
  MS. Egerton 2,615 49, 54
  MS. Royal 17.C.XVII 80
Brockett, Clyde 20
Bronarski, Ludwig 10–11, 13, 20
Bronzino, Agnolo 93, 99
Brown, Carleton 61
Buch, H., *pastor* 180–82
Bukofzer, Manfred 136

Caccini, Giulio 150
Calvin, John 143
Camarata, Florentine 127
Cambridge, Trinity College, MS. 0.3.58 65
Cambridge University Library, MS. MmIIg 64
Campion, Thomas 126, 128

213

Carcopino, Jérôme 195
Carissimi, Giacomo 192
Carolingian reforms 159
Casserio, Giulio 197
Castiglione, Baldesar 93
Chambers, E. K. 50
Chapman, George 113
Charlemagne, *emperor*
    158–61, 163, 210
Chaucer, Geoffrey; *see*
    Prioress' Tale
Christian VI, *king* 179–81
Cicero 84
Cifra, Antonio 131
Cistercian, Order of 36, 38
Cividale, Reale Museo
    Archeologico Nazionale,
    MS. C1 39
Clement of Alexandria 147
Cobb, John 128
Cogan, Robert 11
Collins, Fletcher 38, 40, 44,
    45–46, 52
Comus 126–27, 131
Conrad von Zabern 81–83, 85,
    189
consonants 203, 205–07
Coprario, Giovanni 132, 142
Cosin, John 143
Country Parson, The 134–35
Coussemaker, Edmond de 45,
    49
Crashaw, Richard 137
Cutts, J. P. 101, 112–13

Daniel, Play of 49–59
Dante Alighieri 131
Dart, Thurston 82
De divinis officiis 176
della Robbia, Lucca 78
Dendermonde Manuscript 10
Depositio 32–33

diction 204–07
Diruta, Girolamo 189
Dodecacordon 171–73
Donna del Paradiso 37
Donne, John 92
Dowland, John 75–76,
    102–06, 114
Dronke, Peter 3–4, 15, 18
Dryden, John 137
Dufay, Guillaume 70–71
Dunstable, John 65, 70–71
Durandus (Guillaume Durand),
    bishop 62, 167
Durham, Rites of 33

Eanbald II, *archbishop* 160
Einhard 210
El Greco 92
Eliade, Mircea 162
Elizabeth I, *Queen* 105
Ephraem, St. 155
Etherea 156–57
Eton Choirbook 67
Eusebius of Caesaria 139
Evans, Willa McClung 102
Everyman 13

Fassler, Margot 49, 54
Feast of Fools 49–50
Fellowes, Edmund H. 105,
    108
Finck, Hermann 187, 189
Flanigan, C. Clifford 161
Flete, Fideles animae 38, 41,
    44
Fleury Playbook 173
Fludd, Robert 140–41, fig. 3
Forest, *English composer*
    70–71
Franciscan Order 36–37
Francis of Assisi 37
Frere, W. H. 64

Index

Gaffurius, Francinus 84, 210
Galen 196
Gallican rite 159–62
Ganassi, Silvetro 210
Gaude Maria 71–73
Gesualdo, Carlo, *Prince of Venosa* 91, 131
Glareanus, Henricus 171–73
Greenberg, Noah 49
Greene, Henry Copley 49
Gregory the Great 170
Guido of Arezzo 51
Guilbert of Gembloux 12

Haar, James 92
Haec Dies 20
Hali Abbas 196
Hamilton, Marie Padgett 69–70
Hammermüller, Joseph 183
Hammerstein, Reinhold 13
Harrison, Frank Ll. 69
Hart, Eric Ford 123
Hayes, Albert M. 152
Herbert, George 133–52
Herbert, Magdalen 135
Herbert of Cherbury, Lord 139
Hermannus Contractus 62–63
Herrick, Robert 129
Hessische Landesbibliothek, Cod. 2 (*Riesenkodex*) 5–8, 11, 13
Hilarius 4
Hildegard of Bingen 3–30, 55
Hiley, David 51
Holstein, J. L. 180, 183
Holy Innocents, Mass of 69–70
Hooker, Richard 144, 147–48
Hozeski, Bruce 13
Hucke, Helmut 158
Hugh of St. Victor 183

Hutchinson, F. E. 135, 150

Ignatius, St., *bishop* 155
Improperia 32, 34
Isidore of Seville 76–77, 79, 82, 87
Iversen, Gunilla 9

Jacobus de Voragine 62
Jacopone da Todi 37
James I, *king* 113
Jena, *singing at* 84
Jeppesen, Knut 91
Jerome of Moravia 77, 81, 207–09
Jerome, St. 148
Johannes de Grocheio 46
Johannes de Muris 207–08
Johnson, Rick 5
Jungmann, Josef 161–62

Kade, Otto 170, 179
Katzenellenbogen, Adolf 12, 29
Kepler, Johannes 136, 143
Kircher, Athanasius 197–99, fig. 6
Koehler, G. Stanley 125

Lady of May, The 106
Lambert 163
Lanier, Nicholas 132
Lassus, Ordandus 92
Lawes, Henry 102–08, 123–32
Lazarus, Raising of 42
Legend of St. Anthony 80
Lehmann, Lilli 83, 194, 202, 207
Leonin 75
Liber responsalis 34

Liber usualis 63, 65
Linköping Missal 165
liturgical drama 3–47, 49–59, 161, 173–74
Loomis, Roger 183
Lucidarium 208
Luther, Martin 144, 177–78
Lydgate, John 80

Mace, Thomas 81, 108, 111
Machaut, Guillaume 76, 86
Maffei da Solofra, Camillo 79
maniera 92–93
Marchetto of Padua 85, 207–08
Marenzio, Luca 131
Masque of the Inner Temple 113
Meditations on the Life of Christ 36
Melito, St. 155
Mersenne, Marin 84–85
Milton, John 123–32
Minter, Drew 196
Mishna, *intonation of* 158
Missale Lundense 165, 167, 175
Moberg, C.-A. 168–69
Montecassino Passion play 31
Monteverdi, Claudio 131, 192
Morley, Thomas 128

Neoplatonism 17–18
Newman, Barbara 24
Nicodemus, Gospel of 34
Notker Balbulus 163

Ockeghem, Johannes 70–71
"O, Guds Lam unskyldig" 182
"O Herre Gud benaade mig" 182
Old Arcadia 105–08, 110

Oley, Barnabas 138
Ordo I 176
Ordo Virtutum, by Hildegard of Bingen 3–30
Orientis partibus 54
Origen 139
Ovid 124
Oxford, Christ Church MS. 439 113

Palestrina 91–100
Palisca, Claude 92
Paradise Lost 125
Parmagianino, Francesca Mazzola 93, 99
Pepin 158–59
Perotin 76
Phillips, John 128
Pietism 177, 179–81, 184
Planctus, from Toulouse 34; from Regensburg 44
Planctus Mariae, from Cividale 31, 38–47
Plato 133, 144
Potter, Robert 9
Power, Leonel 70–71
Praetorius, Michael 84
Prioress' Tale, by Geoffrey Chaucer 61–73, 82
Psychomachia, of Prudentius 11–12
Purcell, Henry 132

Quintillian 195
Quitschreiber, Georg 84

Raby, F. J. E. 63
Rankin, Susan 4
Reese, Gustave 63, 139
Regina caeli laetari 71
registers 76, 85–96, 207–09
Rhazes 196

Index

Ridley, Florence 72
Ringler, William 106, 109–10, 112, 114
Ritscher, Maria-Immaculata 8
Robinson, Ian 72
Romanian letters 163–67
Romano, Giulio 93
Romanus 163
Rose, Arnold 193, 202
Roskilde Cathedral, *Passion from* 177–84
Rossetti, Biagio 77–78, 84, 189, 210
Rosso, Fiorentino 93

Sachs, Curt 75–76
St. John Passion 155–84
St. Matthew Passion 179
Salisbury Cathedral, *music at* 143
Salve sancte parens 68
Sandys, Sir Edwin 113
S. Maria Novella, Forence singing at 78
Sarum Antiphonal 64, 67
Sarum Missal 168, 176
Schnabel, Bernhard, *pastor* 180–82
Schütz, Heinrich 179
Schweitzer, Albert 180
Scivias, of Hildegard of Bingen 8, 12, 25, 28–29
Shakespeare, William 150
Shearman, John 92, 99
Sheingorn, Pamela 9
Sidney, Sir Philip 101–22
Skeat, W. W. 61
Smith, Henry Lea, Jr. 127
Smoldon, William L. 4, 42, 44–46, 52
Spener, Philipp Jacob 180
Stabat Mater 37, 44

Stevens, John 51, 53
Sticca, Sandro 35–36
Strabo, Walafrid 159
Sturton, Edmund 67, 70–71
syllables, *rhythmic quality of* 124–27
Symphonia, of Hildegard of Bingen 9–10, 13
Sypher, Wylie 91–92

Taylor, Jerome 50–51
Taylour, Robert 113
Tenebrae 34
Thornton, Barbara 5, 208
Timaeus 133
Tinctoris, Johannes 138
Tovey, Donald 123
Trager, George L. 127
Trisagion 162
Trithemius, Johannes 8
tuning 140, 142
Tuve, Rosamond 151

Uberti, Mauro 78, 86

van der Werf, Hendrik 46
Varchi, Benedetto 92
Vasari, Giorgio 92, 99
Vecchi, Horatio 131
Vesalius 197
vibrato 75–76, 83–85, 207, 209–11
Victimae Paschali 15
Visions of Tundale 80
Visitatio Sepulchri 34–35, 173
Volmar 12
von Ramm, Andrea 75, 80, 83–84, 209–10
vowels 205–06

Waller, Edmund 129
Walther, Johann 179

Walton, Izaak 139, 148
Ward, John 109
Warner, Marina 37
Werner, Eric 158
Wezelen 9, 12
Willetts, Pamela J. 102
Wimsatt, W. K. 125
Worcester Cathedral Library,
  MS. F160 64–65, 67
Worm, C. W., *bishop* 180–82

York Missal 170
Young, Karl 3, 31–32, 36

Zacconi, Lodovico 86
Zamorensis, Rodericus 78

The recipient of a doctorate from the University of Minnesota and an active musician and scholar, **Audrey Ekdahl Davidson** (1930–2006) was a mainstay of the International Congress on Medieval Studies at Kalamazoo almost from its beginning. In 1993 she retired as Professor of Music at Western Michigan University.